THE TERROR OF NEOLIBERALISM

Cultural Politics & the Promise of Democracy
A Series from Paradigm Publishers
Edited by Henry A. Giroux

Empire and Inequality: America and the World Since 9/11
 by Paul Street

The Terror of Neoliberalism
 by Henry A. Giroux

Forthcoming
*Reading and Writing for Civic Literacy: The Critical Citizen's
 Guide to Argumentative Rhetoric*
 by Donald Lazere

Listening Beyond the Echoes: Agency and Ethics in a Mediated World
 by Nick Couldry

Schooling and the Struggle for Public Life, Second Edition
 by Henry A. Giroux

Reading French Feminism
 by Michael Payne

THE TERROR OF NEOLIBERALISM

HENRY A. GIROUX

Paradigm Publishers

Boulder • London

Garamond Press

Aurora, Ontario

Published in the United States by Paradigm Publishers, 3360 Mitchell Lane Suite C, Boulder, Colorado 80301 USA.

Paradigm Publishers is the trade name of Birkenkamp & Company, LLC, Dean Birkenkamp, President and Publisher.
ISBN 1-59451-011-3 (pbk)
ISBN 1-59451-010-5 (cloth)

Library of Congress Cataloging-in-Publication Data
has been applied for.

Published 2004 in Canada by Garamond Press Ltd, 63 Mahogany Court, Aurora, Ontario L4G 6M8 Canada.

Library and Archives Canada Cataloguing in Publication

Giroux, Henry A.
The terror of neoliberalism / Henry A. Giroux.
Includes bibliographical references and index.
ISBN 1-55193-054-4
1. Liberalism.   2. Free enterprise.   3. Democracy.   4. Social problems.
I. Title.
D2003.G57 2004   909.83   C2004-904512-1

Printed and bound in the United States of America on acid-free paper that meets the standards of the American National Standard for Permanence of Paper for Printed Library Materials.

Designed and Typeset by Straight Creek Bookmakers.

09   08   07   06   05   04
5   4   3   2   1

For Susan, my heartbeat, forever.

CONTENTS

Acknowledgments

♧

This book was written at a very dire time in American history. Motivated by both a sense a outrage and hope, it attempts to identify neoliberalism as a threat to democracy at home and abroad as well as and to offer a productive series of analyses of how to stop its poisonous affects on all aspects of public and private life. As one of the most dangerous ideologics of the 21ˢᵗ century, neoliberalism has become a breeding ground for militarism, rapacious profiteering, and dissident profiling, and a new political and religious fundamentalism that undermines the presupposition that democracy is about sharing power and resources. In fact, democracy at the present time looks less like a reachable ideal than a forgotten ideology of the past. The government, as many notable and courageous critics have pointed out, is in the hands of extremists who have shredded civil liberties, lied to the American public to legitimate sending young American troops to Iraq, alienated most of the international community with a blatant exercise of arrogant power, tarnished the highest offices of government with unsavory corporate alliances, used political power to unabashedly pursue legislative polices that favor the rich and punish the poor, and disabled those public spheres not governed by the logic of the market. Closer to home, a silent war is being waged against people of color who are being incarcerated at alarming rates. Academic freedom is increasingly under attack, homophobia has become the poster-ideology of the Republican Party's presidential campaign, and a full-fledged assault on women's reproductive rights is being championed by Bush's evangelical supporters. While people of color, the poor, youth, the middle class, the elderly, gays, and women are being attacked, the current administration (buttressed by Mel Gibson and the media) are supporting a campaign to not only collapse the boundaries between the church and state, but to make it clear that all non-Christians as well as unorthodox Christians will eventually burn in hell.

Fortunately, power is never completely on the side of domination, religious fanaticism, or political corruption. Nor is it entirely in the hands of those who view democracy as an excess or burden. Increasingly, more and more individuals and groups at home and around the globe including students, workers, feminists, educators, writers, environmentalists, senior citizens, artists, and a host of other individuals and movements are organizing to challenge the dangerous slide on the part of the United States into the dredges of an authoritarianism that threatens not only democracy at home but also abroad. This book is composed in solidarity with them and the next generation of young people who hopefully will never let this terrible assault on democracy happen again.

This book would not have been written without the help of many friends who offered invaluable criticisms and support. I would like to especially thank Arif Dirlik, Imre Szeman, John Comaroff, Mike Payne, Michael Brenson, Norman Denzin, Nick Couldry, Robert Ivie, Ted Striphas, Paul Street, Stanley Aronowitz, Jeff Nealon, Doug Kellner, Michael Berube, Roger Simon, Ken Saltman, David Theo Goldberg, Lawrence Grossberg, Paul Youngquist, Sut Jhally, Donaldo Macedo, Robin D. G. Kelley, Peter Trifanos, Ted Striphas, Micaela Amato, Vorris Nunley, Don Schule, Dean Birkenkamp, and David Gamson. Needless to say, I bear the responsibility for the final outcome. I also want to thank Brett, Chris, and Jack for keeping me honest and connected to the world. I want to thank my wonderful mother-in-law, Jessica Marlow, for her deeply appreciated love, generosity, and support. I am deeply indebted to Christopher Robbins, my graduate assistant, who provided detailed editorial suggestions on the entire manuscript and was a pleasure to work with. Once again, I am thankful that Grizz, my aging canine companion, is still around. As usual, I could never have written this book without the help and insight of my Friday study group: Doug Morris, Heidi Hendershot, Leticia Ortega, Chris Robbins, and Anto Sisto. They have been of enormous help in enabling me to think through many of arguments presented in this book. Finally, I would like to thank Peter George, Ken Norrie, and Nasrin Rahimieh for reviving my faith in educational leaders who believe higher education cannot be abstracted from the demands of an inclusive democracy. Some of ideas in these chapters are drawn from work published in other places. Chapter 1, "Living in the Shadow of Authoritarianism" is also being published in a slightly different version in as a Phi Delta Kappa monograph. Chapter 2, "Spectacles of Race and Pedagogies of Denial" appeared in *Communication Education* 52: 3/4 (July/October, 2003), pp. 191–211, available on-line also at: http://www.tandf.co.uk/journals/titles/03634523.asp; a shorter version of chapter 3 appeared in *Workplace: A Journal of Academic Labor* 6:1 (February 2004). Available on-line: http://www.louisville.edu/journal/workplace/issue6p1/giroux04.html; sections of chapter 4 were published in *Parallax*; and chapter 6 was published in slightly different form in *Cultural Studies/Critical Methodologies.*

Preface

❧

In 1945 or 1950, if you had seriously proposed any of the ideas and policies in today's standard neo-liberal toolkit, you would have been laughed off the stage or sent off to the insane asylum.... The idea that the market should be allowed to make major social and political decisions; the idea that the State should voluntarily reduce its role in the economy, or that corporations should be given total freedom, that trade unions should be curbed and citizens given much less rather than more social protection—such ideas were utterly foreign to the spirit of the time. Even if someone actually agreed with these ideas, he or she would have hesitated to take such a position in public and would have had a hard time finding an audience.

—Susan George[1]

Just as the world has seen a more virulent and brutal form of market capitalism, generally referred to as neoliberalism, develop over the last thirty years, it has also seen "a new wave of political activism [which] has coalesced around the simple idea that capitalism has gone too far."[2] Wedded to the belief that the market should be the organizing principle for all political, social, and economic decisions, neoliberalism wages an incessant attack on democracy, public goods, and noncommodified values. Under neoliberalism everything either is for sale or is plundered for profit. Public lands are looted by logging companies and corporate ranchers; politicians willingly hand the public's airwaves over to broadcasters and large corporate interests without a dime going into the public trust; Halliburton gives war profiteering a new meaning as it is granted corporate contracts without any competitive bidding and then bilks the U.S. government for millions; the environment is polluted and despoiled in the name of profit-making just as the government passes legislation to make it easier for corporations to do so; public services are gutted in order to lower the taxes of major corporations; schools increasingly resemble malls or jails, and teachers, forced to raise revenue for classroom materials, increasingly function as circus barkers hawking everything from hamburgers to pizza parties—that is, when they are not reduced to prepping students to get higher test scores. As markets are touted as the driving force of everyday life, big government is disparaged as either incompetent or threatening to individual freedom, suggesting that power should reside in markets and corporations rather than in governments and citizens. Citizenship has increasingly become a function of consumerism, and politics has been restructured as "corporations have been increasingly freed from social control through deregulation, privatization, and other neoliberal measures."[3]

Fortunately, the corporate capitalist fairytale of neoliberalism has been challenged all over the globe by students, labor organizers, intellectuals, community activists, and a host of individuals and groups unwilling to allow democracy to be bought and sold by multinational corporations, corporate swindlers, international political institutions, and government politicians who willingly align themselves with corporate interests and profits. From Seattle to Genoa, people engaged in popular resistance are collectively taking up the challenge of neoliberalism and reviving both the meaning of resistance and the sites where it takes place. Political culture is now global and resistance is amorphous, connecting students with workers, schoolteachers with parents, and intellectuals with artists. Groups protesting the attack on farmers in India, whose land is being destroyed by the government in order to build dams, now find themselves in alliance with young people resisting sweatshop labor in New York City. Environmental activists are joining up with key sections of organized labor as well as with groups protesting Third World debt. The collapse of the neoliberal showcase, Argentina, along with numerous corporate bankruptcies and scandals (notably including Enron), reveals the cracks in neoliberal hegemony and domination. Moreover, the multiple forms of resistance against neoliberal capitalism are not limited by an identity politics focused on particularized rights and interests. On the contrary, identity politics is affirmed within a broader crisis of political culture and democracy that connects the militarization of public life with the collapse of the welfare state and the attack on civil liberties. Central to these new movements is the notion that neoliberalism has to be understood within a larger crisis of vision, meaning, education, and political agency. Democracy in this view is not limited to the struggle over economic resources and power; indeed, it also includes the creation of public spheres where individuals can be educated as political agents equipped with the skills, capacities, and knowledge they need to perform as autonomous political agents. I want to expand the reaches of this debate by arguing that any struggle against neoliberalism must address the discourse of political agency, civic education, and cultural politics as part of a broader struggle over the relationship between democratization (the ongoing struggle for a substantive and inclusive democracy) and the global public sphere.

We live at a time when the conflation of private interests, empire building, and evangelical fundamentalism brings into question the very nature, if not the existence, of the democratic process. Under the reign of neoliberalism, capital and wealth have been largely distributed upward while civic virtue has been undermined by a slavish celebration of the free market as the model for organizing all facets of everyday life. Political culture has been increasingly depoliticized as collective life is organized around the modalities of privatization, deregulation, and commercialization. When the alleged champions of neoliberalism invoke politics, they substitute "ideological certainty for reasonable doubt," and deplete "the national reserves of political intelligence" just as they endorse "the illusion that the future can be bought instead of earned."[4] Under attack is the social contract with its emphasis on enlarging the public good and expanding social provisions—such as access to adequate health care, housing, employment, public transportation, and education—which provided a limited though important safety net and a set of conditions upon which democracy could be experienced and critical citizenship engaged. It has been replaced with a notion of national security based on fear, surveillance, and control rather than on a culture of shared responsibility. Self-reflection and collective empowerment, now reduced to self-promotion and self-interest, are legitimated by a new and ruthless social Darwinism played out nightly on network television as a metaphor for the "naturalness" of downsizing, the celebration of hyper-masculinity, and the promotion of a war of all against all over even the most limited notions of solidarity and collective struggle.

Under neoliberal domestic restructuring and the foreign policy initiatives of the Washington Consensus, motivated by an evangelical belief in free-market democracy at home and open markets abroad, the United States in the last thirty years has witnessed the increasing obliteration of those discourses, social forms, public institutions, and noncommercial values that are central to the language of public commitment, democratically charged politics, and the common good. Civic engagement now appears impotent as corporations privatize public space and disconnect power from issues of equity, social justice, and civic responsibility. Financial investments, market identities, and commercial values take precedence over human needs, public responsibilities, and democratic relations. Proceeding outside of democratic accountability, neoliberalism has allowed a handful of private interests to control as much of social life as possible in order to maximize their personal profit.

Abroad, neoliberal global policies have been used to pursue rapacious free-trade agreements and expand Western financial and commercial interests through the heavy-handed policies of the World Bank, the World Trade Organization, and the International Monetary Fund in order to manage and transfer resources and wealth from the poor and less developed nations to the richest and most powerful nation-states and to the wealthy corporate defenders of capitalism. Third World and semi-peripheral states of Latin America, Africa, and Asia have become client states of the wealthy nations led by the United States. Loans made to the client states by banks and other financial institutions have produced severe dislocations in "social welfare programs such as health care, education, and laws establishing labor standards."[5] For example, the restrictions that the IMF and World Bank impose on countries as a condition for granting loans not only subject them to capitalist values but also undermine the very possibility of an inclusive and substantive democracy. The results have been disastrous, as evidenced by the economic collapse of countries such as Argentina and Nigeria as well as by the fact that "one third of the world's labor force—more than a billion people—are unemployed or underemployed."[6] In tracking twenty-six countries that received loans from the World Bank and the IMF, the *Multinational Monitor* spelled out the conditions that accompanied such loans:

> civil service downsizing, privatization of government-owned enterprises with layoffs required in advance of privatization and frequently following privatization; promotion of labor flexibility—regulatory changes to remove restrictions on the ability of government and private employers to fire or lay off workers; mandated wage reductions, minimum wage reductions of containment, and spreading the wage gap between government

employees and managers; and pension reforms, including privatization, that cut social security benefits for workers.[7]

At home, corporations increasingly design not only the economic sphere but also shape legislation and policy affecting all levels of government, and with limited opposition. As corporate power lays siege to the political process, the benefits flow to the rich and the powerful. Included in such benefits are reform policies that shift the burden of taxes from the rich to the middle class, the working poor, and state governments as can be seen in the shift from taxes on wealth (capital gains, dividends, and estate taxes) to a tax on work, principally in the form of a regressive payroll tax. During the 2002–2004 fiscal years, tax cuts delivered $197.3 billion in tax breaks to the wealthiest 1% of Americans (i.e., households making more than $337,000 a year) while state governments increased taxes to fill a $200 billion budget deficit.[8] Equally alarming, a recent Congressional study revealed that 63% of all corporations in 2000 paid no taxes while "[s]ix in ten corporations reported no tax liability for the five years from 1996 through 2000, even though corporate profits were growing at record-breaking levels during that period."[9] While the rich get tax cuts, 8.2 million people are out of work; some have simply given up even looking for jobs. Moreover, as part of an ongoing effort to destroy public entitlements, the Bush administration has reduced government services, income, and health care; implemented cuts in Medicare and veterans benefits; and trimmed back or eliminated funds for programs for children and for public housing. Neoliberalism has become complicitous with this transformation of the democratic state into a national security state that repeatedly uses its military and political power to develop a daunting police state and military-prison-education-industrial complex to punish workers, stifle dissent, and undermine the political power of labor unions and progressive social movements.

With its debased belief that profit-making is the essence of democracy, and its definition of citizenship as an energized plunge into consumerism, neoliberalism eliminates government regulation of market forces, celebrates a ruthless competitive individualism, and places the commanding political, cultural, and economic institutions of society in the hands of powerful corporate interests, the privileged, and unrepentant religious bigots. Neoliberal global policies also further the broader cultural project of privatizing social services through appeals to "personal responsibility as the proper functions of the state are narrowed, tax and wage costs in the economy are cut, and more social costs are absorbed by civil society and the family."[10] The hard currency of human suffering permeates the social order as health-care costs rise, one out of five children fall beneath the poverty line, and 43 million Americans bear the burden of lacking any health insurance. As part of this larger cultural project fashioned under the sovereignty of neoliberalism, human misery is largely defined as a function of personal choices, and human misfortune is viewed as the basis for criminalizing social problems. Misbehaving children are now put in handcuffs and taken to police stations for violating dress codes. Mothers who test positive for drugs in hospitals run the risk of having their children taken away by police. Young, urban, poor black men who lack employment are targeted by the criminal justice system and, instead of being educated or trained for a job, often end up in jail.

Within the discourse of neoliberalism, democracy becomes synonymous with free markets while issues of equality, social justice, and freedom are stripped of any substantive meaning and used to disparage those who suffer systemic deprivation and chronic punishment. Individual misfortune, like democracy itself, is now viewed as either excessive or in need of radical containment. The media, largely consolidated through corporate power, routinely provide a platform for high-profile right-wing pundits and politicians to remind us of how degenerate the poor have become to reinforce the central neoliberal tenet that all problems are private rather than social in nature. Conservative columnist Ann Coulter captures the latter sentiment with her comment that "[i]nstead of poor people with hope and possibility, we now have a permanent underclass of aspiring criminals knifing one another between having illegitimate children and collecting welfare checks."[11] Radio talk show host Michael Savage, too, exemplifies the unabashed racism and fanaticism that emerges under a neoliberal regime in which ethics and justice appear beside the point. For instance, Savage routinely refers to nonwhite countries as "turd world nations," homosexuality as a "perversion," and young children who are victims of gunfire as "ghetto slime."[12]

As Fredric Jameson has argued in *The Seeds of Time*, it has now become easier to imagine the end of the world than the end of capitalism.[13] The breathless rhetoric of the global victory of free-market rationality spewed forth by the mass media, right-wing intellectuals, and governments alike has found its material expression both in an all-out attack on democratic values and in the growth of a range of social problems including virulent and persistent poverty, joblessness, inadequate health care, racial apartheid in the inner cities, and increasing inequalities between the rich and the poor. Such problems appear to have been either removed from the inventory of public discourse and social policy or factored into talk-show spectacles in which the public becomes merely a staging area for venting private interests and emotions. Within the discourse of neoliberalism that has taken hold of the public imagination, there is no way of talking about what is fundamental to civic life, critical citizenship, and a substantive democracy. Neoliberalism offers no critical vocabulary for speaking about political or social transformation as a democratic project. Nor is there a language for either the ideal of public commitment or the notion of a social agency capable of challenging the basic assumptions of corporate ideology as well as its social consequences. In its dubious appeals to universal laws, neutrality, and selective scientific research, neoliberalism "eliminates the very possibility of critical thinking, without which democratic debate becomes impossible."[14] This shift in rhetoric makes it possible for advocates of neoliberalism to implement the most ruthless economic and political policies without having to open up such actions to public debate and dialogue. Hence, neoliberal policies that promote the cutthroat downsizing of the workforce, the bleeding of social services, the reduction of state governments to police precincts, the ongoing liquidation of job security, the increasing elimination of a decent social wage, the creation of a society of low-skilled workers, and the emergence of a culture of permanent insecurity and fear hide behind appeals to common sense and alleged immutable laws of nature.

When and where such nakedly ideological appeals strain both reason and imagination, religious faith is invoked to silence dissension. Society is no longer defended as a space in which to nurture the most fundamental values and relations necessary to a democracy but has been recast as an ideological and political sphere "where religious fundamentalism comes together with market fundamentalism to form the ideology of American supremacy."[15] Similarly, American imperial ambitions are now legitimated by public relations intellectuals as part of the responsibilities of empire-building, which in turn is now celebrated as a civilizing process for the rest of the globe. Neoconservatives have joined hands with neoliberals and religious fundamentalists in broadcasting to the world at large an American triumphalism in which the United States is arrogantly defined as "[t]he greatest of all great powers in world history."[16] Money, profits, and fear have become powerful ideological elements in arguing for opening up new markets and closing down the possibility of dissent at home. In such a scenario, the police state is celebrated by religious evangelicals like John Ashcroft as a foundation of human freedom. This becomes clear not only in the passage of repressive laws such as the USA PATRIOT Act but also in the work of prominent neoconservatives such as David Frum and Richard Perle who, without any irony intended, insist that "[a] free society is not an un-policed society. A free society is a self-policed society."[17] In what could only be defined as an Adam Smith joins George Orwell in a religious cult in California scenario, markets have been elevated to the status of sacrosanct temples to be worshipped by eager consumers while citizens-turned-soldiers of the Army of God are urged to spy on each other and dissent is increasingly criminalized.[18] Democratic politics is increasingly depoliticized by the intersection of a free-market fundamentalism and an escalating militarism. The consequences can be seen in the commercialization of vibrant public spheres and the attack on civil liberties; it is also evident in a growing militarization at home and abroad organized around the perpetuation of an obsessive culture of fear and the unbridled economic claims of empire, most obvious in the occupation of Iraq. The demise of democracy is also revealed in a policy of anti-terrorism practiced by the Bush administration that mimics the very terrorism it wishes to eliminate. Not only does this policy of all-embracing anti-terrorism exhaust itself in a discourse of moral absolutes, militarism, revenge, and public acts of denunciation, it also strips community of democratic values by configuring politics in religious terms and defining every citizen and inhabitant of the United States as a potential terrorist. Politics becomes empty as it reduces citizens to obedient recipients of power, content to follow orders, while shaming those who make power accountable. Under the dictates of a pseudo-patriotism, dissent is stifled in the face of a growing racism that condemns Arabs and people of color as less than civilized. The recent refusal of the American government to address with any degree of self-criticism or humanity the torture and violation of human rights exercised by American soldiers at Abu Ghraib prison in Iraq offers a case in point. In light of the revelation, captured on camera and video, of the most grotesque brutality, racism, and inhumanity exhibited by American soldiers against Arab prisoners, powerful right-wing politicians and pundits such as Rush Limbaugh and Cal Thomas defend such actions as either a way for young men to "blow some steam off," engage in a form of harmless frat hazing, or give Muslim prisoners what they deserve. It gets worse. Commentators such as Newt Gingrich and Republican Senator James Inhofe have gone so far as to suggest that calling attention to such crimes, not only undermines troop morale in Iraq, but is also unpatriotic. Defending torture and gross sexual humiliations by U.S. troops in Saddam's old jails is not merely insensitive political posturing, it is, more tellingly, indicative of how far the leadership of this country has strayed from any real semblance of democracy.

Political culture, if not the nature of politics itself, has undergone revolutionary changes in the last two decades, reaching its most debased expression under the administration of President George W. Bush. Within this political culture, not only is democracy subordinated to the rule of a market, but corporate decisions are freed from territorial constraints and the demands of public obligations, just as economics is disconnected from its social consequences. Power is now free from territorial constraints, and politics is largely local. Zygmunt Bauman captures what is new about the relationship among power, politics, and the shredding of social obligations:

> The mobility acquired by "people who invest"—those with capital, with money which the investment requires—means the new, indeed unprecedented ... disconnection of power from obligations: duties towards employees, but also towards the younger and weaker, towards yet unborn generations and towards the self-reproduction of the living conditions of all; in short, the freedom from the duty to contribute to daily life and the perpetuation of the community.... Shedding the responsibility for the consequences is the most coveted and cherished gain which the new mobility brings to free-floating, locally unbound capital.[19]

Corporate power increasingly frees itself from any political limitations just as it uses its power through the educational force of the dominant culture to put into place an utterly privatized notion of agency in which it becomes difficult for young people and adults to imagine democracy as a public good, let alone the transformative power of collective action. Democratic politics has become ineffective, if not banal, as civic language is impoverished and genuine spaces for democratic learning, debate, and dialogue, such as schools, newspapers, popular culture, television networks, and other public spheres, are either underfunded, eliminated, privatized, or subject to corporate ownership. Under the politics and culture of neoliberalism (despite its tensions and contradictions), society is increasingly mobilized for the production of violence against the poor, immigrants, dissenters, and others marginalized because of their age, gender, race, ethnicity, and color. At the center of neoliberalism is a new form of politics in the United States—a politics in which radical exclusion is the order of the day, and in which the primary questions no longer concern equality, justice, or freedom but are now about the survival of the slickest in a culture marked by fear, surveillance, and economic deprivation. As Susan George points out, the question that currently seems to define neoliberal "democracy" is "Who has a right to live or does not?"[20]

One of the main arguments of this book is that neoliberalism is not a neutral, technical, economic discourse that can be measured with the precision of a mathematical formula or defended through an appeal to the rules of a presumptively unassailable science that conveniently leaves its own history behind. Nor is it a paragon of economic rationality that offers the best "route to optimum efficiency, rapid economic growth and innovation, and rising prosperity for all who are willing to work hard and take advantage of available opportunities."[21] On the contrary, neoliberalism is an ideology and politics buoyed by the spirit of a market fundamentalism that subordinates the art of democratic politics to the rapacious laws of a market economy that expands its reach to include all aspects of social life within the dictates and values of a market-driven society. More important, it is an economic and implicitly cultural theory—a historical and socially constructed ideology that needs to be made visible, critically engaged, and shaken from the stranglehold of power it currently exercises over most of the commanding institutions of national and global life. As such, neoliberalism makes it difficult for many people either to imagine a notion of individual and social agency necessary for reclaiming a substantive democracy or to theorize the economic, cultural, and political conditions necessary for a viable global public sphere in which public institutions, spaces, and goods become valued as part of a larger democratic struggle for a sustainable future and the downward distribution of wealth, resources, and power.

As a public pedagogy and political ideology, the neoliberalism of Friedrich Hayek and Milton Friedman[22] is far more ruthless than the classic liberal economic theory developed by Adam Smith and David Ricardo in the eighteenth and nineteenth centuries. Neoliberalism has become the current conservative revolution because it harkens back to a period in American history that supported the sovereignty of the market over the sovereignty of the democratic state and the common good. Reproducing the future in the image of the distant past, it represents a struggle designed to roll back, if not dismantle, all of the policies put into place over seventy years ago by the New Deal to curb corporate power and give substance to the liberal meaning of the social contract. The late Pierre Bourdieu captures what is new about neoliberalism in his comment that neoliberalism is

> a new kind of conservative revolution [that] appeals to progress, reason and science (economics in this case) to justify the restoration and so tries to write off progressive thought and action as archaic. It sets up as the norm of all practices, and therefore as ideal rules, the real regularities of the economic world abandoned to its own logic, the so-called laws of the market. It reifies and glorifies the reign of what are called the financial markets, in other words the return to a kind of radical capitalism, with no other law than that of maximum profit, an unfettered capitalism without any disguise, but rationalized, pushed to the limit of its economic efficacy by the introduction of modern forms of domination, such as "business administration," and techniques of manipulation, such as market research and advertising.[23]

Neoliberalism has indeed become a broad-based political and cultural movement designed to obliterate public concerns and liquidate the welfare state, and make politics everywhere an exclusively market-driven project.[24] But neoliberalism does more than make the market "the informing principle of politics"[25] while allocating wealth and resources to those who are most privileged by virtue of their class, race, and power. Its supporting political culture and pedagogical practices also put into play a social universe and cultural landscape that sustain a particularly barbaric notion of authoritarianism, set in motion under the combined power of a religious and market fundamentalism and anti-terrorism laws that suspend civil liberties, incarcerate disposable populations, and provide the security forces necessary for capital to destroy those spaces where democracy can be nourished. All the while, the landscape and soundscape become increasingly homogenized through the spectacle of flags waving from every flowerbox, car, truck, and house, encouraged and supplemented by jingoistic bravado aired by Fox Television News and Clear Channel radio stations. As a cultural politics and a form of economic domination, neoliberalism tells a very limited story, one that is antithetical to nurturing democratic identities, values, and institutions and thereby enables fascism to grow because it has no ethical language for recognizing politics outside the realm of the market, for controlling market excesses, or for challenging the underlying tenets of a growing authoritarianism bolstered by the pretense of religious piety.

Neoliberal ideology, on the one hand, pushes for the privatization of all noncommodified public spheres and the upward distribution of wealth. On the other hand, it supports policies that increasingly militarize facets of public space in order to secure the privileges and benefits of the corporate elite and ultra-rich. Neoliberalism does not merely produce economic inequality, iniquitous power relations, and a corrupt political system; it also promotes rigid exclusions from national citizenship and civic participation. As Lisa Duggan points out, "Neoliberalism cannot be abstracted from race and gender relations, or other cultural aspects of the body politic. Its legitimating discourse, social relations, and ideology are saturated with race, with gender, with sex, with religion, with ethnicity, and nationality."[26] Neoliberalism comfortably aligns itself with various strands of neoconservative and religious fundamentalisms, waging imperial wars abroad as well as at home against those groups and movements that threaten its authoritarian misreading of the meaning of freedom, security, and productiveness.

One controversial example of how big corporations, particularly media conglomerates, use their power to simultaneously support neoliberal values, reactionary policies, and the politicians who produce them took place in 2004 when the Sinclair Broadcast Group, a Maryland-based media company whose holdings include 62 television stations, including several ABC affiliates, refused to air on its stations a special edition of *Nightline* with Ted Koppel. Sinclair was disturbed because Koppel announced that he was going to read the names and show photographs of the faces of the 721 U.S. soldiers killed in Iraq. Sinclair's refusal to air *Nightline* on its ABC stations was based on the argument that Koppel was making a political statement, which allegedly undermined the war effort by drawing attention to its most troubling consequences. Sinclair's rationale for the act of censorship was partly based on the argument that *Nightline* could have read the names of the thousands of citizens killed in terrorists attacks during the events of September 11, 2001. The problem with this accusation, as a statement from ABC made clear shortly after the charge, is that the network did broadcast a list of the 9/11 victims, one year after the gruesome event. What Sinclair did not mention was that it was a generous contributor to the Republican Party and that it has lobbied successfully for policies that have allowed it to own even more stations. Sinclair shares the perspective of many of its corporate allies on the Right who believe that the costs of the war should be hushed up in favor of news that portrays the Bush administration in a favorable light. After all, censoring the news is a small price to pay for the corporate windfalls that reward such acts. Free-market fundamentalism makes it easier for corporate power and political favoritism to mutually inform each other, reinforcing the ideological and political conditions for the perpetuation of a system of profits, money, market-values, and power that allows, as Bill Moyers has pointed out, big corporations and big government to scratch each others's back, while cancelling out the principles of justice and human dignity that inform a real democracy.[27]

The main argument of this book is that neoliberalism has to be understood and challenged as both an economic theory and a powerful public pedagogy and cultural politics. That is, it has to be named and critically understood before it can be critiqued. The common-sense assumptions that legitimate neoliberalism's alleged historical inevitability have to be unsettled and then engaged for the social damage they cause at all levels of human existence. Hence, I attempt to identify and critically examine many of the most salient and powerful ideologies that inform and frame neoliberalism. I am also arguing for making cultural politics and the notion of public pedagogy central to the struggle against neoliberalism, particularly since education and culture now play such a prominent political and economic role in both securing consent and producing capital. In fact, my position is similar to Susan Buck-Morss's argument that "[t]he recognition of cultural domination as just as important as, and perhaps even as the condition of possibility of, political and economic domination is a true 'advance' in our thinking."[28] Of course, this position is meant not to disavow economic and institutional struggles but to supplement them with a cultural politics that connects symbolic power and its pedagogical practices with material relations of power. What I am calling for in this case is a new language for addressing "social and cultural learning and reproduction in the context of globalization and the way in which globalization itself constitutes a problem of and for pedagogy."[29] In addition, I analyze how neoliberal policies work at the level of everyday life through the language of privatization and the lived cultural forms of class, race, gender, youth, and ethnicity. Finally, I attempt in every chapter to employ a language of critique and possibility, engagement and hope, as part of a broader project of viewing democracy as a site of intense struggle over matters of representation, participation, and shared power.

Central to this book is the belief, as Alain Touraine argues, that neoliberal globalization has not "dissolved our capacity for political action."[30] Such action depends on the ability of various groups—the peace movement, the anti-corporate globalization movement, the human rights movement, the environmental justice movement—within and across national boundaries to form alliances in which matters of global justice, community, and solidarity provide a common symbolic space and multiple public spheres where norms are created, debated, and engaged as part of an attempt to develop a new political language, culture, and set of relations. Such efforts must be understood as part of a broader attempt not only to collectively struggle against domination but also to defend all those social advances that strengthen democratic public spheres and services, demand new rights, establish modes of power sharing, and create notions of social justice adequate to imagining and sustaining democracy on a global level. Consider, for example, the anti-corporate globalization movement's slogan "Another World Is Possible!" which demands, as Alex Callinicos insightfully points out, a different kind of social logic, a powerful sense of unity and solidarity.

> Another *world*—that is, a world based on a different social logic, run according to different priorities from those that prevail today. It is easy enough to specify what the desiderata of such an alternative social logic would be—social justice, economic efficiency, environmental sustainability, and democracy—but much harder to spell out how a reproducible social system embodying these requirements could be built. And then there is the question of how to achieve it. Both these questions—What is the alternative to capitalism? What strategy can get us there?—can be answered in different ways. One thing the anti-capitalist movement is going to have to learn is how to argue through the differences that exist and will probably develop around such issues without undermining the very powerful sense of unity that has been one of the movement's most attractive qualities.[31]

Callinicos's insight suggests that any viable struggle against neoliberal capitalism will have to rethink "the entire project of politics within

the changed conditions of a global public sphere, and to do this democratically, as people who speak different political languages, but whose
goals are nonetheless the same: global peace, economic justice, legal
equality, democratic participation, individual freedom, mutual respect."[32]
One of the central tasks facing intellectuals, activists, educators, and
others who believe in an inclusive and substantive democracy is the
need to use theory to rethink the language and possibilities of politics
as a way to imagine a future outside the powerful grip of neoliberalism
and the impending authoritarianism that has a different story to tell
about the future, one that reinvents the past in the image of the crude
exercise of power and the unleashing of unimaginable human suffering. Critical reflection and social action in this discourse must acknowledge how the category of the global public sphere extends the space of
politics beyond the boundaries of local resistance. Global problems
need global institutions, global modes of dissent, global intellectual
work, and global social movements.

In Chapter 1, I examine various debates about the growing authoritarianism in the United States and how neoliberal ideology
becomes complicitous in reproducing the conditions for a new type
of domination and proto-fascism. This chapter chronicles those forces that are not only suspicious of democracy but are aggressively at
work to hollow out its substantive content and undercut its most
basic values and principles. In Chapter 2, I address the ways in which
the discourse of neoliberalism privatizes the language of race while
demonizing and punishing poor blacks and other youth of color as
part of a larger attack on the welfare state. Focusing on race as a
category through which racial exclusions and violence are abstracted
from public issues and considerations, I discuss how public considerations become privatized, reduced to matters of taste, character, and
personal responsibility. In Chapter 3, I look at how a war is being
waged against poor whites and kids of color, and how this war focuses on punishing students in public schools rather than investing
financially and intellectually in their education and future. This chapter explores how various aspects of public life, especially for young
people, are being militarized—a trend that is particularly noticeable
in public schools. In Chapter 4, I address what it means to understand neoliberalism as a form of public pedagogy and discuss how
the latter concept might become theoretically useful in rethinking
strategies necessary to struggle individually and collectively against
its most basic assumptions about the social order, work, education,
and the larger global public sphere. In Chapter 5, I urge intellectuals

to restore an enlightened notion of the future of democratic public life as well as forms of resistance to neoliberalism grounded in the spirit of a militant hope and the creation of broader, more democratic social movements. And in Chapter 6 I conclude by examining the late Edward Said's view of what it means to be an engaged and public intellectual willing to fight against the ravages of the neoliberalism and imperialism at work in the United States and abroad.

I
Living in the Shadow of Authoritarianism

⊸⊝

Introduction

> I submit that neo-liberalism has changed the fundamental nature of pol-
> itics. Politics used to be primarily about who ruled whom and who got
> what share of the pie. Aspects of both these central questions remain, of
> course, but the great new central question of politics is, in my view, "Who
> has a right to live and who does not." Radical exclusion is now the order
> of the day and I mean this deadly seriously.[1]

Following the tragic events of September 11, 2001, the United States
garnered the sympathy and respect of many nations all over the
globe. The killing of 3,000 innocent people by terrorist thugs not
only offered a vivid example of a grotesque assault on human life
and human rights but also underscored the vulnerability of one of
the world's most powerful democracies. Tragedy was followed by
myriad examples of human courage among many Americans, and a
spirit of political resilience gave the federal government a renewed
credibility for a short time. Controversial and albeit "leading apolo-
gist for neoauthoritarian politics,"[2] former New York Mayor Rudolph
Guiliani exhibited a newfound leadership that made all the more
visible the principles, values, and sense of compassion central to a
vibrant democracy. At the same time, the international community
rallied behind the United States whose democracy appeared wounded but whose strength was revealed in its willingness to respond to
an egregious act of terrorism with displays of compassion and national

1

unity. The French newspaper *Le Monde* captured this sense of international solidarity and support when it proclaimed, "We Are All Americans." But within two years, the cache of respect and regard that had been accorded the Bush administration both at home and abroad dwindled considerably as an increasing number of nations and individuals came to regard the United States as a major threat to world peace, if not to democracy itself. As Senator Robert C. Byrd put it, "In some corners of the world, including some corners of Europe and Great Britain, our beloved nation is now viewed as the world bully."[3] The Bush administration's unilateral policy quickly turned America's allies into some of its most severe critics. Even *New York Times* columnist Thomas Friedman, no enemy of dominant power, asserted that "Europeans have embraced President Bush's formulation that an 'axis of evil' threatens world peace. There's only one small problem. President Bush thinks the axis of evil is Iran, Iraq, and North Korea, and the Europeans think it's Donald Rumsfeld, Dick Cheney, and Condi [Condoleezza] Rice."[4]

The events of September 11th hastened a major shift not only in domestic and foreign policy but also "in our nation's self-understanding. It became commonplace to refer to an 'American Empire' and to the United States as 'the world's only superpower.'"[5] Embracing a policy molded largely by fear and bristling with partisan, right-wing ideological interests, the Bush administration took advantage of the tragedy of 9/11 by adopting and justifying a domestic and foreign policy that blatantly privileged security over freedom, the rule of the market over social needs, and militarization over human rights and social justice. Multilateralism in foreign affairs gave way to reckless unilateralism and a gross disregard for international law fueled by a foreign policy that defined itself through the arrogance of unbridled power. Refusing to sign a number of landmark international agreements such as the Antiballistic Missile Treaty, the International Criminal Court, and the Kyoto Protocol, the Bush administration increasingly displayed an "insulting arrogance toward the United Nations in general, and individual members in particular."[6] National security was now delineated as part of a larger policy in which the United States has the right to use preventive military force "to eliminate a perceived threat, even if invented or imagined."[7] Senator Byrd described the unprecedented Bush doctrine of preemptive strike as an irresponsible policy that sets a dangerous precedent, undermines Congress's constitutional authority to declare war, and produces a "rising tide of anti-Americanism across the globe."[8] Global hegemony now became synonymous with national security as official policy proclaimed that any challenge to U.S. power and supremacy would be blocked by military force.[9] After the attack on Afghanistan, Iraq was invaded by American forces and justified through what later was proved to be a series of blatant and misleading arguments by the Bush administration.[10] Empire soon became the requisite term to define American power abroad. What has become clear since the invasion of Iraq is the willingness of the Bush administration to wage a war on terrorism at the expense of civil liberties, just as it scrapped a foreign policy that at least made a gesture toward democratic values for one that unleashed untold violence in the name of combating evil and exercising control over all other global powers. As Robert Jay Lifton points out, war has now taken on a mythic and heroic status under the Bush administration, "carried out for the defense of one's nation, to sustain its special historical destiny and the immortality of its people."[11] Such a doctrine is far from heroic, not only resulting in widespread fear, anxiety, massive suffering, and death but also completely undermining the credibility of the American government as a bastion of democracy. The pictures of U.S. soldiers grinning as they tortured and sexually humiliated Iraqi prisoners at Abu Ghraib has further undermined the moral and political credibility of the United States both in the Arab world and around the globe. Restoring one of Saddam Hussein's most infamous torture chambers to its original use has reinforced the image of the United States as a dangerous, rogue state with despicable imperial ambitions. As columnist Katha Pollitt puts it

> The pictures and stories [from Abu Ghraib] have naturally caused a furor around the world. Not only are they grotesque in themselves, they reinforce the pre-existing impression of Americans as racist, cruel and frivolous. They are bound to alienate—further alienate—Iraqis who hoped that the invasion would lead to secular democracy and a normal life and who fear Islamic rule. Abroad, if not here at home, they underscore how stupid and wrong the invasion of Iraq was in the first place, how predictably the "war of choice" that was going to be a cakewalk has become a brutal and corrupt occupation, justified by a doctrine of American exceptionalism that nobody but Americans believe.[12]

Patricia Williams writing in *The Nation* goes further by linking the criminal abuse of Iraqi detainees at Abu Ghraib prison to a web of secrecy, violation of civil rights, and racist violence that has become commonplace on the domestic front. Referring to the public images of torture and humiliation at Abu Ghraib prison, she writes:

> [I]t's awfully hard not to look at those hoods and think Inquisition; or the piles of naked and sodomized men and think Abner Louima; or the battered corpses and think of Emmett Till. . . . This mess is the predictable byproduct of any authority that starts "sweeping" up "bad guys" and holding them without charge, in solitary and in secret, and presuming them guilty. It flourished beyond the reach of any formal oversight by Congress, by lawyers or by the judiciary, a condition vaguely rationalized as "consistent with" if not "precisely" pursuant to the Geneva Conventions. Bloodied prisoners were moved around to avoid oversight by international observers, a rather too disciplined bit of sanitizing.[13]

On the domestic front, a strange mixture of neoconservative ideologues, free-market right-wingers, and evangelical Christians began to wage another kind of war, not only against the social contract that had been put in place by Franklin Delano Roosevelt's New Deal and Lyndon Johnson's Great Society, but also against the secular government and the long-standing division between church and state, secular reason and religious beliefs. The needs of poor, working-class, and middle-class Americans are now under siege by the federal government, which instituted tax cuts for the richest 1 percent, increased corporate welfare, bankrolled a massive military machine, and turned a 2001 government surplus of $127 billion into a deficit of $521 billion by 2004.[14] In short, public assets have been hijacked by those at the top of the economic pyramid, leaving few public resources for financially strapped state and local governments to use for addressing new problems or long-term improvements. One specific—and intended—outcome of this policy is that there is very little money or assistance available for those Americans most in need. The rich get tax handouts and corporate relief while the most basic health-care services for children, the elderly, and the disabled are either cut or dramatically reduced.[15] For example, "about 270,000 children of low-income, working parents have been barred from health insurance programs in the nine states where estimates are available."[16] The Center on Budget and Policy Priorities reports that with thirty-four states making cuts over the last two years in public health insurance programs, "[s]ome 1.2 million to 1.6 million low-income people— including 490,000 to 650,000 children and large numbers of parents, seniors, and people with disabilities—have lost public-funded health coverage as a result."[17] Over 37 percent of all children lack health insurance in the world's wealthiest nation. Under President Bush's 2004 budget, it has been estimated that about "600,000 children will lose child-care and after-school services."[18] The long-standing social contract that was central to American democracy is not simply deteriorating, it is under sustained attack by free-market extremists and right-wingers. In what is truly one of the most glaring contradictions of the current Republican-led government, vast numbers of people are now being cut by the Bush administration from the most basic social provisions and public resources at the same time that Bush and his aids are increasingly using the hyped-up language of religious morality and "compassionate conservatism" to defend the discourse of free-market fundamentalism and a politics that largely caters to the rich and powerful. Congressman Bernie Sanders, in an exchange in 2003 with FED Chairman Alan Greenspan, provides a more specific indication of the social costs incurred by the neoconservative and right-wing free-market policies recently put into place:

> You [Greenspan] talk about an improving economy while we have lost 3 million private sector jobs in the last two years, long-term unemployment is more than tripled, unemployment is higher than it's been since 1994. We have a $4 trillion national debt, 1.3 million Americans have lost their health insurance, millions of seniors can't afford prescription drugs, middle-class families can't send their kids to college because they don't have the money to do that, bankruptcy cases have increased by a record-breaking 23 percent, business investment is at its lowest level in more than 50 years, CEOs make more than 500 times what their workers make, the middle class is shrinking, we have the greatest gap between the rich and the poor of any industrialized nation, and this is an economy that is improving?[19]

President George W. Bush sees no irony in proclaiming in one speech after another, largely to highly selected groups of conservatives, that he is a "born again" Christian, all the while ruthlessly passing legislation that weakens environmental laws such as the Clean Air Act, opposes a U.N. resolution to fund global AIDS education and prevention, undermines the stability of Medicare, wages a budget war against disadvantaged children, denies millions of poor working adults a child tax credit, squanders the federal surplus on tax cuts for the rich, and increases corporate welfare to the tune of $125 billion as he decreases social benefits for millions of Americans, especially those who are poverty-stricken, old, young, and disabled.[20]

Religious fundamentalism appears to be growing in the United States, and the movement has received an enormous boost from those in power who think of themselves as "chosen." At the same time, this mounting religious fervor, with its Manichean division of the world into the modalities of good and evil, remains inhospitable to dissent and reinforces a distinctly undemocratic view of patriotism. The slide into self-righteousness and intolerance appears to be on the rise in American life as politicians and moralists lay claim to an alleged monopoly on the truth, based on their religious conviction—an outlandish presumption matched only by utter disdain for those who do not share their worldview.[21] Under the Bush administration patriotism is now legitimated through the physics of unaccountable power and unquestioned authority, defined crudely in the dictum "Either you are with us or with the terrorists."[22] When millions all over the world (including numerous international allies) protested the U.S. invasion of Iraq, Bush and his evangelical counselors simply dismissed such criticism as evidence of weakness and a refusal to acknowledge evil. As Gary Wills sums it up: "Question the policy, and you no longer believe in evil—which is the same, in this context, as not believing in God. That is the religious test on which our president is grading us."[23]

This culture of intolerance and patriotic jingoism is readily shared and legitimated by the corporate controlled media and an army of intellectual cheerleaders, largely bankrolled by a powerful conservative money machine including the Olin, Heritage, Coors, and Scaife Family Foundations. Such absolutes, of course, have little respect for difference, dissent, or even democracy itself. Politics in this instance has much less in common with public engagement, dialogue, and democratic governance than with a heavy reliance on institutions that rule through fear and, if necessary, brute force. Right-wing media favorite Ann Coulter not only asserts in her book *Treason* that "liberals are either traitors or idiots"[24] but argues elsewhere as well that John Walker, the young American captured in Afghanistan, should be given the death penalty "in order to physically intimidate liberals, by making them realize that they can be killed too. Otherwise they can be turned into outright traitors."[25] Kathleen Parker, a conservative columnist, published an article in which she cites, without challenging, a quote from "a friend" who suggested that a number of Democratic Party candidates "should be lined up and shot."[26] On the syndicated radio talk show, *Savage Nation,* which was aired on May 10–11, 2004, conservative host, Michael Savage referred to Abu Ghraib prison as "Grab-an-Arab prison" and stated that "We need more of the humiliation, not less.... [T]here should be no mercy shown to the sub-humans. I believe that a thousand of them should be killed tomorrow. I think a thousand of them held in the Iraqi prison should be [put on] trial and executed.... They should put dynamite in their behinds and drop them from 35,000 feet, the whole pack of scum out of that jail."[27]

Such rhetorical interventions are about more than eliminating the critical function of dissent or thinking itself, both vital to the democratic health of a society; they embody a kind of violence that suggests that critics and "others" seen as enemies of the United States should be targeted and punished. Such polemic is characteristic of a distrust of not only Muslims and people of color but also the intellectual world and Enlightenment thought now viewed as the "beginning of modern depravity." Moreover, this "disagreement is treason" bravado has a lot in common with traditional fascist movements that attacked critical thinking as a way of "exploiting and exacerbating the natural fear of difference."[28] Put differently, the embrace of anti-intellectualism and distrust of critical thought and intellectuals supports authoritarianism over and against democracy. Such rhetoric cannot be dismissed as an aberration. Unfortunately, this kind of extreme language is not only found among eccentric right-wing intellectuals; it is also on prominent display in mainstream Republican Party rhetoric. For example, when the Republican Party launched its 2004 campaign to reelect George W. Bush, it produced an ad that stated "Some are now attacking the president for attacking the terrorists." As rhetorically dishonest as it is opportunistic, the ad both misrepresents the complexity of a post–9/11 world and suggests that critics of Bush's policies support terrorism. Critics are not supporting terrorism. Instead, they are pointing out that the Bush administration has squandered much-needed funds by invading Iraq and in doing so has lost sight of the real threats posed by terrorists while seriously "undermining the campaign against terrorism."[29]

I am not suggesting that all conservatives support this kind of sophistry or believe in these deeply undemocratic sentiments and actions, though I am concerned by the refusal of many prominent conservatives to condemn the McCarthyite, if not fascistic ranting of the likes of Ann Coulter, Rush Limbaugh, Pat Robertson, and Michael Savage, among others. I do think the right-wing takeover of the Republican Party and its relentless appeal to the moral high ground—coupled with its ongoing demonization and punishment of those on the Right and Left who dare to question its policies—shut down the possibility for dialogue and exchange, thereby silencing those who wish to make power visible as well as politically and morally account-able in a democracy. But this type of politics does more than cele-brate its own intolerance; it also lays the groundwork for a kind of authoritarianism that views democracy as both a burden and a threat.

As the federal government is restructured under the Bush admin-istration, it relies more heavily on its militarizing functions, giving free rein to the principle of security at the expense of public service, and endorsing property rights over human rights. As a consequence, democracy is imperiled as the emerging security state offers the Amer-ican people the false choice between being safe or free.[30] In the name of security, the distinction between government power and "laws governing the rights of people accused of a crime"[31] is lost. A web of secrecy has emerged under the Bush administration that gives it the opportunity to abuse democratic freedoms and at the same time make itself unaccountable for its actions by using national security to its legal advantage. Under the veil of legislated secrecy, the U.S. government can now name individuals as terrorists without offering them a public hearing and break into the private homes and tap the phones of U.S. citizens without a warrant. As if this were not bad enough, constitutional freedoms and civil liberties are fur-ther compromised by the power of government agents to subpoena anybody's telephone, medical, bookstore, library, or university records "simply by certifying that the records are needed for an investigation of international terrorism."[32] The CIA and Pentagon are allowed to engage in domestic intelligence work, and the USA PATRIOT Act allows government to detain people secretly and indefinitely without access to either lawyers or a jury trial.[33] Even children as young as 14 have been held without legal representation as enemy combatants in possibly inhumane conditions at the military's infamous Camp Delta at Guantanamo Bay, Cuba. Under such circumstances, as Arundhati Roy argues, "the fundamental governing principles of democracy are not just being subverted but deliberately sabotaged. This kind of democracy is the problem, not the solution."[34] Dissent does not come easy in a country where people can be detained, deported, tried without representation, and held indefinitely in a jail under a legal policy of enforced secrecy.

One recent example can be found in the willingness of the gov-ernment to serve subpoenas to four activists who attended an anti-war conference at Drake University on November 15, 2003. Not only were the students ordered to appear before a grand jury investiga-tion, but Drake University was ordered by a federal judge to provide information about the anti-war conference, specifically the records of those who were in control of the conference as well as those who attended.[35] In this instance, there is strong evidence to suggest that the USA PATRIOT Act is being used to target certain forms of political activities, intimidate protesters, and stifle the free-speech rights of those protesting the policies of the Bush administration.[36] Authoritarianism's shadow becomes increasingly darker as society is organized relentlessly around a culture of unquestioned obedience, fear, cynicism, and unbridled self-interest—a society in which the government promotes legislation urging neighbors to spy on each other and the president endorses a notion of patriotism based on moral absolutes and an alleged Christian mandate to govern (with a little help, of course, from Jeb Bush and the U.S. Supreme Court).[37] The arrogance of power is on full display as both the president and the attorney general, in the name of national security, refuse to give congressional committees information they have requested about a range of government actions, including Vice President Cheney's meetings in the White House with representatives of the energy industry and materials related to the government's anti-terrorist policies prior to the tragic events of 9/11. The Bush administration's obsession with secrecy was shamelessly invoked when the President and Vice-President agreed to appear before the 9/11 Commission only if the meeting took place behind closed doors. They did not have to testify under oath, and it was agreed that the session would not be recorded.

The New Rhetoric Against Extremism and Proto-Fascism

It is against the restructuring of American power and ideology that a number of critics at home and across the globe have begun to suggest that a new form of political tyranny is emerging in the United States that threatens not only its underlying democratic values but also peace abroad.[38] The chorus of complaints and criticisms is disturbing. One of the world's most respected elder statesman, South African leader Nelson Mandela, claimed in an interview with *Newsweek* that George W. Bush's rhetoric about democracy is a sham and that U.S. foreign policy is motivated by a "desire to please the arms and oil industries in the United States." He further argued that a foreign policy built on the unilateral right to invade alleged enemies both undermines the United Nations and sets a dangerous standard in foreign affairs for the enemies of democracy. In light of the U.S. invasion of Iraq, Mandela insisted that "the United States has become a threat to world peace."[39] He is not alone in thinking this. In a recent survey of 7,500 Europeans, the United States was ranked second, above even Kim Jong Il's nuclear-armed North Korea and terrorist-sponsoring Iran, as the greatest threat to world peace.[40] Ken Livingston, the mayor of London, denounced George W. Bush as "the greatest threat to life on this planet that we've most probably ever seen."[41] An equally disturbing critique has emerged, suggesting that the U.S. government not only poses a danger to world peace but has completely abdicated its democratic traditions—and its "conserving" values—in favor of radical extremism. As George Soros, respected philanthropist and multibillionaire, puts it: "The Republican Party has been captured by a bunch of extremists."[42] U.S. Senator Robert Byrd, on the floor of the Congress in October 2003, went so far as to compare Bush's use of the media to the propaganda techniques employed by the leaders of the Third Reich. Drawing comparisons between the Bush administration and the infamous Nazi murderer Herman Goering, Byrd offered a biting criticism of the growing extremism in the Bush administration.[43] In his book *Made in Texas,* Michael Lind argues that Bush is one of the worst presidents in American history and that his mission is to carry out the economic and foreign policy agenda of the far Right.[44] The notion of extremism has also been raised by former national security advisor to President Jimmy Carter, Zbiginiew Brzezinski, who claims that the Bush administration's "war on terrorism" represents "a rather narrow and extremist vision of foreign policy of the world's primary superpower."[45] Administration insiders such as Karen Kwiatowski, a former Air Force lieutenant and specialist in the office of the Undersecretary of Defense for Policy, claims that "the country has been hijacked" by neoconservatives who are running a shadow government.[46] And in response to Bush's radical market fundamentalism and neoliberal ideology, American Nobel Prize laureate for economics George A. Akerlof stated in an interview with *Der Spiegel* magazine that

> this is the worst government the US has ever had in its more than 200 years of history. It has engaged in extraordinarily irresponsible policies not only in foreign and economic but also in social and environmental policy. This is not normal government policy. Now is the time for people to engage in civil disobedience.[47]

An even more serious attack against the Bush administration has emerged among a number of critics who claim that the United States is increasingly abandoning democracy altogether, as it descends into the icy political waters of a new form of authoritarianism. Two critics who have received attention in the popular press for such arguments are Arundhati Roy, Indian novelist and social activist, and Sheldon Wolin, emeritus professor of politics at Princeton University. Both individuals have argued that the specter of a creeping fascism is becoming a reality in the United States and that democracy is not just being challenged but transformed by a form of authoritarianism that, almost unnoticed, is shaping political culture and daily life. According to Roy, the commanding institutions of American life have now been sold to the highest bidder, largely subverted by neoliberal capitalists who have "mastered the technique of infiltrating the instruments of democracy—the 'independent' judiciary, the 'free' press[—] … and molding them to their purpose."[48] Roy is particularly concerned about corporate control of the media in the United States and the role it plays in perpetuating an ultra-patriotic fervor that shuts down dissent and renders dominant power free from responsibility for its actions. She points in particular to Clear Channel Communications, the largest radio broadcaster in the United States; reaching more than 200 million people, it has organized pro-war rallies, refused to give airtime to artists critical of the war, and engaged in ongoing efforts to manufacture not only consent but the news itself.[49] Citing how democracy is undermined by the commercialization of public space, the control of the media, the ongoing erosion of civil liberties, the rise of repressive state power, and the emergence of an era of systemic automated surveillance—all of which is reinforced by the war against terrorism—Roy argues that the price of alleged new democracy in Iraq and other countries is the "death of real democracy at home."[50] In light of these dramatic shifts away from democratic principles and social relations, she asserts that American society has entered an historical period when dominant economic and state power has removed itself from the dynamics of political constraint and public accountability. The overall result is that the space of freedom is undermined, constituting a step toward fascism. She writes:

> The incipient, creeping fascism of the past few years has been groomed by many of our "democratic" institutions. Everyone has flirted with it—[Congress], the press, the police, the administration, the public. Even "secularists" have been guilty of helping to create the right climate. Each time you defend the right of an institution, any institution (including the Supreme Court), to exercise unfettered, unaccountable power that must

never be challenged, you move toward fascism. To be fair, perhaps not everyone recognized the early signs for what they were.[51]

Roy was heavily criticized in the American media for opposing the war in Iraq, the implication being that such criticism amounted to supporting terrorism. This position was legitimated in the highest reaches of the government of the United States and stated publicly by Attorney General John Ashcroft[52]—a charge I've already established as routine. She was also roundly condemned for suggesting that the United States was increasingly behaving like a fascist state.[53] Roy's use of the term *fascism* was intended not so much to imply a crude parallel between the Bush administration and Hitler's Nazi Germany as to suggest how extremist the Republican Party has become since the appointment of George W. Bush in 2000.

Sheldon Wolin, a world-renowned political theorist, wrote a much more damning article about the growing authoritarianism in the United States. Refusing to engage in rhetorical excesses, Wolin argues that "[w]e are facing forms of domination that exceed the old vocabulary and so we have to try to find language that corresponds to this condition."[54] Rather than argue that the United States has become an authoritarian regime in the manner of Nazi Germany or fascist Italy during the 1930s and '40s, Wolin, like Roy, argues that the United States exhibits both similarities with and differences from these regimes. Specifically, the United States shares with both of these totalitarian societies an administration and political party whose aim is "to promote empire abroad and corporate [interests] at home," while at the same time "seeking total power."[55] Wolin argues that the Bush administration is moving toward an "inverted totalitarianism"; in sharing the Nazi "aspiration toward unlimited power and aggressive expansionism, their methods and actions seem upside down."[56] Whereas the Nazis filled the streets with thugs in their drive toward unlimited power, the Bush administration centers its power in the unbridled reach of government and the massively concentrated power of a corporate-controlled media. And whereas the Nazis subordinated big business to the political regime, under the Bush regime corporate power shapes political policy. In addition, "[w]hile Nazi totalitarianism strove to give the masses a sense of collective power and strength, *Kraft durch Freude* ("Strength Through Joy"), inverted totalitarianism promotes a sense of weakness, of collective futility."[57] For Wolin, these differences suggest a departure in the way political power is mobilized and a reconfiguration of the institutional and social agents at the heart of such struggle. But, in both cases, the aim is the same: the elimination of democracy and the concentration of power and control in the hands of a single party and the ruling corporate elite. According to Wolin, all of the elements are in place for what he calls the "attempted transformation of a tolerably free society into a variant of the extreme regimes of the past century." He writes:

> Thus the elements are in place: a weak legislative body, a legal system that is both compliant and repressive, a party system in which one party, whether in opposition or in the minority, is bent upon reconstituting the existing system so as to permanently favor a ruling class of the wealthy, the well-connected and the corporate, while leaving the poorer citizens with a sense of helplessness and political despair, and, at the same time, keeping the middle classes dangling between fear of unemployment and expectations of fantastic rewards once the new economy recovers. That scheme is abetted by a sycophantic and increasingly concentrated media; by the integration of universities with their corporate benefactors; by a propaganda machine institutionalized in well-funded think tanks and conservative foundations; by the increasingly closer cooperation between local police and national law enforcement agencies aimed at identifying terrorists, suspicious aliens and domestic dissidents.[58]

The most public rebuke to Wolin came from James Traub writing in the *New York Times Magazine*. Traub denounced critics such as Roy and Wolin as "Weimar Whiners" and argued that any comparison between the Bush administration and the Hitler regime "constitutes a gross trivialization of the worst event in modern history."[59] According to Traub, *fascism* is a term that was abused by the Left in the 1960s and is being used recklessly once again by those criticizing the Bush regime. His argument suggests that fascism is a historically specific movement whose ideology cannot be applied outside of the conditions in which it emerged. In short, Traub implies that any suggestion that the United States is becoming a fascist state is simply preposterous. Perfectly at ease with the increasing repressions established under the Bush administration as well as the violations of civil liberties put into place by John Ashcroft, Traub cites Norman Siegel, the former head of the New York Civil Liberties Union, to suggest that the USA PATRIOT Act has nothing to do with a creeping fascism and may be well-justified as part of the current war on terrorism. If Traub is to be believed, democracy in the United States is as strong as ever. However, Traub's argument is informed by the mistaken

13

notion "that the collapse of fascist regimes represented the death of fascism; it mistakes the regime for the ideology and movement." No critic is saying that the United States now mimics the fascism of the 1930s; rather, the point is that it appears to be developing a number of characteristics that are endemic to fascist ideology. Traub has no sense of different degrees or gradations of authoritarianism, of fascism as an ideology that can always reconstitute itself in different ideas, practices, and arguments. Instead, he clings to both a reductive understanding of fascism and a simplistic binary logic which holds that a country is either authoritarian or democratic. He has no language for entertaining either a mixture of both systems or a degree of unaccountable power that might suggest a more updated, if not different, form of authoritarianism.

Emerging Elements of Authoritarianism and Proto-Fascism in the United States

In what follows, I argue that fascism and authoritarianism are important categories that need to be mined in order to explore the changing nature of power, control, and rule in the United States and the challenge that such changes pose to a democracy clearly under siege. I want to make clear from the outset that I am not suggesting the United States is engaged in a process of genocidal terror against racialized populations—though the increase in police brutality in the last decade against people of color, coupled with the rise of a prison-industrial-military complex that primarily punishes black men, cannot be overlooked.[60] Nor can the increased attack by the American government on the rights of many innocent Arabs, Muslims, and immigrants be understood as anything other than a kind of totalitarian time-warp in which airport terminals now resemble state prisons as foreign nationals are fingerprinted, photographed, and interrogated.[61] Rather, I am arguing that the United States has many earmarks of a growing authoritarianism, the characteristics of which I spell out below. Fascism is not an ideological apparatus frozen in a particular historical period but a theoretical and political signpost for understanding how democracy can be subverted, if not destroyed. Bertram Gross in the 1980s wrote a book titled *Friendly Fascism* in which he argued that if fascism came to the United States it would not embody the fascist characteristics that were associated with its legacies in the past.[62] There would be no Nuremberg rallies, doctrines of racial superiority, government-sanctioned book burnings, death camps, or the abrogation of the constitution. In short, fascism would not take the form of an ideological grid from the past simply downloaded onto another country under different historical conditions. On the contrary, he believed that fascism is an eternal danger and has the ability to become relevant under new conditions, taking on familiar forms of thought that resonate with nativist traditions, experiences, and political relations. Umberto Eco, in his discussion of "eternal fascism," argues that an updated version of fascism will not openly assume the mantle of historical fascism; rather, new forms of authoritarianism will appropriate some of its elements. Like Gross, Eco asserts that fascism, if it comes to America, will have a different guise, though it will be no less destructive of democracy. He writes:

> Ur-Fascism [a term meaning "eternal fascism"] is still around us, sometimes in plainclothes. It would be much easier for us if there appeared on the world scene somebody saying, "I want to reopen Auschwitz, I want the Blackshirts to parade again in the Italian squares." Life is not that simple. Ur-Fascism can come back under the most innocent of disguises. Our duty is to uncover it and to point our finger at any of its new instances—everyday, in every part of the world. Franklin Roosevelt's words of November 4, 1938, are worth recalling: 'If American democracy ceases to move forward as a living force, seeking day and night by peaceful means to better the lot of our citizens, fascism will grow in strength in our land.' Freedom and liberation are an unending task.[63]

In order to make a distinction between the old and new forms of fascism, I want to use the term *proto-fascism*, not only because it suggests a different constellation of elements and forms pointing toward its reconstitution but also because it has "the beauty of familiarity, and rightly in many cases reveals a deliberate attempt to make fascism relevant in new conditions."[64] The point here is not to obscure the distinctiveness of the nature, force, or consequences of the old fascism but to highlight how some of its central elements are emerging in contemporary forms. Precise accounts of the meaning of *fascism* abound, and I have no desire, given its shifting nature, to impose a rigid definition with universal pretensions. But most scholars agree that fascism is a mass movement that emerges out of a failed democracy and that its ideology is extremely anti-liberal, anti-democratic, and anti-socialistic. It is also marked by an "elaborate ideology which covers all aspects of man's existence and which contains a powerful chiliastic [messianic or religious] moment."[65] As a political philosophy, fascism exalts the nation and race—or some purified form of national identity—over the individual, supports centralized dictatorial power, demands blind obedience from the masses, and promotes a top-down revolution. As a social order, it is generally characterized by a system of terror directed against perceived enemies of the state; a monopolistic control of the mass media; an expanding prison system; a state monopoly of weapons; the existence of privileged groups and classes; control of the economy by a limited number of people; unbridled corporatism; "the appeal to emotion and myth rather than reason; the glorification of violence on behalf of a national cause; the mobilization and militarization of civil society; [and] an expansionist foreign policy intended to promote national greatness."[66] Robert Paxton provides a working definition of fascism that points to both its anti-democratic moments and those elements that link it to both the past and the present. Paxton's point is not to provide precise definitions of fascism but to understand the conditions which enabled fascism to work and enable its development in the future. He writes:

> A form of political behavior marked by obsessive preoccupation with community decline, humiliation or victimhood and by compensatory cults of unity, energy and purity, in which a mass-based party of committed nationalist militants, working in uneasy but effective collaboration with traditional elites, abandons democratic liberties and pursues with redemptive violence and without ethical or legal restraints goals of internal cleansing and external expansion.[67]

I argue in this chapter that the specter of fascism resides in the lived relations of a given social order and the ways in which such relations exacerbate the material conditions of inequality, undercut a sense of individual and social agency, hijack democratic values, and promote a deep sense of hopelessness and cynicism. Proto-fascism as both an ideology and a set of social practices emerges within the contradictions that mark such relations, scorning the present while calling for a revolution that rescues a deeply anti-modernist past as a way to revolutionize the future. Mark Neocleous touches on the anti-modernist nature of fascist ideology in his discussion of a "reactionary modernism" that is typical of the New Right and whose project is essentially ultraconservative. He writes:

> [The New Right] pitted itself against the existing order—the post-war "consensus" regarding welfarism and the quasi corporate management of capitalism—in the light of an image of past national glory (a mythic and

contradictory image, but no less powerful for that). The central elements of New Right politics—an aggressive leadership, uncompromising stance on law and order, illiberal attitude on moral questions generally and certain political questions such as race and immigration, an attack on the labor movement and a defense of private property, and a forthright nationalism—all combine in a politics of reaction: a reassertion of the principle of private property and capital accumulation as the *raison d'être* of modern society, alongside an authoritarian moralism requiring excessive state power as a means of policing civil society. If there is such a thing as the New Right distinct from "traditional" conservatism, then it lies in its being a reactionary modernism of our times.[68]

The emerging proto-fascism that threatens American democracy can best be understood by examining a number of characteristics that relate it to both an older form of fascism and a set of contemporary conditions that give it a distinctive character. After documenting and analyzing these central, though far from exhaustive, features of proto-fascism, I want to conclude by examining how neoliberalism provides a unique set of conditions for both producing and legitimating the central tendencies of proto-fascism.

The cult of traditionalism and a reactionary modernism are central features of proto-fascism and are alive and well in Bush's America. The alliance of neoconservatives, extremist evangelical Christians, and free-market advocates on the political Right imagine a social order modeled on the presidency of William McKinley and the values of the robber barons. The McKinley presidency lasted from 1897 to 1901 and "had a consummate passion to serve corporate and imperial power."[69] This was an age when blacks, women, immigrants, and minorities of class "knew their place," big government served the exclusive interests of the corporate monopolists, commanding institutions were under the sway of narrow political interests, welfare was a private enterprise, and labor unions were kept in place by the repressive forces of the state. All of these conditions are being reproduced under the leadership of an extremist element of the Republican Party that holds sway over all branches of government. William Greider, writing in *The Nation,* comments on the cult of traditionalism and anti-modernism that characterizes this administration and its return to a past largely defined through egregious inequality,[70] corporate greed, hyper-commercialism, political corruption, and an utter disdain for economic and political democracy. According to Greider, the overall ambition of the Bush administration and his right-wing allies is to roll back the twentieth century, quite literally. That is, defenestrate the federal government and reduce its scale and powers to a level well below what it was before the New Deal's centralization. With that accomplished, movement conservatives envision a restored society in which the prevailing values and power relationships resemble the America that existed around 1900, when William McKinley was President.... [Under such circumstances] governing authority and resources are dispersed from Washington, returned to local levels and also to individuals and private institutions, most notably corporations and religious organizations. The primacy of private property rights is re-established over the shared public priorities expressed in government regulation. Above all, private wealth—both enterprises and individuals with higher incomes—are permanently insulated from the progressive claims of the graduated income tax.[71]

A second feature connecting the old fascism to its updated version is the ongoing corporatization of civil society and the diminishing of public space. The latter refers to the fact that corporate space is destroying democratic public spheres, eliminating those public spaces where norm-establishing communication takes place. Viewed primarily as an economic investment rather than as a central democratic sphere for fostering the citizen-based processes of deliberation, debate, and dialogue, public space is being consistently diminished through the relentless dynamic of privatization and commercialization. The important notion that space can be used to cultivate citizenship is now transformed by a new "common sense" that links it almost entirely to the production of consumers. The inevitable correlate to this logic is that providing space for democracy to grow is no longer a priority. As theorists such as Jürgen Habermas and David Harvey have argued, the space of critical citizenship cannot flourish without the reality of public space.[72] Put differently, "the space of citizenship is as important as the idea of citizenship."[73] As a political category, space is crucial to any critical understanding of how power circulates, how disciplinary practices are constructed, and how social control is organized. But, as Margaret Kohn points out in her landmark study on radical space, "spatial practices can also contribute to transformative politics."[74] Moreover, space as a political category performs invaluable theoretical work in connecting material struggles to ideas, theories to concrete practices, and political operations to the concerns of everyday life. Without public space, it becomes more difficult for individuals to imagine themselves as political agents or to understand the necessity for developing a discourse capable of defending civic institutions. Public space confirms the idea of individuals and groups having a public voice, thus drawing a distinction between civic liberty and market liberty. The demands of citizenship affirm the social as a political concept in opposition to it being understood as simply an economic category; the sanctity of the town hall or public square in American life is grounded in the crucial recognition that citizenship has to be cultivated in noncommercialized spaces. Indeed, democracy itself needs public spheres where education as a condition for democracy can flourish, where people can meet and democratic identities, values, and relations have the time "to grow and flourish."[75] Zygmunt Bauman captures the historical importance of public spaces for nourishing civic discourses and engaging citizens as well as the ethical consequences of the current disappearances of noncommodified spheres. He writes:

> These meeting places ... public spaces—agoras and forums in their various manifestations, places where agendas are set, private affairs are made public ...—were also the sites in which *norms were created*—so that justice could be done, and apportioned horizontally, thus re-forging the conversationalists into a *community*, set apart and integrated by the shared criteria of evaluation. Hence a territory stripped of public space provides little chance for norms being debated, for values to be confronted, to clash and to be negotiated. The verdicts of right and wrong, beauty and ugliness, proper and improper, useful and useless may only descend from on high, from regions never to be penetrated by any but a most inquisitive eye; the verdicts are unquestionable since no questions may be meaningfully addressed to the judges and since the judges left no address—not even an e-mail address—and no one can be sued where they reside. No room is left for the "local opinion leaders"; no room is left for the "local opinion" as such.[76]

A third feature of the emerging proto-fascism is the relationship between the constructions of an ongoing culture of fear and a form of patriotic correctness designed to bolster a rampant nationalism and a selective popularism. Fear is mobilized through both the war on terrorism and "the sovereign pronouncement of a 'state of emergency' [which] generates a wild zone of power, barbaric and violent, operating without democratic oversight in order to combat an 'enemy' that threatens the existence of not merely and not mainly its citizens, but its sovereignty."[77] As Stanley Aronowitz points out, the national security state is now organized through "a combination of internal terrorism and the threat of external terrorism," which reinforces "its most repressive functions."[78] The threat of outside terrorism redefines the rules of war since there is no traditional state or enemy to fight. One consequence is that all citizens and noncitizens are viewed as potential terrorists and must prove their innocence through either consent or complicity with the national security state. Under such circumstances, patriotic fervor marks the line between terrorists and nonterrorists. Jingoistic patriotism is now mobilized in the highest reaches of government, in the media, and throughout society, put on perpetual display through the rhetoric of celebrities, journalists, and nightly television news anchors, and relentlessly buttressed by the never-ending waving of flags—on cars, trucks, clothes, houses, and the lapels of TV anchors—as well as through the use of mottoes, slogans, and songs. As a rhetorical ploy to silence dissent, "patriotism" names as unpatriotic any attempt either to make governmental power and authority responsive to its consequences at home or to question how the appeal to nationalism is being used to legitimate the U.S. government's bad-faith aspirations to empire-building overseas. As I mentioned earlier, this type of anti-liberal thinking is deeply distrustful of critical inquiry, mistakes dissent for treason, constructs politics on the moral absolutes of "us and them," and views difference and democracy as threats to consensus and national identity. Such patriotic fervor fuels a system of militarized control that not only repudiates the authority of international law but also relies on a notion of preventive war in order to project the fantasies of unbridled American power all over the globe. Richard Falk argues that it is precisely this style of imperial control—fed by the desire for incontestable military preeminence in the world—and the use of authoritarian modes of regulation by the state at home that have given rise to what he describes as the threat of global fascism posed by the current administration. He writes:

> But why fascist? ... First of all, the combination of unchallengeable military preeminence with a rejection by the US Government of the restraining impact of international law and the United Nations.... Secondly, the US government in moving against terrorism has claimed sweeping power to deal with the concealed Al Qaeda network.... [T]he character of the powers claimed include secret detentions, the authority to designate American citizens as "enemy combatants" without any rights, the public consideration of torture as a permissible police practice in anti-terrorist work, the scrutiny applied to those of Muslim faith, the reliance on assassination directed at terrorist suspects wherever they are found, and numerous invasions of privacy directed at ordinary people.... The slide toward fascism at home is given tangible expression by these practices, but it is

also furthered by an uncritical and chauvinistic patriotism, by the release of periodic alarmist warnings of mega-terrorist imminent attacks that fail to materialize, and by an Attorney General, John Ashcroft, who seems to exult in the authoritarian approach to law enforcement.[79]

A fourth feature of proto-fascism is the attempt to control the mass media through government regulation, consolidated corporate ownership, or sympathetic media moguls and spokespeople. The use of government regulation is evident in the Bush-appointed FCC's attempts to pass legislation favoring media monopolies that would undermine opposition and organize consent through a "capillary network of associations with vast powers of social and cultural persuasion."[80] Indeed, media regulation has promoted rather than limited the consolidation of media ownership in the United States. As a powerful form of public pedagogy, the media set the agenda for what information is included or excluded; they provide the narratives for understanding the past and present, distinguish between high- and low-status knowledge, provide subject positions, legitimate particular values, and have the power to deeply influence how people define the future. The media do not merely manufacture consent; they go so far as to produce the news and offer up the knowledge, skills, and values through which citizenship is lived and democracy defined. In the process, the media have assumed a major role in providing the conditions necessary for creating knowledgeable citizens capable of participating fully in shaping and governing society by having access to a wide range of knowledge and information. At the risk of exaggerating this issue, I must stress that in the twenty-first century the media as well as the culture they produce, distribute, and sanction have become the most important educational forces in creating citizens and social agents capable of putting existing institutions into question and making democracy work—or doing just the opposite.

Unfortunately, the power of the media along with the agenda they set are now in the hands of a limited number of transnational corporations, and the number of owners is actually getting smaller. Robert McChesney and John Nichols argue that "the U.S. media system is dominated by about ten transnational conglomerates including Disney, AOL TimeWarner, News Corporation, Viacom, Vivendi Universal, Sony, Liberty, Bertelsmann, AT&T Comcast, and General Electric (NBC)."[81] Before the Telecommunications Act of 1996, a single firm could own no more than twenty-eight radio stations nationally. But with the passage of the law and the relaxation of restrictions, the radio industry has been in a state of upheaval as hundreds of stations have been sold. Three firms in the largest radio market now control access to more than half of the listening audience. One of these firms, Clear Channel Communications, owns 1,225 stations in the United States "and reaches ... more than 70 percent of the American public."[82] Under proto-fascism, the marketplace of ideas has almost nothing to do with what is crucial for citizens to know in order to be active participants in shaping and sustaining a vibrant democracy. On the contrary, the media largely serve to target audiences for advertising, to pander to the anti-liberal ideologies of the political elite, to reinforce the conventional wisdom of corporate interests, and to promote cynical withdrawal by a populace adrift in a sea of celebrity scandal and mindless info-tainment. In a proto-fascist state, they basically deteriorate into a combination of commercialism, propaganda, and entertainment.[83] Under such circumstances, the media neither operate in the interests of the public good nor provide the pedagogical conditions necessary for producing critical citizens or defending a vibrant democracy. Instead, as McChesney and Nichols point out, concentrated media depoliticize the culture of politics, commercially carpet-bomb its citizens, and denigrate public life.[84] Rather than perform an essential public service, they have become the primary tool for promoting a culture of consent in which citizens are misinformed and public discourse is debased. Media concentration restricts the range of views to which people have access and, in doing so, does a disservice to democracy itself. For example, the staff at *NOW with Bill Moyers* did a radio survey in which they discovered that "the top-rated talk radio stations across the country ran 310 hours of conservative talk each day and only five hours of views that were not right-wing."[85]

A fifth element of proto-fascism in the United States is the rise of an Orwellian version of Newspeak, or what Umberto Eco labels as the language of "eternal fascism," whose purpose is to produce "an impoverished vocabulary, and an elementary syntax [whose consequence is] to limit the instruments for complex and critical reasoning."[86] Under the Bush administration, especially since the horrible events of September 11th, the tools of language, sound, and image are increasingly being appropriated in an effort to diminish the capacity of the American public to think critically. As the critical power of language is reduced in official discourse to the simulacra of communication, it becomes more difficult for the American public to engage in critical debates, translate private considerations into public concerns, and recognize the distortions and lies that underlie many of the current government policies. What happens to critical language under the emergence of official Newspeak can be seen in the various ways in which the Bush administration and its official supporters misrepresent by misnaming government policies and engage in lying to cover up their own regressive politics and policies.[87]

Many people have pointed to Bush himself as a mangler of the English language, but this charge simply repeats the obvious while privatizing a much more important issue connecting language to power. Bush's discursive ineptness may be fodder for late-night comics, but such analyses miss the more strategic issue of how the Bush administration actually manipulates discourse. For instance, Bush describes himself as a "reformer" while he promotes policies that expand corporate welfare, give tax benefits to the rich, and "erode the financial capacity of the state to undertake any but the most minimal welfare functions.[88] He defines himself as a "compassionate conservative," but he implements policies that result in "billions of dollars in cuts ... proposed for food stamp and child nutrition programs, and for health care for the poor."[89] Bush's public speeches, often mimicked in the media, are filled with what Renana Brooks has called "empty language"—that is, statements that are so abstract as to be relatively meaningless, except to reinforce in simplistic terms an often reactionary ideological position. Brooks cites the example of Bush's comment on the complex relationship between malpractice suits and skyrocketing health care, which he reduces to "No one has ever been healed by a frivolous lawsuit."[90] While Bush's own ideological position becomes clear in this comment, the complexity of the issue is completely trivialized and removed from public discussion. Sometimes the distortions of official language are hard to miss, even among the media guards so quick to invoke patriotic correctness. One glaring example happened in an interview between Terry Gross, host of National Public Radio's *Fresh Air*, and Grover Norquist, president of Americans for Tax Reform, also considered to be the chief architect of President Bush's tax plan. The topic for discussion was the estate tax, reviled as the "death tax" by conservative elites to gain popular support for its repeal, though the vast majority of Americans will not be affected by this tax. Gross suggested that since the estate tax affects only a small minority of people who get over $2 million in inheritance, the law eliminating it clearly privileges the rich, not the average American. Norquist responded by arguing that the morality behind her argument was comparable to the same type of morality that resulted in the deaths of millions of Jews under the Holocaust. When Gross challenged this specious analogy, Norquist argued illogically that people (read "liberals") who attacked the estate tax could now be placed on the same moral plane as the Nazis who killed over 6 million Jews and untold others.[91] Under this logic, any critique of a minority group, but especially the rich, can be dismissed as comparable to the kind of discrimination waged by the perpetrators of one of the worst mass murders in human history. Of course, there is the further implication that liberal critics should be punished for these views just as the Nazis were punished in Nuremberg for their crimes against humanity. This is not just a matter of using a desperate logic to dismiss counterarguments or of silencing one's critics through distortion; such Newspeak actually demonizes those who hold the "wrong" views. Norquist's position is a contortion that fails to hide the fundamentalism that often drives this type of language.

Official Newspeak also trades in the rhetoric of fear in order to manipulate the public into a state of servile political dependency and unquestioning ideological support. Fear and its attendant use of moral panics create not only a rhetorical umbrella to promote other agendas but also a sense of helplessness and cynicism throughout the body politic. Hence, Bush's increased dependency upon issuing terror and security alerts and panic-inducing references to 9/11 is almost always framed in Manichean language of absolute good and evil. Bush's doublespeak also employs the discourse of evangelicalism, with its attendant suggestion that whatever wisdom Bush has results from his direct communion with God—a position not unlike that of Moses on Mount Sinai, which, of course, cannot be challenged by mere mortals.[92]

While all governments sometimes resort to misrepresentations and lies, Bush's doublespeak makes such actions central to its maintenance of political power and its manipulation of the media and the public. Language is used in this context to say one thing but to actually mean its opposite.[93] This type of discourse mimics George Orwell's dystopian world of *1984*, in which the Ministry of Truth produces lies and the Ministry of Love is used to torture people. Ruth Rosen argues that the Bush administration engages in a kind of doublespeak right out of Orwell's novel. For instance, Bush's Healthy Forest Initiative "allows increased logging of protected wilderness. The 'Clear Skies' initiative permits greater industrial air pollution."[94] With respect to the latter, the Bush administration has produced Spanish-language public-service commercials hawking "Clear Skies" legislation, using ads that claim such legislation promotes "cleaner air," when in fact it has weakened restrictions on corporate polluters and eased regulations on some toxic emissions such as mercury. In fact, J. P. Suarez, the Environmental Protection Agency's chief of enforcement, recently notified his staff that "the agency would stop pursuing Clean Air Act enforcement cases against coal-burning power plants."[95] Eric Pianin reported in the *Washington Post* that "[t]he Bush administration has decided to allow thousands of the nation's dirtiest coal-fired power plants and refineries to upgrade their facilities without installing costly anti-pollution equipment as they now must do."[96] In addition, the Bush administration has weakened federal programs for cleaning up dirty waters and has removed scientific studies offering evidence of global warming from government reports.[97] Even when it comes to children, Bush is undaunted in his use of deceptive language. In arguing for legislation that would shift financial responsibility to the states for the highly successful Head Start program, which provides over 1 million poor children with early educational, health, and nutrition services, Bush employed the phrase "opt in" to encourage Congress to pass new legislation reforming Head Start. While "opt in" sounds as if it refers to expanding the program, it actually undermines it because the states that are facing crushing deficits do not have the money to fund the program. Hence, the legislation would drastically weaken Head Start. Such language calls to mind the Orwellian logic that "war is peace, freedom is slavery, and ignorance is strength."

There is also abundant evidence that the Bush administration manipulated intelligence to legitimate his claim for a preemptive war with Iraq. The list of misrepresentations and rhetorical contortions includes the claims that Iraq was building nuclear weapons and was engaged in the production of biological and chemical agents, and that Saddam Hussein was working with Osama bin Laden and had direct ties to Al Qaeda.[98] Even after the CIA reported that the charge that Saddam Hussein had bought uranium from the African country of Niger in pursuit of developing a nuclear weapon was fabricated, Bush included the assertion in his 2003 State of the Union Address.[99] Moreover, charges of Newspeak do not come exclusively from the Left or from cantankerous critics. *New York Times* op-ed writer and economist Paul Krugman asserts that "misrepresentation and deception are standard operating procedure for [the Bush] administration, which—to an extent never before seen in U.S. history—systematically and brazenly distorts the facts." And, referring to Bush's record on the selling of the Iraqi war, he argues that it "is arguably the worst scandal in American political history—worse than Watergate, worse than Iran-Contra. Indeed, the idea that we were deceived into war makes many commentators so uncomfortable that they refuse to admit the possibility."[100]

In what has to rank as one of the most egregious distortions to have emerged from the Bush administration (or maybe just one of the most delusional ravings, as the *New York Daily News* suggests),[101] President Bush in an interview with *New Yorker* reporter Ken Auletta claimed that "[n]o president has ever done more for human rights than I have."[102] Such a statement is extraordinary given that Amnesty International condemned the United States in 2002 for being one of the world leaders in human rights violations. Similarly, a number of organizations such as Human Rights Watch, U.S. Human Rights Network, the ACLU, the Center for Constitutional Rights, and Amnesty International have accused the Bush administration itself of engaging in various human rights violations, including preventing foreign nationals held as prisoners at Guantanamo Bay from gaining access to U.S. courts; executing juvenile offenders; engaging in the racial profiling, detention, inhumane treatment, and deportation of Muslim immigrants after September 11, 2001; and refusing to ratify the American Convention on Human Rights, the Geneva Conventions, the International Covenant on Civil and Political Rights, the Convention on the Rights of the Child, and numerous other international agreements aimed at protecting human rights. The atrocities and torture carried out by U.S. soldiers and personnel at Abu Ghraib provide further proof that the Bush administration represents a threat to human rights, a threat now largely recognized by most other countries.

A sixth element of proto-fascism is the growing collapse of the separation between church and state, on the one hand, and the increasing use of religious rhetoric as a marker of political identity and the shaping of public policy, on the other. Religion has always played a powerful role in the daily lives of Americans. But it has never wielded such influence in the highest levels of American government as it does under Bush's presidency. Moreover, the religious conservative movement that has come into political prominence with the election of George W. Bush views him as its earthly leader. As *Washington Post* staff writer Dana Milbank puts it:

For the first time since religious conservatism became a modern political movement, the president of the United States has become the movement's de facto leader—a status even Ronald Reagan, though admired by religious conservatives, never earned. Christian publications, radio and television shower Bush with praise, while preachers from the pulpit treat his leadership as an act of providence. A procession of religious leaders who have met with him testify to his faith, while Web sites encourage people to fast and pray for the president.[103]

Considered the leader of the Christian Right, Bush is viewed by many of his aides and followers as a leader with a higher purpose. Bush aide Tim Goeglein echoes this view: "I think President Bush is God's man at this hour, and I say this with a great sense of humility."[104] Ralph Reed, a longtime crusader against divorce, single-parent families, and abortion and current head of Georgia's Republican Party, assesses Bush's relationship with the Christian Right in more sobering political terms. He argues that the role of the religious conservative movement has changed, in that it is no longer on the outskirts of power since it has helped to elect leaders who believe in its cause. Referring to the new-found role of the religious Right, he asserted: "You're no longer throwing rocks at the building; you're in the building."[105] Bush has not disappointed his radical evangelical Christian following.

Believing he is on a direct mission from God, President Bush openly celebrates the virtues of evangelical Christian morality, prays daily, and expresses his fervent belief in Christianity in both his rhetoric and policy choices. For example, while running as a presidential candidate in 2000, Bush proclaimed that his favorite philosopher was Jesus Christ. Further, in a speech in which he outlined the dangers posed by Iraq, he stated: "We do not claim to know all the ways of Providence, yet we can trust in them, placing our confidence in the loving God behind all of life, and all of history. May He guide us now."[106] Stephen Mansfield, in his book *The Faith of George W. Bush,* claims that Bush told James Robinson, a Texas preacher: "I feel like God wants me to run for president. I can't explain it, but I sense my country is gong to need me.... I know it won't be easy on me or my family, but God wants me to do it."[107] Surrounded by born-again missionaries and directing his appeals to God, rather than looking to the basic tenets of American democracy as sources of leadership, Bush has relentlessly developed policies based less on social needs than on a highly personal and narrowly moral sense of divine purpose. Using the privilege of executive action, he has aggressively attempted to evangelize the realm of social services. For example, to a greater extent than any other president, he has made federal funds available to Christian religious groups that provide a range of social services. He has also eased the rules "for overtly religious institutions to access $20-billion in federal social service grants and another $8-billion in Housing and Urban Development money. Tax dollars can now be used to construct and renovate houses of worship as long as the funds are not used to build the principal room used for prayer, such as the sanctuary or chapel."[108] He has also provided over $60 billion in federal funds for faith-based initiatives organized by religious charitable groups.[109] Not all religious groups, however, receive equal funding. The lion's share of federal monies goes to Christian organizations, thus undermining, via state sanction of some religions over others, the very idea of religious freedom. In addition, he has promised that such agencies can get government funds "without being forced to change their character or compromise their mission."[110] This means that such organizations and groups can now get federal money even though they discriminate on religious grounds in their hiring practices. The two programs that Bush showcased during his January 2003 State of the Union speech both "use religious conversion as treatment."[111] Bush has also created an office in the White House entirely dedicated to providing assistance to faith-based organizations applying for federal funding. Moreover, Bush is using school voucher programs to enable private schools to receive public money, and refusing to fund schools that "interfere with or fail to accommodate 'prayer for bible study' by teachers or students."[112] Secretary of Education Rod Paige made clear how he feels about the separation of church and state when he told a Baptist publication that he believed that schools should teach Christian values. When asked to resign by a number of critics, Paige refused and his office declined to clarify, if not repudiate, his suggestion that either public schools should teach Christian values or parents should take their kids out of such schools and send them to parochial schools. His office replied curtly: "The quotes are the quotes."[113] The Bush administration has also refused to sign a U.N. declaration on children's rights, unless it eliminates sexual health services such as providing teenage sex education in which contraception or reproductive rights are discussed. On the domestic front, Bush has passed legislation halting "late-term" abortion, tried to pass legislation stopping the distribution of the morning-after pill, and eliminated financial support for international charities that provide advice on abortion. Such

measures not only call into question the traditional separation between church and state; they also undercut public services and provide a veneer of government legitimacy to religious-based
organizations that prioritize religious conversion over modern scientific techniques. As Winnifred Sullivan, a senior lecturer at the University of Chicago Divinity School, puts it, the conservative evangelical
proponents of the faith-based initiative "want government funds to
go to the kinds of churches that regard conversion as part of your
rehabilitation. It's a critique of secular professional social service
standards."[114]

Unfortunately, Bush's religious fervor appears more indebted to
the God of the Old Testament—the God who believes in an eye-for-
an-eye, the God of vengeance and retribution. Hence, Bush appears
indifferent to the seeming contradiction between his claim to religious piety and his willingness as the governor of Texas to execute
"more prisoners (152) than any governor in modern U.S. history."[115]
Nor does he see the contradiction between upholding the word of
God and imposing democracy on the largely Muslim population of
Iraq through the rule of force and the barrel of a gun. Indeed, while
Bush and his religious cohorts claim they are working to exercise
great acts of charity, it appears that the poor are being punished and
the only charity available is the handout being given to the rich. For
instance, as funds were being distributed for faith-based initiatives,
Congress not only passed legislation that eliminated a child tax credit that would have benefited about 2 million children but also agreed
to a $350 billion tax cut for the rich while slashing domestic spend-
ing for programs that benefit the poor, elderly, and children.

Bush is not the only one in his administration who combines
evangelical morality with dubious ethical actions and undemocratic
practices. Attorney General John Ashcroft, a Christian fundamental-
ist who holds morning-prayer sessions in his Washington office, add-
ed another layer to this type of religious fervor in February 2002
when he told a crowd at the National Religious Broadcasters Convention in Nashville, Tennessee, that the freedoms Americans enjoy
appear to have little to do with the men who wrote the U.S. Constitution since such freedoms are made in Heaven. Ashcroft argues
that "[w]e are a nation called to defend freedom—a freedom that is
not the grant of any government or document but is our endow-
ment from God."[116] Without any irony intended, Ashcroft further
exhibited his rigid Christian morality by having the "Spirit of Justice"
statue draped so as to cover up her marble breasts; yet, at the same

time, he has violated the constitutional rights of thousands of Muslims and Arabs who, since September 11, 2001, he has arrested, held in secret, and offered no legal recourse or access to their families. Such harsh treatment rooted in a Manichean notion of absolute good and evil represents more than an act of capricious justice; it actually undermines "the presumption of innocence, as well as the constitutional rights to due process, to counsel, and to a speedy and public trial." And in legitimating such treatment "the Bush administration has weakened these protections for all, citizens and aliens alike. In the process, it has tarnished American democracy."[117]

Behind the rhetoric of religious commitment is the reality of permanent war, the further immiseration of the poor, and the ongoing attacks on the notion of the secular state. There is also the force of intolerance and bigotry, the refusal to recognize the multiplicity of religious, political, linguistic, and cultural differences—those vast and diverse elements that constitute the democratic global sphere at its best. Hints of this bigotry are visible not only in the culture of fear and religious fundamentalism that shapes the world of Bush and Ashcroft but also in those who serve them with unquestioning loyalty. This became clear when the national press revealed that a high-ranking Defense Department official called the war on terrorism a Christian battle against Satan. Lieutenant General William Boykin, in his capacity as Deputy Under Secretary of Defense for Intelligence, and while standing in front of pictures of Osama bin Laden, Saddam Hussein, and Kim Jung Il, asked the parishioners of the First Baptist Church of Broken Arrow, Oklahoma, the following question: "Why do they hate us? ... The answer to that is because we are a Christian nation. We are hated because we are a nation of believers." He continued, "Our spiritual enemy will only be defeated if we come against them in the name of Jesus."[118] For Boykin, the war being fought in Iraq, in Afghanistan, and maybe eventually at home against other nonbelievers, is a holy war. Boykin appears dead serious when claiming that other countries "have lost their morals, lost their values. But America is still a Christian nation."[119] This language is not merely the ranting of a religious fanatic; it is symptomatic of a deeper strain of intolerance and authoritarianism that is emerging in this country. It can be heard in the words of Reverend Jerry Falwell, who claimed on the airwaves that the terrorist attack of 9/11 was the result of God's judgment on the secularizing of America. He stated: "I really believe that the pagans, and the abortionists, and the feminists, and the gays and lesbians, the ACLU, People for the

American Way—all of them who have tried to secularize America—I point the finger in their face and say, 'You helped this happen.'"[120] It can be heard in the diatribes of the founder of the Christian Coalition, Pat Robertson, who argues that Islam is not a peaceful religion, and in the claims of many other Christian fundamentalists in America. The emergence of a government-sanctioned religious fundamentalism has its counterpart in a political authoritarianism that undermines not only the most basic tenets of religious faith but also the democratic tenets of social justice and equality. Of course, this type of religious fundamentalism, supported largely by politicians and evangelical missionaries who run to the prayer groups and Bible study cells sprouting up all over the Bush White House, has little to do with genuine religion or spirituality. Those who believe that biblical creationism rather than evolution should be taught in the schools, or that the United States "must extend God's will of liberty for other countries, by force if necessary,"[121] do not represent the prophetic traditions in Islam, Christianity, or Judaism. These traditions foster belief in a God who is giving and compassionate, who rejects secular policies that bankrupt the government in order to benefit the rich or that produce laws that disadvantage the poor and impose more suffering on those already in need. It is a tradition espoused by the Reverend James Forbes Jr., head of the Riverside Church in New York City, and captured in his assertion that "poverty is a weapon of mass destruction."[122] Joseph Hough, the head of Union Theological Seminary, speaks for many religious leaders when he argues that what passes as Christianity in the Bush administration is simply a form of political machination masquerading as religion, making a grab for power. He writes:

> I'm getting tired of people claiming they're carrying the banner of my religious tradition when they're doing everything possible to undercut it. And that's what's happening in this country right now. The policies of this country are disadvantaging poor people every day of our lives and every single thing that passes the Congress these days is disadvantaging poor people more.... And anybody who claims in the name of God they're gonna run over people of other nations, and just willy-nilly, by your own free will, reshape the world in your own image, and claim that you're acting on behalf of God, that sounds a lot like Caesar to me.[123]

Apocalyptic Biblical prophesies fuel more than the likes of John Ashcroft, who opposes dancing on moral grounds, or David Hager, appointed by Bush to the FDA's Advisory Committee for Reproductive Health Drugs, "who refuses to prescribe contraceptives to unmarried women (and believes the Bible is an antidote for premenstrual syndrome)";[124] they also fuel a world view in which immigrants, African-Americans, and others marked by differences in class, race, gender, and nationality are demonized, scapegoated, and subjected to acts of state violence. Such rhetoric and the policies it supports need to be recognized as a crisis of democracy itself. What progressives and others need to acknowledge is that the Bush administration's attempt to undo the separation between church and state is driven by a form of fundamentalism that both discredits democratic values, public goods, and critical citizenship and spawns an irrationality evident in the innumerable contradictions between its rhetoric of "compassionate conservative" religious commitment and its relentless grab for economic and political power—an irrationality that is the hallmark of both the old fascism and proto-fascism.

While there are other elements central to proto-fascism, I want to conclude in substantial detail with a discussion of the growing militarization of public space and the social order in American society. Of course, the militarization of public space was a central feature of the old fascism. But it is particularly important in the United States today because it poses the greatest risk to our civil liberties and any semblance of democracy, and it has been a crucial force in the rise of the national security state.

The Politics of Militarization at Home and Abroad

Militarization refers to related instances of the increasing centrality of the military in American society, the militarization of U.S. culture, and the increased propensity to suppress dissent. The process of militarization has a long history in the United States and is varied rather than static, changing under different historical conditions.[125] The militarizing of public space at home contributes to the narrowing of community, the increasing suppression of dissent, and a growing escalation of concentrated, unaccountable political power that threatens the very foundation of democracy in the United States. Militarization is no longer simply the driving force of foreign policy, it has become a defining principle for social changes at home. Catherine Lutz captures the multiple registers and complex processes of militarization that have extensively shaped social life during the 20th century.

By militarization, I mean ... an intensification of the labor and resources allocated to military purposes, including the shaping of other institutions in synchrony with military goals. Militarization is simultaneously a discursive process, involving a shift in general societal beliefs and values in ways necessary to legitimate the use of force, the organization of large standing armies and their leaders, and the higher taxes or tribute used to pay for them. Militarization is intimately connected not only to the obvious increase in the size of armies and resurgence of militant nationalisms and militant fundamentalisms but also to the less visible deformation of human potentials into the hierarchies of race, class, gender, and sexuality, and to the shaping of national histories in ways that glorify and legitimate military action.[126]

Lutz's definition of militarization is inclusive, attentive to its discursive, ideological, and material relations of power in the service of war and violence. But militarization is also a powerful cultural politics that works its way through everyday life spawning particular notions of masculinity, sanctioning war as a spectacle, and using fear as a central formative component in mobilizing an affective investment in militarization. In other words, the forces of militarization, with its emphasis on the discursive production of violence and the material practices it entails has produced a pervasive culture of militarization, which "inject[s] a constant military presence in our lives."[127] Unlike the old style of militarization in which all forms of civil authority are subordinate to military authority, the new ethos of militarization is organized to engulf the entire social order, legitimating its values as a central rather than peripheral aspect of American public life. Moreover, the values of militarism no longer reside in a single group or are limited to a particular sphere of society. On the contrary, as Jorge Mariscal points out:

In liberal democracies, in particular, the values of militarism do not reside in a single group but are diffused across a wide variety of cultural locations. In twenty-first century America, no one is exempt from militaristic values because the processes of militarization allow those values to permeate the fabric of everyday life.[128]

The growing influence of the military presence and ideology in American society is visible, in part, because the United States has more police, prisons, spies, weapons, and soldiers than at any other time in its history. This radical shift in the size, scope, and influence of the military can be seen, on the one hand, in the redistribution of domestic resources and government funding away from social programs into military-oriented security measures at home and war abroad. As Richard Falk has pointed out, "The US Government is devoting huge resources to the monopolistic militarization of space, the development of more usable nuclear weapons, and the strengthening of its world-girdling ring of military bases and its global navy, as the most tangible way to discourage any strategic challenges to its preeminence."[129] And according to journalist George Monbiot, the U.S. federal government "is now spending as much on war as it is on education, public health, housing, employment, pensions, food aid and welfare put together."[130] On the other hand, the state is being radically transformed into a national security state, increasingly put under the sway of the military-corporate-industrial-educational complex, just as the military logic of fear, surveillance, and control is gradually permeating our public schools, universities, streets, popular culture, and criminal justice system.

Since the events of 9/11 and the wars in Afghanistan and Iraq, the military has assumed a privileged place in American society. President Bush not only celebrates the military presence in American culture, he cultivates it by going out of his way to give speeches at military facilities, talk to military personnel, and address veterans groups. He often wears a military uniform when speaking to "captive audiences at military bases, defense plants, and on aircraft carriers."[131] He also takes advantage of the campaign value of military culture by using military symbolism as a political prop in order to attract the widest possible media attention. One glaring instance occurred on May 1, 2003, when Bush landed in full aviator flight uniform on the USS *Abraham Lincoln* in the Pacific Ocean, where he officially proclaimed the end of the Iraqi war. There was also his secret trip to Baghdad to spend Thanksgiving day (2003) with the troops, an event that attracted worldwide coverage in all the media. But Bush has done more than take advantage of the military as a campaign prop to sell his domestic and foreign policies: His administration and the Republican Party, which now controls all three branches of government, have developed a new, if not dangerous, "and unprecedented confluence of our democratic institutions and the military."[132]

Writing in *Harper's Magazine*, Kevin Baker claims that the military "has become the most revered institution in the country."[133] Soon after the Iraqi war, a Gallup Poll reported that over 76 percent of Americans "expressed 'a great deal' or 'quite a lot' of confidence in their nation's military." Among a poll of 1,200 students conducted by

Harvard University, 75 percent believed that the military most of the time would "do the right thing." In addition, the students "characterized themselves as hawks over doves by a ratio of two to one."[134] Popular fears about domestic safety and internal threats accentuated by endless terror alerts have created a society that increasingly accepts the notion of a "war without limits" as a normal state of affairs. But fear and insecurity do more than produce a collective anxiety among Americans, exploited largely to get them to believe that they should vote Republican because it is the only political party that can protect Americans. In addition to producing manufactured political loyalty, such fears can also be manipulated into a kind of "war fever." The mobilization of war fever, intensified through a politics of fear, carries with it a kind of paranoid edge, endlessly stroked by government alerts and repressive laws and used "to create the most extensive national security apparatus in our nation's history."[135] But it is also reproduced in the Foxified media, which—in addition to constantly marketing the flag and interminably implying that critics of American foreign policy are traitors—offers up seemingly endless images of brave troops on the front line, heroic stories of released American prisoners, and utterly privatized commentaries on those wounded or killed in battle.[136] *Time* magazine embodied this representational indulgence in military culture by naming "The American Soldier" as the "person of the year" for 2003. Not only have such ongoing and largely uncritical depictions of war injected a constant military presence in American life, they have also helped to create a civil society that has become more aggressive in its warlike enthusiasms. But there is more at work here than simple exploitation of the troops for higher ratings or attempts by right-wing political strategists to keep the American public in a state of permanent fear so as to remove pressing domestic issues from public debate. There is also the Bush administration's persistent effort to convince as many Americans as possible that under the current "state of emergency" the use of the military internally in domestic affairs is perfectly acceptable, evident in its increasing propensity to use the military establishment "to incarcerate and interrogate suspected terrorists and 'enemy combatants' and keep them beyond the reach of the civilian judicial system, even if they are American citizens."[137] It is also evident in the federal government's attempts to try terrorists in military courts, and to detain prisoners "outside the provisions of the Geneva Convention on prisoners of war … at the U.S. Marine Corps base at Guantanamo, Cuba because that facility is outside of the reach of the American courts."[138]

As the military becomes more popular in American life, its underlying values, social relations, ideology, and hyper-masculine aesthetic begin to spread into other aspects of American culture. Citizens are recruited as foot soldiers in the war on terrorism, urged to spy on their neighbors' behavior, to watch for suspicious-looking people, and to supply data to government sources. As permanent war becomes a staple of everyday life, flags, as I've already noted, increasingly appear on storefront windows, lapels, cars, houses, SUVs, and elsewhere as a show of support for both the expanding interests of empire abroad and the increasing militarization of the culture and social order at home. Major universities more intensively court the military establishment for Defense Department grants and, in doing so, become less open to either academic subjects that do not generate revenue or programs that encourage rigorous debate, dialogue, and critical thinking. Public schools not only have more military recruiters, they also have more military personnel teaching in the classrooms. J.R.O.T.C. programs are increasingly becoming a conventional part of the school day. And as a result of the No Child Left Behind Act, President Bush's educational law, "schools risk losing all federal aid if they fail to provide military recruiters full access to their students; the aid is contingent with complying with federal law."[139] Schools were once viewed as democratic public spheres that would teach students how to resist the militarization of democratic life, or at least how to peacefully engage in solutions to domestic and international problems. Now they serve as recruiting stations for students to fight enemies at home and abroad.

Militarization abroad cannot be separated from the increasing militarization of society at home. War takes on a new meaning in American life as wars are waged on drugs, social policies are criminalized, youth are tried as adults, incarceration rates soar among the poor (especially people of color), and schools are increasingly modeled after prisons. Indeed, schools represent one of the most serious public spheres to come under the influence of military culture and values. Tough love now translates into zero-tolerance policies that turn public schools into prison-like institutions, as students' rights increasingly diminish under the onslaught of military-style discipline. Students in many schools, especially those in poor urban areas, are routinely searched, frisked, subjected to involuntary drug tests, maced, and carted off to jail. Elissa Gootman, writing about schools in New York City, asserts: "In some places, schools are resorting to zero-tolerance policies that put students in handcuffs for dress code violations."[140] As educators turn over their responsibility for school safety to the police, the new security culture in public schools has turned them into "learning prisons,"[141] most evident in the ways in which schools are being "reformed" through the addition of armed guards, barbed-wired security fences, and lock-down drills. Recently, in Goose Creek, South Carolina, police conducted an early-morning drug-sweep at Stratford High School. When the police arrived they drew guns on students, handcuffed them, and made them kneel facing the wall.[142] No drugs, weapons, or even cigarettes were found in the raid. Though this incident was aired on the national news, there was barely any protest from the public.

The rampant combination of fear and insecurity that is so much a part of the permanent-war culture in the United States seems to bear down particularly hard on children. In many poor school districts, specialists are being laid off and crucial mental health services are being cut back. Indeed, as Sandra Rimer recently pointed out in the *New York Times,* much-needed student-based services and traditional, if not compassionate, ways of dealing with student problems are now being replaced by the juvenile justice system, which functions "as a dumping ground for poor minority kids with mental health and special-education problems.... The juvenile detention center has become an extension of the principal's office."[143] For example, in some cities, ordinances have been passed that "allow for the filing of misdemeanor charges against students for anything from disrupting a class to assaulting a teacher."[144] Children are no longer given a second chance for minor behavior infractions, nor are they simply sent to the guidance counselor, the principal, or detention. They now come under the jurisdiction of the courts and juvenile justice system.

The militarization of public high schools has become so commonplace that even in the face of the most flagrant disregard for children's rights, such acts are justified by both administrators and the public on the grounds that they keep kids safe. In Biloxi, Mississippi, surveillance cameras have been installed in all of its 500 classrooms. The school's administrators call this "school reform," but none of them have examined the implications of what they are teaching kids who are put under constant surveillance. The not-so-hidden curriculum here is that kids can't be trusted and that their rights are not worth protecting. At the same time, they are being educated to passively accept military-sanctioned practices organized around maintaining control, surveillance, and unquestioned authority, all conditions central to a police state and proto-fascism. It gets worse. Some schools are actually using sting operations in which undercover agents pretend to be students in order to catch young people suspected of selling drugs or committing school infractions. The consequences of such actions are far-reaching. As Randall Beger points out:

> Opponents of school-based sting operations say they not only create a climate of mistrust between students and police, but they also put innocent students at risk of wrongful arrest due to faulty tips and overzealous police work. When asked about his role in a recent undercover probe at a high school near Atlanta, a young-looking police officer who attended classes and went to parties with students replied: "I knew I had to fit in, make kids trust me and then turn around and take them to jail."[145]

Instances of domestic militarization and the war at home can also be seen in the rise of the prison-industrial-educational complex and the militarization of the criminal justice system. The traditional "distinctions between military, police, and criminal justice are blurring."[146] The police now work in close collaboration with the military. This takes the form of receiving surplus weapons, arranging technology/ information transfers, introducing SWAT teams modeled after the Navy Seals (such teams are experiencing a steep growth in police departments throughout the United States), and becoming more dependent on military models of crime control.[147] The increasing use of such military models in American life has played a crucial role in the paramilitarizing of the culture, which provides both a narrative and a legitimation "for recent trends in corrections, including the normalization of special response teams, the increasingly popular Supermax prisons, and drug war boot camps."[148] In the paramilitaristic perspective, crime is no longer seen as a social problem; it is now viewed as both an individual pathology and a matter of punishment rather than rehabilitation. Unsurprisingly, paramilitary culture increasingly embodies a racist and class-specific discourse and "reflects the discrediting of the social and its related narratives."[149] This is particularly evident in the singling-out of America's inner-cities as dangerous enclaves of crime and violence. The consequences for those communities have been catastrophic, especially in terms of the cataclysmic rise of the prison-industrial complex. As is widely reported, the United States is now the biggest jailer in the world. Between 1985 and 2002 the total number of prison inmates grew from 744,206 to 2.1 million (approaching the combined populations of Idaho, Wyoming, and Montana), and prison budgets jumped from $7 billion in 1980 to $40 billion in 2000.[150] As Sanho Tree points out:

> With more than 2 million people behind bars (there are only 8 million prisoners in the entire world), the United States—with one-twenty-second of the world's population—has one-quarter of the planet's prisoners. We operate the largest penal system in the world, and approximately one-quarter of all our prisoners (nearly half a million people) are there for nonviolent drug offenses.[151]

Yet, even as the crime rate plummets dramatically, more people, especially those of color, are being arrested, harassed, punished, and put in jail.[152] Of the 2 million people behind bars, 70 percent of the inmates are people of color: 50 percent are African-American and 17 percent are Latino.[153]

Under the auspices of the national security state and owing to the militarization of domestic life, the most trivial social infractions are now criminalized in the schools. Students are subjected to containment policies that undermine their ability to question power, exercise self-determination, and become empowered citizens, while schools increasingly function as zoning mechanisms to separate students marginalized by class and color and, as such, are modeled after prisons. This observation follows the argument of David Garland, who points out that "[l]arge-scale incarceration functions as a mode of economic and social placement, a zoning mechanism that segregates those populations rejected by the depleted institutions of family, work, and welfare and places them behind the scenes of social life."[154]

And judging from the 2004 State of the Union Address, the Bush administration will continue to allocate funds for "educational reform" intended to strip young people of the capacity to think critically both by teaching them that learning is largely about test taking and by preparing them for a culture in which punishment has become the central principle of reform. Bush cannot fully fund his own educational reform act, but in the address he pledged an additional $23 million to promote drug testing of students in public schools and $350 million to purchase security technologies. In short, fear, punishment, and containment continue to override the need to provide health care for 9.3 million uninsured children, increase the ranks of new teachers by at least 100,000, fully support Head Start programs, repair deteriorating schools, and improve those youth services that for many poor students would provide an alternative to the direct pipeline between school and the local police station, the courts, or prison.

Domestic militarization, also widespread in the realm of culture, functions as a mode of public pedagogy, instilling the values and the aesthetic of militarization through a variety of pedagogical sites and cultural venues. For instance, Humvees offer up the fantasy of military glamour through advertisements suggesting that ownership of these vehicles first used in Desert Storm not only guarantees virility for its owners but promotes a mixture of fear and admiration from everyone else. One of the fastest-growing sports for middle-class suburban youth is the game of paintball "in which teenagers stalk and shoot each other on 'battlefields.' (In San Diego, paintball participants pay an additional $50 to hone their skills at the Camp Pendleton Marine Base.)"[155] And military recruitment ads flood all modes of entertainment using sophisticated marketing tools that resonate powerfully with the appeal to particular forms of masculinity that serve as an enticement for recruitment. For example, the Marine Corps' website, www.marines.com, opens with the sound of gunfire and then provides the following message:

> We are the warriors, one and all. Born to defend, built to conquer. The steel we wear is the steel within ourselves, forged by the hot fires of discipline and training. We are fierce in a way no other can be. We are the Marines.

From video games to Hollywood films to children's toys, popular culture is increasingly bombarded with militarized values, symbols, and images. Video games such as *Doom* have a long history of using violent graphics and shooting techniques that appeal to hyper-modes of masculinity. The Marine Corps was so taken with *Doom* in the mid-1990s that it produced its own version of the game, *Marine Doom*, and made it available to download for free. One of the developers of the game, Lieutenant Scott Barnett, claimed at the time that it was a useful game to keep marines entertained. The interface of military and popular culture is valuable not only in providing video game technology for diverse military uses but also in allowing the armed forces to develop partnerships "with the video game industry to train and recruit soldiers."[156] The military uses the games to train recruits and the video game makers offer products that have the imprimatur

40

of a first-class fighting machine. And the popularity of militarized war games is on the rise. Nick Turse argues that as the line between entertainment and war disappears, a "'military-entertainment complex' [has] sprung up to feed both the military's desire to bring out ever-more-realistic computer and video combat games. Through video games, the military and its partners in academia and the entertainment industry are creating an arm of media culture geared toward preparing young Americans for armed conflict."[157] Combat teaching games offer a perfect fit between the Pentagon, with its accelerating military budget, and the entertainment industry, with annual revenues of $479 billion—including $40 billion from the video game industry. The entertainment industry offers a stamp of approval for the Pentagon's war games, and the Defense Department provides an aura of authenticity for corporate America's war-based products. Collaboration between the Defense Department and the entertainment industry has been going on since 1997, but the permanent-war culture that now grips the United States has given this partnership a new life and greatly expanded its presence in popular culture.

The military has found numerous ways to take advantage of the intersection between popular culture and the new electronic technologies. Such technologies are being employed not only to train military personnel but also to attract recruits, tapping into the realm of popular culture with its celebration of video games, computer technology, the Internet, and other elements of visual culture used by teenagers.[158] For instance, the army has developed on-line software that appeals to computer-literate recruits, and the most attractive feature of the software is a shooting game "that actually simulates battle and strategic-warfare situations."[159] When asked about the violence being portrayed, Brian Ball, the lead developer of the game, was crystal clear about the purpose of the video. "We don't downplay the fact that the Army manages violence. We hope that this will help people understand the role of the military in American life."[160] Capitalizing on its link with industry, the military now has a host of new war games in production. For instance, there is *America's Army*, one of the most popular and successful recruiting video games. This game teaches young people how "to kill enemy soldiers while wearing your pajamas [and also provides] plenty of suggestions about visiting your local recruiter and joining the real US Army."[161] Using the most updated versions of satellite technology, military-industry collaboration has also produced *Kuma: War*, a game developed by the Department of Defense and Kuma Reality Games that is slated for release in 2004. It is a subscription-based product that "prepares gamers for actual missions based on real-world conflicts," updated weekly.[162] The game allows players to re-create actual news stories such as the raid that American forces conducted in Mosul, Iraq, in which Saddam Hussein's two sons, Uday and Qusay, were killed. Gamers can take advantage of real "true-to-life satellite imagery and authentic military intelligence, to jump from the headlines right into the frontlines of international conflict."[163] Of course, certain realities—carrying 80-pound knapsacks in 120-degree heat, dealing with the panic-inducing anxiety and fear of real people shooting real bullets or planting real bombs to kill or maim you and your fellow soldiers, and spending months, if not years, away from family—are not among the experiences reproduced for instruction or entertainment. Young people no longer learn military values either in training camp or in military-oriented schools; instead, these values are now disseminated through the pedagogical force of popular culture itself, which has become a major tool used by the armed forces to educate young people about the ideology and social relations that inform military life—minus a few of the unpleasantries. The collaboration between the military and the entertainment industry offers up a form of public pedagogy that "may help to produce great battlefield decision makers, but ... strike from debate the most crucial decisions young people can make in regard to the morality of a war—choosing whether or not to fight and for what cause."[164]

In light of the militaristic transformation of the country, attitudes toward war play have changed dramatically and can be observed in the major increase in the sales, marketing, and consumption of military toys, games, videos, and clothing. Corporations recognize that there are big profits to be made at a time when military symbolism gets a boost from the war in Iraq and the upsurge in patriotic jingoism. The popularity of militarized culture is apparent not only in the sales of video combat games but also in the sales of children's war-related toys. Major retailers and chain stores across the country are selling out of such toys. KB Toys stores in San Antonio, Texas, sold out in one day an entire shipment of fatigue-clad plush hamsters that dance to military music, and managers at these stores were instructed "to feature military toys in the front of their stores."[165] Sales of action figures have also soared. As Hasbro has reported, for example, "between 2001 and 2002, sales of *G.I. Joe* increased by 46 percent." And when toy retailer Small Blue Planet launched a series of figures called "Special Forces: Showdown with Iraq, two of the four models sold out immediately."[166] KB Toys took advantage of the infatuation with action toys related to the war in Iraq by marketing a doll that is a pint-sized model of George W. Bush dressed in the U.S. pilot regalia he wore when he landed on the USS *Abraham Lincoln* on May 1, 2003. Japanese electronic giant SONY attempted to cash in on the war in Iraq by patenting the phrase "Shock and Awe" for use with video and computer games. This phrase was used by Pentagon strategists as part of a scare tactic to be used against Iraq. It referred to the massive air bombardment planned for Baghdad in the initial stages of the war. In addition, the *New York Times* reported that after September 11, 2001, "nearly two-dozen applications were filed for the phrase 'Let's Roll.'" The term was made famous by one of the passengers on the ill-fated abducted plane that crashed in a field in Pennsylvania.

Even in the world of fashion, the ever-spreading chic of militarization and patriotism is making its mark. Army-navy stores are doing a brisk business selling, not only American flags, gas masks, aviator sun glasses, night-vision goggles, and other military equipment, but also clothing with the camouflage look.[167] Even top designers are getting into the act. For instance, at a recent fashion show in Milan, Italy, many designers were "drawn to G.I. uniforms [and were] fascinated by the construction of military uniforms." One designer "had beefy models in commando gear scramble over tabletops and explode balloons."[168]

Proto-fascism views life as a form of permanent warfare and, in doing so, subordinates society to the military rather than subordinating the military to the needs of a democratic social order. Militarism in this scenario diminishes both the legitimate reasons for a military presence in society and the necessary struggle for the promise of democracy itself. As Umberto Eco points out, proto-fascist ideology, under the rubric of its aggressive militarism, maintains that "there is no struggle for life but, rather, life is lived for struggle."[169] The ideology of militarization is central to any understanding of proto-fascism since it appeals to a form of irrationality that is at odds with any viable notion of democracy. For instance, militarization uses fear to drive human behavior, and the values it promotes are mainly distrust, patriarchy, and intolerance. Within this ideology, masculinity is associated with violence, and action is often substituted for the democratic processes of deliberation and debate. Militarization as an ideology is about the rule of force and the expansion of repressive state power. In fact, democracy appears as an excess in this logic and is often condemned by militarists as being a weak system of government. Echoes of this anti-democratic sentiment can be found in the passage of the USA PATRIOT Act with its violation of civil liberties, in the rancorous patriotism that equates dissent with treason, and in the discourse of public commentators who in the fervor of a militarized culture fan the flames of hatred and intolerance. One example that has become all too typical emerged after the September 11 attacks. Columnist Ann Coulter, in calling for a holy war on Muslims, wrote: "We should invade their countries, kill their leaders and convert them to Christianity. We weren't punctilious about locating and punishing only Hitler and his top officers. We carpet-bombed German cities; we killed civilians. That's war. And this is war."[170] While this statement does not reflect mainstream American opinion, the uncritical and chauvinistic patriotism and intolerance that informs it have not only become standard fare among conservative radio hosts in the United States but are increasingly being legitimated in a variety of cultural venues. As militarization spreads through the culture, it produces policies that rely more on force than on dialogue and compassion, offers up modes of identification that undermine democratic values and tarnish civil liberties, and makes the production of both symbolic and material violence a central feature of everyday life. As Kevin Baker points out, we are quickly becoming a nation that "substitute[s] military solutions for almost everything, including international alliances, diplomacy, effective intelligence agencies, democratic institutions—even national security."[171] By blurring the lines between military and civilian functions, militarization deforms our language, debases democratic values, celebrates fascist modes of control, defines citizens as soldiers, and diminishes our ability as a nation to uphold international law and support a democratic global public sphere. Unless militarization is systematically exposed and resisted at every place where it appears in the culture, it will undermine the meaning of critical citizenship and do great harm to those institutions that are central to a democratic society.

Neoliberalism and the Eclipse of Democracy

It is virtually impossible to understand the rise of such multifaceted authoritarianism in American society without analyzing the importance of neoliberalism as the defining ideology of the current historical moment.[172] While fascism does not need neoliberalism to develop, neoliberalism creates the ideological and economic conditions that can promote a uniquely American version of fascism.[173] Neoliberalism not only undermines the vital economic and political institutions and public spaces central to a democracy, it also has no vocabulary for recognizing anti-democratic forms of power. Even worse, it accentuates a structural relationship between the state and the economy that produces hierarchies, concentrates power in relatively few hands, unleashes the most brutal elements of a rabid individualism, destroys the welfare state, incarcerates large numbers of its disposable populations, economically disenfranchises large segments of the lower and middle classes, and reduces entire countries to pauperization.[174]

Under neoliberalism, the state now makes a grim alignment with corporate power, transnational corporations, and the forces of militarization. Gone are the days when the state "assumed responsibility for a range of social needs."[175] Instead, agencies of government now pursue a wide range of "'deregulations,' privatizations, and abdications of responsibility to the market and private philanthropy."[176] Deregulations, in turn, promote "widespread, systematic disinvestment in the nation's basic productive capacity."[177] Flexible production encourages wage slavery at home. And the search for ever greater profits leads to outsourcing, which accentuates the flight of capital and jobs abroad. Neoliberalism has now become the prevailing logic in the United States; indeed, according to Stanley Aronowitz, "the neoliberal economic doctrine proclaiming the superiority of free markets over public ownership, or even public regulation of private economic activities, has become the conventional wisdom, not only among conservatives but among social progressives."[178] The ideology and power of neoliberalism also cuts across national boundaries. Throughout the globe, the forces of neoliberalism are on the march, dismantling the historically guaranteed social provisions provided by the welfare state, defining profit-making as the essence of democracy, and equating freedom with the unrestricted ability of markets to "govern economic relations free of government regulation."[179] Transnational in scope, neoliberalism now imposes its economic regime and market values on developing and weaker nations through structural adjustment policies enforced by powerful financial institutions such as the World Bank, the International Monetary Fund (IMF), and the World Trade Organization (WTO). Secure in its dystopian vision that there are no alternatives, as Margaret Thatcher once put it, neoliberalism obviates issues of contingency, struggle, and social agency by celebrating the inevitability of economic laws in which the ethical ideal of intervening in the world gives way to the idea that we "have no choice but to adapt both our hopes and our abilities to the new global market."[180] Coupled with a new culture of fear, market freedoms seem securely grounded in a defense of national security, capital, and property rights.

In its capacity to dehistoricize and depoliticize society, as well as in its aggressive attempts to destroy all of the public spheres necessary for the defense of a genuine democracy, neoliberalism reproduces the conditions for unleashing the most brutalizing forces of capitalism and accentuating the central elements of proto-fascism. As the late Pierre Bourdieu argued, neoliberalism is a policy of depoliticization, attempting to liberate the economic sphere from all government controls:

> Drawing shamelessly on the lexicon of liberty, liberalism, and deregulation, it aims to grant economic determinisms a fatal stranglehold by liberating them from all controls, and to obtain the submission of citizens and governments to the economic and social forces thus liberated.... [T]his policy has imposed itself through the most varied means, especially juridical, on the liberal—or even social democratic—governments of a set of economically advanced countries, leading them gradually to divest themselves of the power to control economic forces.[181]

At the same time, neoliberalism uses the breathless rhetoric of the global victory of free-market rationality to cut public expenditures and undermine those noncommodified public spheres that serve as the repository for critical education, language, and public intervention. Spewed forth by the mass media, right-wing intellectuals, and governments alike, neoliberal ideology, with its ongoing emphasis on deregulation and privatization, has found its material expression in an all-out attack on democratic values and on the very notion of the public sphere. Within the discourse of neoliberalism, the notion of the public good is devalued and, where possible, eliminated as part of a wider rationale for a handful of private interests to control as much of social life as possible in order to maximize their personal profit. Public services such as health care, child care, public assistance, education, and transportation are now subject to the rules of the market. Construing the public good as a private good and the needs of the corporate and private sector as the only source of investment, neoliberal ideology produces, legitimates, and exacerbates the existence of persistent poverty, inadequate health care, racial apartheid in the inner cities, and growing inequalities between the rich and the poor.[182]

As Aronowitz points out, the Bush administration has made neoliberal ideology the cornerstone of its program, actively supporting and implementing the following policies:[183]

> deregulation of business at all levels of enterprise and trade; tax reduction for wealthy individuals and corporations; the revival of the near-dormant nuclear energy industry; limitations and abrogation of labor's right to organize and bargain collectively; a land policy favoring commercial and industrial development at the expense of conservation and other proenvironment policies; elimination of income support to the chronically unemployed; reduced federal aid to education and health; privatization of the main federal pension program, Social Security; limitation on the right of aggrieved individuals to sue employers and corporations who provide services; in addition, as social programs are reduced, [Republicans] are joined by the Democrats in favoring increases in the repressive functions of the state, expressed in the dubious drug wars in the name of fighting crime, more funds for surveillance of ordinary citizens, and the expansion of the federal and local police forces.[183]

Central to both neoliberal ideology and its reinforcement by the Bush administration is the ongoing attempts by free-market fundamentalists and right-wing politicians to view government as the enemy of freedom (except when it aids big business) and to discount it as a guardian of the public interest. The call to eliminate big government is neoliberalism's great unifying idea and has broad popular appeal in the United States because it is a principle deeply embedded in the country's history and tangled up with its notion of political freedom. And yet, the right-wing appropriation of this tradition is racked with contradictions in terms of neoliberal policies. As William Greider points out:

> "Leave me alone" is an appealing slogan, but the right regularly violates its own guiding principle. The antiabortion folks intend to use government power to force their own moral values on the private lives of others. Free-market right-wingers fall silent when Bush and congress intrude to bail out airlines, insurance companies, banks—whatever sector finds itself in desperate need. The hard-right conservatives are downright enthusiastic when the Supreme Court and Bush's Justice Department hack away at our civil liberties. The "school choice" movement seeks not smaller government but a vast expansion of taxpayer obligations.[184]

The advocates of neoliberalism have attacked what they call big government when it has provided essential services such as crucial safety nets for the less fortunate, but they have no qualms about using the government to bail out the airline industry after the economic nosedive that followed the 2000 election of George W. Bush and the events of 9/11. Nor are there any expressions of outrage from the cheerleaders of neoliberalism when the state engages in promoting various forms of corporate welfare by providing billions of dollars in direct and indirect subsidies to multinational corporations. In short, government bears no obligation either for the poor and dispossessed or for the collective future of young people.

As the laws of the market take precedence over the laws of the state as guardians of the public good, the government offers increasingly little help in mediating the interface between the advance of capital and its rapacious commercial interests. Neither does it aid noncommodified interests and nonmarket spheres that create the political, economic, and social spaces and discursive conditions vital for critical citizenship and democratic public life. Within the discourse of neoliberalism, it becomes difficult for the average citizen to speak about political or social transformation, or even to challenge, outside of a grudging nod toward rampant corruption, the ruthless downsizing, the ongoing liquidation of job security, and the elimination of benefits for people now hired on a part-time basis.

The liberal democratic vocabulary of rights, entitlements, social provisions, community, social responsibility, living wage, job security, equality, and justice seems oddly out of place in a country where the promise of democracy has been replaced by casino capitalism, a winner-take-all philosophy suited to lotto players and day traders alike. As corporate culture extends ever deeper into the basic institutions of civil and political society, buttressed daily by a culture industry largely in the hands of concentrated capital, it is reinforced even further by the pervasive fear and insecurity of the public, by its deep-seated skepticism that the future holds nothing beyond a watered-down version of the present. As the prevailing discourse of neoliberalism seizes the public imagination, there is no vocabulary for progressive social change, democratically inspired visions, or critical notions of social agency to expand the meaning and purpose of democratic public life. Against the reality of low-wage jobs, the erosion of social provisions for a growing number of people, and the expanding war against young people of color at home and empire-building abroad, the market-driven juggernaut of neoliberalism continues to mobilize desires in the interest of producing market identities and market relationships that ultimately sever the link between education and social change while reducing agency to the obligations of consumerism.

As the influence of neoliberal ideology and corporate culture deepens, there is a simultaneous diminishing of noncommodified public spheres—public schools, independent bookstores, churches, noncommercial public broadcasting stations, libraries, trade unions, and voluntary institutions engaged in dialogue, education, and learning—that address the relationship of the individual to public life, foster social responsibility, and provide a robust vehicle for public participation and democratic citizenship. As media theorists Edward Herman and Robert McChesney observe, noncommodified public spheres have historically played an invaluable role "as places and forums where issues of importance to a political community are discussed and debated, and where information is presented that is essential to citizen participation in community life."[185] Without these critical public spheres, corporate power often goes unchecked and politics becomes dull, cynical, and oppressive.[186] Moreover, in the vacuum left by diminishing democracy, religious zealotry, cultural chauvinism, xenophobia, and racism have become the dominant tropes of neoconservatives and other extremist groups eager to take advantage of the growing insecurity, fear, and anxiety that result from increased joblessness, the war on terror, and the unraveling of communities. In this context, neoliberalism creates the economic, social, and political instability that helps feed both the neoconservative and religious Right movements and their proto-fascist policy initiatives.

Especially troubling under the rule of neoliberalism is not simply that ideas associated with freedom and agency are defined through the prevailing ideology and principles of the market, but that neoliberal ideology wraps itself in what appears to be an unassailable appeal to conventional wisdom. Defined as the paragon of modern social relations by Friedrich A. von Hayek, Milton Friedman, Robert Nozick, Francis Fukuyama, and other market fundamentalists, neoliberalism attempts to eliminate any engaged critique about its most basic principles and social consequences by embracing the "market as the arbiter of social destiny."[187] Neoliberalism empties the public treasury, privatizes formerly public services, limits the vocabulary and imagery available to recognize anti-democratic forms of power, and reinforces narrow models of individual agency. Equally important is its role in undermining the critical functions of a viable democracy by undercutting the ability of individuals to engage in the continuous translation between public considerations and private interests, which it accomplishes, in part, by collapsing public issues into the realm of the private. As Bauman observes, "It is no longer true that the 'public' is set on colonizing the 'private.' The opposite is the case: it is the private that colonizes the public space, squeezing out and chasing away everything which cannot be fully, without residue, translated into the vocabulary of private interests and pursuits."[188] Divested of its political possibilities and social underpinnings, freedom offers few opportunities for people to translate private worries into public concerns and collective struggle.[189]

The good life, in this discourse, "is construed in terms of our identities as consumers—we are what we buy."[190] For example, some neoliberal advocates argue that the health-care and education crises faced by many states can be solved by selling off public assets to private interests. Blatantly demonstrating neoliberal ideology's contempt for noncommodified public spheres and democratic values, the Pentagon even considered, if only for a short time, turning the war on terror and security concerns over to futures markets, subject to on-line trading. In this exhibition of market logic and casino capitalism, neoliberalism reveals its dream of a social order dominated by commercial spheres. At the same time, it aggressively attempts to empty the substance of critical democracy and replace it with a democracy of goods available to those with purchasing power and the ability to expand the cultural and political power of corporations throughout the world. As a result of the consolidated corporate attack on public life, the maintenance of democratic public spheres from which to launch a moral vision or to engage in a viable struggle over politics loses all credibility—not to mention monetary support. As the alleged objectivity of neoliberal ideology remains largely unchallenged within dominant public spheres, individual critiques and collective political struggles become more difficult.[191] It gets worse. Dominated by extremists, the Bush administration is driven by an arrogance of power and an inflated sense of moral righteousness mediated largely by a false sense of certitude and a never-ending posture of triumphalism. As George Soros points out, this rigid ideology and inflexible sense of mission allow the Bush administration to believe that "because we are stronger than others, we must know better and we must have right on our side. This is where religious fundamentalism comes together with market fundamentalism to form the ideology of American supremacy."[192]

As public space is increasingly commodified and the state becomes more closely aligned with capital, politics is defined largely by its policing functions rather than as an agency for peace and social reform. Its ideological counterpart is a public pedagogy that mobilizes power in the interest of a social order marked by the progressive removal of autonomous spheres of cultural production such as journalism, publishing, and film; by the destruction of collective structures capable of counteracting the widespread imposition of commercial values and effects of the pure market; by the creation of a global reserve army of the unemployed; and by the subordination of nation-states to the real masters of the economy. Bourdieu emphasized the effects of neoliberalism on this dystopian world:

> First is the destruction of all the collective institutions capable of counteracting the effects of the infernal machine, primarily those of the state, repository of all of the universal values associated with the idea of the public realm. Second is the imposition everywhere, in the upper spheres of the economy and the state as at the heart of corporations, of that sort of moral Darwinism that, with the cult of the winner, schooled in higher mathematics and bungee jumping, institutes the struggle of all against all and cynicism as the norm of all action and behaviour.[193]

Besides the destruction of collective solidarities, though never without opposition, neoliberalism refigures the relationship between the state and capital. As the state abandons its social investments in health, education, and the public welfare, it becomes progressively reduced to its repressive functions. Theorists such as George Steinmetz, Pierre Bourdieu, Stanley Aronowitz, Howard Zinn, and Noam Chomsky have argued that as the state is hollowed out, it increasingly takes on the functions of an enhanced police state or security state, the signs of which are most visible in the ongoing use of the state apparatus to spy on and arrest its subjects, the incarceration of individuals considered disposable (primarily poor people of color), and the ongoing criminalization of social policies. Examples of the latter include anti-begging and anti-loitering ordinances that fine or punish the homeless for sitting or lying down too long in public places.[194] An even more despicable instance of the barbaric nature of neoliberalism, with its emphasis on profits over people and its willingness to punish rather than serve the poor and disenfranchised, can be seen in the growing tendency of many hospitals across the country to have patients arrested and jailed if they cannot pay their medical bills. This policy, right out of the pages of George Orwell's *1984*, represents a return to debtors prisons. Now chillingly called "body attachment," it is " basically a warrant for ... the patient's arrest."[195]

Neoliberalism is not simply an economic policy designed to cut government spending, pursue free-trade policies, and free market forces from government regulations; it is also a political philosophy and ideology that affects every dimension of social life. Indeed, neoliberalism has heralded a radical economic, political, and experiential shift that now largely defines the citizen as a consumer, disbands the social contract in the interests of privatized considerations, and separates capital from the context of place. Within this discourse, as Jean and John Comaroff have argued, "the personal is the only politics there is, the only politics with a tangible referent or emotional valence. It is in these privatized terms that action is organized, that the experience of inequity and antagonism takes meaningful shape."[196] Under such circumstances, neoliberalism portends the death of politics as we know it, strips the social of its democratic values, reconstructs agency in terms that are utterly privatized, and provides the conditions for an emerging form of proto-fascism that must be resisted at all costs. Neoliberalism not only enshrines unbridled individualism as a central feature of proto-fascism, as Herbert Marcuse reminds us,[197] it also destroys any vestige of democratic society by undercutting its "moral, material, and regulatory moorings;"[198] and in doing so it offers no language for understanding how the future might be grasped outside of the narrow logic of the market. But there is even more at stake here than the obliteration of public concerns, the death of the social, the emergence of a market-based fundamentalism that undercuts the ability of people to understand how to translate the privately experienced misery into collective action, and the elimination of the gains of the welfare state: There is also the growing threat of displacing "political sovereignty with the sovereignty of the market, as if the latter has a mind and morality of its own."[199] As democracy becomes a burden under the reign of neoliberalism, civic discourse disappears and the reign of unfettered social Darwinism with its survival-of-the-slickest philosophy emerges as the template for a new form of proto-fascism. None of this will happen in the face of sufficient resistance, nor is the increasing move toward proto-fascism inevitable; but the conditions exist for democracy to lose all semblance of meaning in the United States. Against this encroaching form of fascism, a new language is needed for redefining the meaning of politics and the importance of public life.

Educators, parents, activists, workers, and others can address this challenge by building local and global alliances and engaging in struggles that acknowledge and transcend national boundaries, but also engage in modes of politics that connect with people's everyday lives. Democratic struggles cannot underplay the special responsibility of intellectuals to shatter the conventional wisdom and myths of neoliberalism with its stunted definition of freedom and its depoliticized and dehistoricized definition of its own alleged universality. As Bourdieu argued, any viable politics that challenges neoliberalism must refigure the role of the state in limiting the excesses of capital and providing important social provisions.[200] At the same time, social movements must address the crucial issue of education as it develops throughout the cultural sphere because the "power of the dominant order is not just economic, but intellectual—lying in the realm of beliefs," and it is precisely within the domain of ideas that a sense of utopian possibility can be restored to the public realm.[201] Most specifically, democracy necessitates forms of education that provide a new ethic of freedom and a reassertion of collective identity as central preoccupations of a vibrant democratic culture and society. Such a task, in part, suggests addressing the crucial pedagogical challenge of educating individuals and groups as social actors while refusing to allow them to be portrayed simply as victims. Pondering the devastation following decades of European fascism, the theorist Theodor Adorno once wrote that "the premier demand upon all education is that Auschwitz not happen again."[202] While recognizing that the particularity of Auschwitz as a specific historical event should never be generalized, I believe that Adorno's comment extends beyond the reality of Auschwitz and speaks to the need to grasp the deeper meaning of education as a political and ethical intervention into what it means to shape the future. Every debate about education should address the important responsibility it has in preventing any relapse into barbarism from happening again. The time to act is now because the stakes have never been so high and the future so dark.

2
Spectacles of Race and Pedagogies of Denial

❧

Race relations in the United States have changed considerably since W.E.B. Du Bois famously predicted in *The Souls of Black Folk* that "the problem of the 20th century is the problem of the color line."[1] This is not to suggest that race has declined in significance, or that the racial conditions, ideologies, and practices that provided the context for Du Bois' prophecy have been overcome; rather, the point is that they have been transformed, mutated, and recycled and have taken on new and in many instances more covert modes of expression.[2] Du Bois recognized that the color line was not fixed—its forms of expression changed over time, as a response to different contexts and struggles—and that one of the great challenges facing future generations would be not only to engage the complex structural legacy of race but also to take note of the plethora of forms in which it was expressed and experienced in everyday life. For Du Bois, race fused power and ideology and was deeply woven into both the public pedagogy of American culture and its geography, economics, politics, and institutions.

The great challenge Du Bois presents to this generation of students, educators, and citizens is to acknowledge that the future of democracy in the United States is inextricably linked "to the outcomes of racial politics and policies, as they develop both in various national societies and the world at large."[3] In part, this observation implies

This chapter is reprinted with permission from Henry A. Giroux, "Spectacles of Race and Pedagogies of Denial," *Communication Education* 52:3/4 pp. 19–21 (2003).

that how we experience democracy in the future will depend on how we name, think about, experience, and transform the interrelated modalities of race, racism, and social justice. It also suggests that the meaning of race and the challenges of racism change for each generation, and that the new challenges we face demand a new language for understanding how the symbolic power of race as a pedagogical force as well as a structural and materialist practice redefines the relationship between the self and the other, the private and the public. It is this latter challenge in particular that needs to be more fully addressed if racism is not to be reduced to an utterly privatized discourse that erases any trace of racial injustice by denying the very notion of the social and the operations of power through which racial politics are organized and legitimated.

When Du Bois wrote *The Souls of Black Folk,* racism was a visible and endemic part of the American political, cultural, and economic landscape. The racial divide was impossible to ignore, irrespective of one's politics. As we move into the new millennium, the politics of the color line and representations of race have become far more subtle and complicated than they were in the Jim Crow era when Du Bois made his famous pronouncement. And though far from invisible, the complicated nature of race relations in American society no longer appears to be marked by the specter of Jim Crow. A majority of Americans now believe that anti-black racism is a thing of the past, since it is assumed that formal institutions of segregation no longer exist. Yet, surveys done by the National Opinion Research Center at the University of Chicago have consistently found "that most Americans still believe blacks are less intelligent than whites, lazier than whites, and more likely than whites to prefer living on welfare over being self-supporting."[4] Contradictions aside, conservatives and liberals alike now view America's racial hierarchy as an unfortunate historical fact that has no bearing on contemporary society. Pointing to the destruction of the Southern caste system, the problematizing of whiteness as a racial category, the passing of civil rights laws, a number of successful lawsuits alleging racial discrimination against companies such as Texaco and Denny's, and the emergence of people of color into all aspects of public life, the color line now seems in disarray, a remnant of another era that Americans have fortunately moved beyond. Best-selling books such as Dinesh D'Souza's *The End of Racism,* Jim Sleeper's *Liberal Racism,* and Stephan and Abigail Thernstrom's *America in Black and White: One Nation, Indivisible* all proclaim racism as an obsolete ideology and practice.[5]

And a large number of white Americans seem to agree. In fact, poll after poll reveals that a majority of white Americans believe that people of color no longer face racial discrimination in American life. For example, a recent Gallup Poll on "Black-White Relations" observes that "7 out of 10 whites believe that blacks are treated equally in their communities.... Eight in ten whites say blacks receive equal educational opportunities, and 83% say blacks receive equal housing opportunities in their communities. Only a third of whites believe blacks face racial bias from police in their areas."[6] For many conservative and liberal intellectuals, the only remaining remnant of racist categorization and policy in an otherwise color-blind society is affirmative action, which is ironically alleged to provide blacks with an unfair advantage in higher education, the labor force, "entitlement programs," and "even summer scholarship programs."[7]

The importance of race and the enduring fact of racism are relegated to the dustbin of history at a time in American life when the discourses of race and the spectacle of racial representations saturate the dominant media and public life. The color line is now mined for exotic commodities that can be sold to white youth in the form of rap music, hip-hop clothing, and sports gear. African-American celebrities such as Michael Jordan, Etta James, and George Foreman are used to give market legitimacy to everything from gas grills to high-end luxury cars to clothes. Black public intellectuals such as Patricia Williams, Cornel West, Michael Dyson, and Henry Louis Gates command the attention of the *New York Times* and other eye-catching media. African-Americans now occupy powerful positions on the Supreme Court and at the highest levels of political life. The alleged collapse, if not transformation, of the color line can also be seen in the emergence of the black elite, prominently on display in television sitcoms, fashion magazines, Hollywood movies, and music videos. On the political scene, however, the supposedly race-transcendent public policy is complicated by ongoing public debates over affirmative action, welfare, crime, and the prison-industrial complex. All of which suggests that whereas the color line has been modified and dismantled in places, race and racial hierarchies still exercise a profound influence on how most people in the United States experience their daily lives.[8] Popular sentiment aside, race—rather than disappearing—has retained its power as a key signifier in structuring all aspects of American life. As Michael Omi keenly observes: "Despite legal guarantees of formal equality and access, race continues to be a fundamental organizing principle of individual identity and collective action. I would argue that, far from declining in significance (as William Julius Wilson would have us believe), the racial dimensions of politics and culture have proliferated."[9]

Representations of race and difference are everywhere in American society, and yet racism as both a symbol and a condition of American life is either ignored or relegated to an utterly privatized discourse, typified in references to individual prejudices or to psychological dispositions such as expressions of "hate." As politics becomes more racialized, the discourse about race becomes more privatized. While the realities of race permeate public life, they are engaged less as discourses and sites where differences are produced within iniquitous relations of power than as either unobjectionable cultural signifiers or desirable commodities. The public morality of the marketplace works its magic in widening the gap between political control and economic power while simultaneously reducing political agency to the act of consuming. One result is a growing cynicism and powerlessness among the general population as the political impotence of public institutions is reinforced through the disparaging of any reference to ethics, equity, justice, or other normative principles that prioritize democratic values over market considerations. Similarly, as corporate power undermines all notions of the public good and increasingly privatizes public space, it obliterates those public spheres in which there might emerge criticism that acknowledges the tensions wrought by a pervasive racism that "functions as one of the deep, abiding currents in everyday life, in both the simplest and the most complex interactions of whites and blacks."[10] Indifference and cynicism breed contempt and resentment as racial hierarchies now collapse into power-evasive strategies such as blaming minorities of class and color for not working hard enough, refusing to exercise individual initiative, or practicing reverse-racism. In short, marketplace ideologies now work to erase the social from the language of public life so as to reduce all racial problems to private issues such as individual character and cultural depravity.

Black public intellectuals such as Shelby Steele and John McWhorter garner national attention by asserting that the subject and object of racism have been reversed. For Steele, racism has nothing to do with soaring black unemployment, failing and segregated schools for black children, a criminal justice system that resembles the old plantation system of the South, or police brutality that takes its toll largely on blacks in urban cities such as Cincinnati and New York. On the contrary, according to Steele, racism has produced white guilt, a burden that white people have to carry as part of the legacy of the civil rights movement. To remove this burden from white shoulders, blacks now have to free themselves from their victim status and act responsibly by proving to whites that *their* suffering is unnecessary.[11] They can do so through the spirit of principled entrepreneurialism—allowing themselves to be judged on the basis of hard work, individual effort, a secure family life, decent values, and property ownership.[12] It gets worse. John McWhorter, largely relying on anecdotes from his own limited experience in the academy at UCLA–Berkeley, argues that higher education is filled with African-American students who are either mediocre or simply lazy, victims of affirmative action programs that coddle them because of their race while allowing them to "dumb down" rather than work as competitively as their white classmates. The lesson here is that the color line now benefits blacks rather than whites and that, in the end, for McWhorter, diversity rather than bigotry is the enemy of a quality education and functions largely to "condemn black students to mediocrity."[13]

Within this discourse, there is a glimmer of a new kind of racial reference, one that can imagine public issues only as private concerns. This is a racism that refuses to "translate private sufferings into public issues,"[14] a racism that works hard to remove issues of power and equity from broader social concerns. Ultimately, it imagines human agency as simply a matter of individualized choices, the only obstacle to effective citizenship and agency being the lack of principled self-help and moral responsibility. In what follows, I want to examine briefly the changing nature of the new racism by analyzing how some of its central assumptions evade notions of race, racial justice, equity, and democracy altogether. In the process, I analyze some elements of the new racism, particularly the discourse of color-blindness and neoliberal racism. I then address the ways in which the controversial Trent Lott affair demonstrated neoliberal racism as well as the racism of denial. I will conclude by offering some suggestions about how the new racism, particularly its neoliberal version, can be addressed as both a pedagogical and a political issue.

Neoliberalism and the Culture of Privatization

The public morality of American life and social policy regarding matters of racial justice are increasingly subject to a politics of denial. Denial in this case is not merely about the failure of public memory or the refusal to know, but an active ongoing attempt on the part of many conservatives, liberals, and politicians to rewrite the discourse of race so as to deny its valence as a force for discrimination and exclusion either by translating it as a threat to American culture or relegating it to the language of the private sphere. The idea of race and the conditions of racism have real political effects, and eliding them only makes those effects harder to recognize. And yet, the urgency to recognize how language is used to name, organize, order, and categorize matters of race not only has academic value, it also provides a location from which to engage difference and the relationship between the self and the other and between the public and private. In addition, the language of race is important because it strongly affects political and policy agendas as well. One only has to think about the effects of Charles Murray's book *Losing Ground* on American welfare policies in the 1980s.[15] But language is more than a mode of communication or a symbolic practice that produces real effects; it is also a site of contestation and struggle. Since the mid-1970s, race relations have undergone a significant shift and acquired a new character as the forces of neoliberalism have begun to shape how Americans understand notions of agency, identity, freedom, and politics itself.[16]

Part of this shift has to be understood within the emerging forces of transnational capitalism and a global restructuring in which the economy is separated from politics and corporate power is largely removed from the control of nation-states. Within the neoliberal register, globalization "represents the triumph of the economy over politics and culture ... and the hegemony of capital over all other domains of life."[17] Under neoliberal globalization, capital removes itself from any viable form of state regulation, power is uncoupled from matters of ethics and social responsibility, and market freedoms replace long-standing social contracts that once provided a safety net for the poor, the elderly, workers, and the middle class. The result is that public issues and social concerns increasingly give way to a growing culture of insecurity and fear regarding the most basic issues of individual livelihood, safety, and survival. Increasingly, a concern with either the past or the future is replaced by uncertainty, and traditional human bonds rooted in compassion, justice, and a respect for others are now replaced by a revitalized social Darwinism, played out nightly in the celebration of reality-based television, in which rabid self-interest becomes the organizing principle for a winner-take-all society. As insecurity and fear grip public consciousness, society is no longer identified through its allegiance to democratic values but through a troubling freedom rooted in a disturbing emphasis on individualism and competitiveness as the only normative measures to distinguish between what is a right or wrong, just or unjust, proper or improper action. Zygmunt Bauman captures this deracinated notion of freedom and the insecurity it promotes in his observation that

> [s]ociety no longer guarantees, or even promises, a collective remedy for individual misfortunes. Individuals have been offered (or, rather, have been cast into) freedom of unprecedented proportions—but at the price of similarly unprecedented insecurity. And when there is insecurity, little time is left for caring for values that hover above the level of daily concerns—or, for that matter, for whatever lasts longer than the fleeting moment.[18]

Within this emerging neoliberal ethic, success is attributed to thriftiness and entrepreneurial genius while those who do not succeed are viewed either as failures or as utterly expendable. Indeed, neoliberalism's attachment to individualism, markets, and antistatism ranks human needs as less important than property rights and subordinates "the art of politics ... to the science of economics."[19] Racial justice in the age of market-based freedoms and financially driven values loses its ethical imperative to a neoliberalism that embraces commercial rather than civic values, private rather than pubic interests, and financial incentives rather than ethical concerns. Neoliberalism negates racism as an ethical issue and democratic values as a basis for citizen-based action. Of course, neoliberalism takes many forms as it moves across the globe. In the United States, it has achieved a surprising degree of success but is increasingly being resisted by labor unions, students, and environmentalists. Major protests against economic policies promoted by the World Bank, International Monetary Fund, and World Trade Organization have taken place in Seattle, Prague, New York, Montreal, Genoa, and other cities around the world. In the United States, a rising generation of students is protesting trade agreements like GATT and NAFTA as well as sweat-shop labor practices at home and abroad and the corporatization of public and higher education. Unfortunately, anti-racist theorists have not said enough about either the link between the new racism and neoliberalism, on the one hand, or the rise of a race-based carceral state, on the other. Neither the rise of the new racism nor any viable politics of an anti-racist movement can be understood outside the power and grip of neoliberalism in the United States. Hence, at the risk of oversimplification and repetition within other chapters, I want to be a bit more specific about neoliberalism's central assumptions and how it frames some of the more prominent emerging racial discourses and practices.

Neoliberalism and the Politics of the New Racism

As mentioned in the preface, under the reign of neoliberalism in the United States, society is largely defined through the privileging of market relations, deregulation, privatization, and consumerism. Central to neoliberalism is the assumption that profit-making be construed as the essence of democracy and consuming as the most cherished act of citizenship. Strictly aligning freedom with a narrow notion of individual interest, neoliberalism works hard to privatize all aspects of the public good and simultaneously narrow the role of the state as both a gatekeeper for capital and a policing force for maintaining social order and racial control. Unrestricted by social legislation or government regulation, market relations as they define the economy are viewed as a paradigm for democracy itself. Central to neoliberal philosophy is the claim that the development of all aspects of society should be left to the wisdom of the market. Similarly, neoliberal warriors argue that democratic values be subordinated to economic considerations, social issues be translated as private dilemmas, part-time labor replace full-time work, trade unions be weakened, and everybody be treated as a customer. Within this market-driven perspective, the exchange of capital takes precedence over social justice, the making of socially responsible citizens, and the building of democratic communities. There is no language here for recognizing anti-democratic forms of power, developing nonmarket values, or fighting against substantive injustices in a society founded on deep inequalities, particularly those based on race and class. Hence, it is not surprising that under neoliberalism, language is often stripped of its critical and social possibilities as it becomes increasingly difficult to imagine a social order in which all problems are not personal, in which social issues provide the conditions for understanding private considerations, critical reflection becomes the essence of politics, and matters of equity and justice become crucial to developing a democratic society.

It is under the reign of neoliberalism that the changing vocabulary about race and racial justice has to be understood and engaged.

As freedom is increasingly abstracted from the power of individuals and groups to actively participate in shaping society, it is reduced to the right of the individual to be free from social constraints. In this view, freedom is no longer linked to a collective effort on the part of individuals to create a democratic society. Instead, freedom becomes an exercise in self-development rather than social responsibility, reducing politics to either the celebration of consumerism or the privileging of a market-based notion of agency and choice that appears quite indifferent to how power, equity, and justice offer the enabling conditions for real individual and collective choices to be both made and acted upon. Under such circumstances, neoliberalism undermines those public spaces where noncommercial values and crucial social issues can be discussed, debated, and engaged. As public space is privatized, power is disconnected from social obligations and it becomes more difficult for isolated individuals living in consumption-oriented spaces to construct an ethically engaged and power-sensitive language capable of accommodating the principles of ethics and racial justice as a common good rather than as a private affair. According to Bauman, the elimination of public space and the subordination of democratic values to commercial interests narrows the discursive possibilities for supporting notions of the public good and creates the conditions for "the suspicion against others, the intolerance of difference, the resentment of strangers, and the demands to separate and banish them, as well as the hysterical, paranoiac concern with 'law and order.'"[20] Positioned within the emergence of neoliberalism as the dominant economic and political philosophy of our times, neoracism can be understood as part of a broader attack not only on difference but on the value of public memory, public goods, and democracy itself.

The new racism represents both a shift in how race is defined and a symptom of the breakdown of a political culture in which individual freedom and solidarity maintain an uneasy equilibrium in the service of racial, social, and economic justice. Individual freedom is now disconnected from any sense of civic responsibility or justice, focusing instead on investor profits, consumer confidence, the downsizing of governments to police precincts, and a deregulated social order in which the winner takes all. Freedom is no longer about either making the powerful responsible for their actions or providing the essential political, economic, and social conditions for everyday people to intervene in and shape their future. Under the reign of neoliberalism, freedom is less about the act of intervention than about the process of withdrawing from the social and enacting one's sense of agency as an almost exclusively private endeavor. Freedom now cancels out civic courage and social responsibility while it simultaneously translates public issues and collective problems into tales of failed character, bad luck, or simply indifference. As Amy Elizabeth Ansell points out:

> The disproportionate failure of people of color to achieve social mobility speaks nothing of the justice of present social arrangements, according to the New Right worldview, but rather reflects the lack of merit or ability of people of color themselves. In this way, attention is deflected away from the reality of institutional racism and towards, for example, the "culture of poverty," the "drug culture," or the lack of black self-development.[21]

Appeals to freedom, operating under the sway of market forces, offer no signposts theoretically or politically for engaging racism as an ethical and political issue that undermines the very basis of a substantive democracy. Freedom in this discourse collapses into self-interest and as such is more inclined to organize any sense of community around shared fears, insecurities, and an intolerance of those "others" who are marginalized by class and color. But freedom reduced to the ethos of self-preservation and brutal self-interest makes it difficult for individuals to recognize the forms that racism often takes when draped in the language of either denial, freedom, or individual rights. In what follows, I want to explore two prominent forms of the new racism—color-blindness and neoliberal racism—and their connection to the New Right, corporate power, and neoliberal ideologies.

Unlike the old racism, which defined racial difference in terms of fixed biological categories organized hierarchically, the new racism operates in various guises proclaiming among other things race-neutrality, asserting culture as a marker of racial difference, or marking race as a private matter. Unlike the crude racism with its biological referents and pseudo-scientific legitimations, buttressing its appeal to white racial superiority, the new racism cynically recodes itself within the vocabulary of the civil rights movement, invoking the language of Martin Luther King, Jr., to argue that individuals should be judged by the "content of their character" and not by the color of their skin. Ansell, a keen commentator on the new racism, notes both the recent shifts in racialized discourse away from more rabid and overt forms of racism and its appropriation particularly by the New Right in the United States and Britain:

> The new racism actively disavows racist intent and is cleansed of extremist intolerance, thus reinforcing the New Right's attempt to distance itself from racist organizations such as the John Birch Society in the United States and the National Front in Britain. It is a form of racism that utilizes themes related to culture and nation as a replacement for the now discredited biological referents of the old racism. It is concerned less with notions of racial superiority in the narrow sense than with the alleged "threat" people of color pose—either because of their mere presence or because of their demand for "special privileges"—to economic, socio-political, and cultural vitality of the dominant (white) society. It is, in short, a new form of racism that operates with the category of "race." It is a new form of exclusionary politics that operates indirectly and in stealth via the rhetorical inclusion of people of color and the sanitized nature of its racist appeal.[22]

What is crucial about the new racism is that it demands an updated analysis of how racist practices work through the changing nature of language and other modes of representation. One of the most sanitized and yet most pervasive forms of the new racism is evident in the language of color-blindness. Within this approach, it is argued that racial conflict and discrimination are things of the past and that race has no bearing on an individual's or group's location or standing in contemporary American society. Color-blindness does not deny the existence of race but, rather, claims that race is responsible for alleged injustices that reproduce group inequalities, privilege whites, and negatively impact on economic mobility, the possession of social resources, and the acquisition of political power. Put differently, inherent in the logic of color-blindness is the central assumption that race has no valence as a marker of identity or power when factored into the social vocabulary of everyday life and the capacity for exercising individual and social agency. As Charles Gallagher observes, "Within the color-blind perspective it is not race per se which determines upward mobility but how much an individual chooses to pay attention to race that determines one's fate. Within this perspective race is only as important as you allow it to be."[23] As Jeff, one of Gallagher's interviewees, puts it, race is simply another choice: "[Y]ou know, there's music, rap music is no longer, it's not a black thing anymore.... [W]hen it first came out it was black music, but now it's just music. It's another choice, just like country music can be considered like white hick music, you know it's just a choice."[24]

64

Hence, in an era "free" of racism, race becomes a matter of taste, lifestyle, or heritage but has nothing to do with politics, legal rights, educational access, or economic opportunities. Veiled by a denial of how racial histories accrue political, economic, and cultural weight to the social power of whiteness, color-blindness deletes the relationship between racial differences and power. In doing so it reinforces whiteness as the arbiter of value for judging difference against a normative notion of homogeneity.[25] For advocates of color-blindness, race as a political signifier is conveniently denied or seen as something to be overcome, allowing whites to ignore racism as a corrosive force for expanding the dynamics of ideological and structural inequality throughout society.[26] Color-blindness, then, is a convenient ideology for enabling whites to disregard the degree to which race is tangled up with asymmetrical relations of power, functioning as a potent force for patterns of exclusion and discrimination including but not limited to housing, mortgage loans, health care, schools, and the criminal justice system. If one effect of color-blindness functions is to deny racial hierarchies, another is that it offers whites the belief not only that America is now a level playing field but also that the success that whites enjoy relative to minorities of color is largely due to individual determination, a strong work ethic, high moral values, and a sound investment in education. In short, color-blindness offers up a highly racialized (though paraded as race-transcendent) notion of agency, while also providing an ideological space free of guilt, self-reflection, and political responsibility, despite the fact that blacks have a disadvantage in almost all areas of social life: housing, jobs, education, income levels, mortgage lending, and basic everyday services.[27] In a society marked by profound racial and class inequalities, it is difficult to believe that character and merit—as color-blindness advocates would have us believe—are the prime determinants for social and economic mobility and a decent standard of living. The relegation of racism and its effects in the larger society to the realm of private beliefs, values, and behavior does little to explain a range of overwhelming realities—such as soaring black unemployment, decaying cities, and segregated schools. Paul Street puts the issue forcibly in a series of questions that register the primacy of and interconnections among politics, social issues, and race:

Why are African-Americans twice as likely to be unemployed as whites? Why is the poverty rate for blacks more than twice the rate for whites? Why do nearly one out of every two blacks earn less than $25,000 while only one in three whites makes that little? Why is the median black household income ($27,000) less than two thirds of the median white household income ($42,000)? Why is the black family's median household net worth less than 10 percent that of whites? Why are blacks much less likely to own their own homes than whites? Why do African-Americans make up roughly half of the United States' massive population of prisoners (2 million) and why are one in three young, black male adults in prison or on parole or otherwise under the supervision of the American criminal justice system? Why do African-Americans continue in severe geographic separation from mainstream society, still largely cordoned off into the nation's most disadvantaged communities thirty years after the passage of the civil rights fair housing legislation? Why do blacks suffer disproportionately from irregularities in the American electoral process, from problems with voter registration to the functioning of voting machinery? Why does black America effectively constitute a Third World enclave of sub-citizens within the world's richest and most powerful state?[28]

Add to this list the stepped-up resegregation of American schools and the growing militarization and lock-down status of public education through the widespread use of zero-tolerance policies.[29] Or the fact that African-American males live on average six years less than their white counterparts. It is worth noting that nothing challenges the myth that America has become a color-blind post-racist nation more than the racialization of the criminal justice system since the late 1980s. As the sociologist Loic Wacquant has observed, the expansion of the prison-industrial complex represents a "de facto policy of 'carceral affirmative action' towards African-Americans."[30] This is borne out by the fact that while American prisons house over 2 million inmates, "roughly half of them are black even though African-Americans make up less than 13 percent of the nation's population.... According to the Justice Policy Institute there are now more black men behind bars than in college in the United States. One in ten of the world's prisoners is an African-American male."[31]

As one of the most powerful ideological and institutional factors for deciding how identities are categorized and power, material privileges, and resources distributed, race represents an essential political category for examining the relationship between justice and a democratic society. But color-blindness is about more than the denial of how power and politics operate to promote racial discrimination and exclusion; it is also an ideological and pedagogical weapon powerfully mobilized by conservatives and the Right for arguing that because of the success of the civil rights movement, racism has been eliminated as an institutional and ideological force, thus eradicating the need for government-based programs designed to dismantle the historical legacy and effects of racism in all dimensions of the social order.

Within the last twenty years, a more virulent form of the new racism has appeared that also affirms the basic principles of color-blindness; but instead of operating primarily as a discourse of denial regarding how power and politics promote racial discrimination and exclusion, neoliberal racism is about the privatization of racial discourse. It is also proactive, functioning aggressively in the public arena as an ideological and pedagogical weapon powerfully mobilized by various conservatives and right-wing groups. Neoliberal racism asserts the insignificance of race as a social force and aggressively roots out any vestige of race as a category at odds with an individualistic embrace of formal legal rights. Focusing on individuals rather than on groups, neoliberal racism either dismisses the concept of institutional racism or maintains that it has no merit. In this context, racism is primarily defined as a form of individual prejudice while appeals to equality are dismissed outright. For instance, racial ideologues Richard J. Herrnstein and Charles Murray write in *The Bell Curve:* "In everyday life, the ideology of equality censors and strait-jackets everything from pedagogy to humor. The ideology of equality has stunted the range of moral dialogue to triviality.... It is time for America once again to try living with inequality, as life is lived."[32] Arguing that individual freedom is tarnished if not poisoned by the discourse of equality, right-wing legal advocacy groups such as the Center for Individual Rights (CIR) and the Foundation for Individual Rights in Education argue that identity politics and pluralism weaken rather than strengthen American democracy because they pose a threat to what it means for the United States "to remain recognizably American."[33] But such groups do more than define American culture in racist and retrograde terms; they also aggressively use their resources—generously provided by prominent right-wing conservative organizations such as the Lynde and Harry Bradley Foundation, the John M. Olin Foundation, the Adolph Coors Foundation, and the Scaife Family Foundation—to challenge racial preference policies that are not based on a "principle of state neutrality."[34] With ample resources at their disposal, advocates of neoliberal racism have successfully challenged a number of cases before the Supreme Court over the legality of affirmative action programs, campus speech codes, hiring practices, the Violence Against Women Act, and the elimination of men's sports teams in higher education.[35] Hence, neoliberal racism provides the ideological and legal framework for asserting that since American society is now a meritocracy, government should be race neutral, affirmative action programs dismantled, civil rights laws discarded, and the welfare state eliminated. As Nikhil Aziz observes, "The Right argues that, because racism has been dealt with as a result of the Civil Rights Movement, race should not be a consideration for hiring in employment or for admission to educational institutions, and group identities other than 'American' are immaterial."[36]

Neoliberal racism is unwilling to accept any concept of the state as a guardian of the public interest. Motivated by a passion for free markets that is matched only by an anti-government fervor, neoliberal racism calls for a hollowing out of the social welfare functions of the state, except for its role in safeguarding the interests of the privileged and the strengthening of its policing functions. Rejecting a notion of the public good for private interest, advocates of neoliberal racism want to limit the state's role in public investments and social programs as a constraint on both individual rights and the expression of individual freedom. In this view, individual interests override any notion of the public good, and individual freedom operates outside of any ethical responsibility for its social consequences. The results of this policy are evident in right-wing attacks on public education, health care, environmental regulations, public housing, race-based scholarships, and other public services that embrace notions of difference. Many of these programs benefit the general public, though they are relied on disproportionately by the poor and people of color. As Zsuza Ferge points out, what becomes clear about neoliberal racism is that "the attack on the big state has indeed become predominantly an attack on the welfare functions of the state.... The underlying motif is the conviction that the supreme value is economic growth to be attained by unfettered free trade equated with freedom *tout court*.... The extremely individualist approach that characterizes this ethic justifies the diagnosis of many that neoliberalism is about the 'individualization of the social.'"[37] By preventing the state from addressing or correcting the effects of racial discrimination, state agencies are silenced, thus displacing "the tensions of contemporary racially charged relations to the relative invisibility of private spheres, seemingly out of reach of public policy intervention."[38]

The relentless spirit of self-interest within neoliberal racism offers an apology for a narrow market-based notion of freedom in which individual rights and choices are removed from any viable notion of social responsibility, critical citizenship, and substantive democracy. By distancing itself from any notion of liberal egalitarianism, civic obligation, or a more positive notion of freedom, neoliberal racism does more than collapse the political into the personal—invoking character against institutional racism and individual rights against social wrongs. Indeed, it claims, as Jean and John Comaroff argue, that

[t]he personal is the only politics there is, the only politics with a tangible referent or emotional valence. It is in these privatized terms that action is organized, that the experience of inequity and antagonism takes meaningful shape.... [Neoliberalism] is a culture that ... re-visions persons not as producers from a particular community, but as consumers in a planetary marketplace.[39]

Neoliberalism devitalizes democracy because it has no language for defending a politics in which citizenship becomes an investment in public life rather than an obligation to consume, relegated in this instance to an utterly privatized affair. The discourse of neoliberal racism has no way of talking about collective responsibility, social agency, or a defense of the public good. But the absences in its discourse are not innocent because they both ignore and perpetuate the stereotypes, structured violence, and massive inequalities produced by the racial state, the race-based attack on welfare, the destruction of social goods such as schools and health care, and the rise of the prison-industrial complex. And its attack on the principles of equality, liberty, economic democracy, and racial justice, in the final analysis, represents "a heartless indifference to the social contract, or any other civic-minded concern for the larger social good."[40] In fact, neoliberalism has played a defining role in transforming the social contract to the carceral contract, which substitutes punishment for social investment. Hence, it is not surprising how neoliberal arguments embracing the primacy of individual solutions to public issues such as poverty or the ongoing incarceration of black males are quick to defend public policies that are both punitive and overtly racist such as workfare for welfare recipients or the public shaming rituals of prison chain gangs, with an overabundance of black males always on display. Neoliberal racism's "heartless indifference" to the plight of the poor is often mirrored in an utter disdain for human suffering, as in Shelby Steele's nostalgic longing for a form of social

Darwinism in which "failure and suffering are natural and necessary elements of success."[41]

It is interesting that whenever white racism is invoked by critics in response to the spectacle of racism, advocates of color-blindness and neoliberal racism often step outside of the privatizing language of rights and have little trouble appropriating victim status for whites while blaming people of color for the harsh conditions under which so many have to live in this country. And in some cases, this is done in the name of a civility that is used to hide both the legacy and the reality of racism and a commitment to equality as a cornerstone of racial progress. A classic example of the latter can be found in *The End of Racism* by Dinesh D'Souza. He writes:

> Nothing strengthens racism in this country more than the behavior of the African-American underclass which flagrantly violates and scandalizes basic codes of responsibility and civility.... [I]f blacks as a group can show that they are capable of performing competitively in schools and the workforce, and exercising both the rights and responsibilities of American citizenship, then racism will be deprived of its foundation in experience.[42]

Spectacles of Race

Scripted denials of racism coupled with the spectacle of racial discourse and representations have become a common occurrence in American life. Power-evasive strategies wrapped up in the language of individual choice and the virtues of self-reliance provide the dominant modes of framing through which the larger public can witness in our media-saturated culture what Patricia Williams calls "the unsaid filled by stereotypes and self-identifying illusion, the hierarchies of race and gender circulating unchallenged," enticing audiences who prefer "familiar drama to the risk of serious democratization."[43] In what follows, I want to address the controversy surrounding the racist remarks made by Trent Lott at Strom Thurmond's centennial birthday celebration and how the Lott affair functions as an example of how controversial issues often assume the status of both a national melodrama and a scripted spectacle. I also want to analyze how this event functioned largely to privatize matters of white racism while rendering invisible the endorsement of systemic and state-fashioned racism. The Lott affair functions as a public transcript in providing a context for examining the public pedagogy of racial representations in media and print culture that are often framed within the ideology of the new racism in order to displace any serious discussion of racial exclusion in the United States. Finally, I offer some suggestions about how to respond politically to neoliberal racism and what the implications might be for a critical pedagogical practice aimed at challenging and dismantling it.

While attending Strom Thurmond's 100th birthday party on December 5, 2002, the then Senate majority leader, Trent Lott, offered the following salute to one of the most legendary segregationists alive: "I want to say this about my state: When Strom Thurmond ran for President, we voted for him. We're proud of it. And if the rest of the country had followed our lead, we wouldn't have had all these problems over all these years, either."[44] Of course, for the historically aware, the meaning of the tribute was clear since Thurmond had run in 1948 on a racist Dixiecrat ticket whose official campaign slogan was "Segregation Forever!"

It took five days before the incident got any serious attention in the national media. But once the story broke, Lott offered an endless series of apologies that included everything from saying he was just "winging it"(until it was revealed that he made an almost identical remark as a congressman at a Reagan rally a few decades earlier), to having found "Jesus," to proclaiming he was now "an across the board" advocate of affirmative action.[45] The Lott story evoked a range of opinions in the media extending from a craven defense provided by conservative columnist Bob Novak (who argued that Lott's racist comments were just a slip of the tongue) to vociferous moral condemnation from all sides of the ideological spectrum. Once Lott's voting record on civil rights issues was made public, he became an embarrassment and liability to those politicians who denounced open racial bigotry but had little to say about structural, systemic, and institutional racism.[46] Under pressure from his Republican party colleagues, Lott eventually resigned as Senate majority leader, though he retained his Senate seat, and the story passed in the national media from revelation to spectacle to irrelevance. The shelf-life of the spectacle in the dominant culture is usually quite long—witness the Gary Condit affair—except when it offers the possibility for revealing how racist expressions privately license relations of power that reproduce a wide range of racial exclusions in the wider social order.

Lott's remarks cast him as a supporter of the old racism—bigoted, crude, and overtly racist. And, for the most part, the wrath his remarks engendered from the Republican Party and its media cheerleaders was mainly of the sort that allowed the critics to reposition themselves in keeping with the dictates of the logic of color-blindness and neoliberal racism. In doing so they distanced themselves from Lott's comments as a safe way to attest their disdain for the old racist bigotry and to provide a display of their moral superiority and civility while at the same time distancing themselves from what Robert Kuttner has called some "inconvenient truths" when it came to talking about race. As Kuttner observes, "His stated views made it more difficult for the Republican party to put on minstrel shows and offer speeches dripping with compassion, while appointing racist judges, battling affirmative action, resisting hate crimes legislation, and slashing social outlays that help minorities. Lott made it harder to hold down black voting in the name of 'ballot security' while courting black voters, and disguising attacks on public education as expanded 'choice' for black parents and stingy welfare reform as promoting self-sufficiency."[47] Of course, singling out Lott also suggested that he was, as an editorial in the *Wall Street Journal* claimed, a one-of-a-kind bad apple, an unfortunate holdover from the Jim Crow era that no longer exists in America. David Brooks, the editor of the conservative *National Review,* proclaimed with great indignation that Lott's views were not "normal Republican ideas" and, to prove the point, asserted that after hanging out with Republicans for two decades he had "never heard an overtly racist comment."[48]

Brooks, like many of his fellow commentators, seems to have allowed his ode to racial cleansing to cloud his sense of recent history. After all, it was only about a decade ago that Kirk Fordice, a right-wing Republican, ended his victorious campaign for governor—orchestrated largely as an attack on crime and welfare cheaters—with a "still photograph of a Black woman and her baby."[49] And of course this was just a few years after George H.W. Bush ran his famous Willie Horton ad and a short time before Dan Quayle in the 1992 presidential campaign used the racially coded category of welfare to attack a sitcom character, Murphy Brown. Maybe David Brooks was just unaware of the interview that John Ashcroft had given in 1999 to the neoconfederate magazine, *Southern Partisan,* "in which he 'vowed to do more' to defend the legacy of Jefferson Davis."[50] Or, as *New York Times* writer Frank Rich puts it in response to the apparent newfound historical amnesia about the overt racism displayed by the Republican Party in more recent times:

Tell that to George W. Bush, who beat John McCain in the 2000 South Carolina primary after what *Newsweek* called "a smear campaign" of leaflets, e-mails and telephone calls calling attention to the McCains' "black child" (an adopted daughter from Bangladesh). Or to Sonny Perdue, the new Republican governor of Georgia, elected in part by demagoguing the sanctity of the confederate flag.[51]

One telling example of how the Trent Lott affair was removed from the historical record of racialized injustices, the realm of political contestation, and, indeed, any critical understanding of how racializing categories actually take hold in the culture can be found in the December 23, 2002, issue of *Newsweek*, which was devoted in entirety to the public uproar surrounding Lott's racist remarks.[52] *Newsweek* featured a 1962 picture of Lott on its cover with the caption "The Past That Made Him—and May Undo Him: Race and the Rise of Trent Lott." The stories that appeared in the magazine portrayed Lott either as an odd and totally out-of-touch symbol of the past ("A Man Out of Time," as one story headline read) or as an unrepentant symbol of racism that was no longer acceptable in American public life or in national politics. *Newsweek* ended its series on Lott with a short piece called "Lessons of the Trent Lott Mess."[53] The author of the article, Ellis Cose, condemned Lott's long history of racist affiliations, as did many other writers, but said nothing about why they were ignored by either the major political party or the dominant media over the last decade, especially given Lott's important standing in national politics. It is interesting to note that Lott's affiliation with the Council of Conservative Citizens (CCC)—a neo-confederate group that succeeded the notorious white Citizens Council, once referred to as the "uptown Klan"—was revealed in a 1998 story by Stanley Crouch, a writer for the *New York Daily News*. Surprisingly, the article was ignored at the time both by prominent politicians and by the dominant media. At issue here is the recognition that the history of racism in which Trent Lott participated is not merely his personal history but the country's history and, hence, should raise far more serious considerations about how the legacy of racism works through its cultural, economic, and social fabric. While Lott has to be held accountable for his remarks, his actions cannot be understood strictly within the language of American individualism—that is, as a bad reminder that the legacy of racism lives on in some old-fashioned politicians who cannot escape their past. In fact,

Lott's remarks as well as the silence that allowed his racist discourse to be viewed in strictly personal and idiosyncratic terms must be addressed as symptomatic of a larger set of racist historical, social, economic, and ideological influences that still hold sway over American society. Collapsing the political into the personal, and serious reporting into talk-show clichés, Cose argues that the reason a person like Lott is serving and will continue to serve in the Senate, sharing power with America's ruling elite, is that "Americans are very forgiving folks."[54] This response is more than simply inane; it is symptomatic of a culture of racism that has no language for or interest in understanding systemic racism, its history, or how it is embodied in most ruling political and economic institutions in the United States. Or, for that matter, why it has such a powerful grip on American culture. The Trent Lott affair is important not because it charts an influential senator's fall from grace and power in the wake of an unfortunate racist remark made in public, but because it is symptomatic of a new racism that offers no resources for translating private troubles into public considerations.

The public pedagogy underlying the popular response to Trent Lott's racist remarks reveals how powerful the educational force of the culture is in shaping dominant conventions about race. Mirroring the logic of neoliberalism, the overall response to Lott both privatized the discourse of racism and attributed a racist expression to an unfortunate slip of the tongue, a psychological disposition, or the emotive residue of a man who is out of step with both his political party and the spirit of the country. But such an expression is not simply the assertion of a prejudiced individual; it is also a mode of exclusion, rooted in forms of authority largely used to name, classify, order, and devalue people of color. As David Theo Goldberg observes:

> As a mode of exclusion, racist expression assumes authority and is vested with power, literally and symbolically, in bodily terms. They are human bodies that are classified, ordered, valorized, and devalued.... When this authority assumes state power, racialized discourse and its modes of exclusion become embedded in state institutions and normalized in the common business of everyday institutional life.... As expressions of exclusion, racism appeals either to inherent superiority or to differences. These putative differences and gradations may be strictly physical, intellectual, linguistic, or cultural. Each serves in two ways: They purport to furnish the basis for justifying differential distributions or treatment, and they represent the very relations of power that prompted them.[55]

As part of the discourse of denial, the Trent Lott episode reveals how racism is trivialized through a politics of racial management in which racism is consigned to an outdated past, a narrow psychologism, the private realm of bad judgment or personal indiscretion. But racial discourse is not simply about private speech acts or individualized modes of communication; it is also about contested histories, institutional relations of power, ideology, and the social gravity of effects. Racist discourses and expressions should alert us to the workings of power and the conditions that make particular forms of language possible and others seemingly impossible, as well as to the modes of agency they produce and legitimate—an issue almost completely ignored in the mainstream coverage of the Lott affair. What was missing from such coverage is captured by Teun A. Van Dijk in his analysis of elite discourse and racism:

> Racism, defined as a system of racial and ethnic inequality, can survive only when it is daily reproduced through multiple acts of exclusion, inferiorization, or marginalization. Such acts need to be sustained by an ideological system and by a set of attitudes that legitimate difference and dominance. Discourse is the principal means for the construction and reproduction of this sociocognitive framework.[56]

Conclusion

Any attempt to address the politics of the new racism in the United States must begin by reclaiming the language of the social and affirming the project of an inclusive and just democracy. This suggests addressing how the politics of the new racism is made invisible under the mantle of neoliberal ideology—that is, raising questions about how neoliberalism works to hide the effects of power, politics, and racial injustice. What is both troubling and must increasingly be made problematic is that neoliberalism wraps itself in what appears to be an unassailable appeal to common sense. As Jean and John Comaroff observe:

> [T]here is a strong argument to be made that neoliberal capitalism, in its millennial moment, portends the death of politics by hiding its own ideological underpinnings in the dictates of economic efficiency: in the fetishism of the free market, in the inexorable, expanding "needs" of business, in the imperatives of science and technology. Or, if it does not conduce to the death of politics, it tends to reduce them to the pursuit of pure interest, individual or collective.[57]

75

Defined as the paragon of all social relations, neoliberalism attempts to eliminate an engaged critique about its most basic principles and social consequences by embracing the "market as the arbiter of social destiny."[58] More is lost here than neoliberalism's willingness to make its own assumptions problematic. Also lost is the very viability of politics itself. Not only does neoliberalism in this instance empty the public treasury, hollow out public services, and limit the vocabulary and imagery available to recognize anti-democratic forms of power and narrow models of individual agency, it also undermines the socially discursive translating functions of any viable democracy by undercutting the ability of individuals to engage in the continuous translation between public considerations and private interests by collapsing the public into the realm of the private.[59] Divested of its political possibilities and social underpinnings, freedom finds few opportunities for rearticulating private worries into public concerns or individual discontent into collective struggle.[60] Hence, the first task in engaging neoliberalism is to reveal its claim to a bogus universalism and make clear how it functions as a historical and social construction. Neoliberalism hides the traces of its own ideology, politics, and history either by rhetorically asserting its triumphalism as part of the "end of history" or by proclaiming that capitalism and democracy are synonymous. What must be challenged is neoliberalism's "future-tense narrative of inevitability, demonstrating that the drama of world history remains wide open."[61]

But the history of the changing economic and ideological conditions that gave rise to neoliberalism must be understood in relation to the corresponding history of race relations in the United States and abroad. Most importantly, since the history of race is either left out or misrepresented by the official channels of power in the United States, it is crucial that the history of slavery, civil rights, racial politics, and ongoing modes of struggle at the level of everyday life be remembered and used pedagogically to challenge the historical amnesia that feeds neoliberalism's ahistorical claim to power and the continuity of its claims to common sense. The struggle against racial injustice cannot be separated from larger questions about what kind of culture and society is emerging under the imperatives of neoliberalism, what kind of history it ignores, and what alternatives might point to a substantive democratic future.

Second, under neoliberalism all levels of government have been hollowed out and largely reduced either to their policing functions or to maintaining the privileges of the rich and the interests of corporate power holders—both largely white. In this discourse, the state is not only absolved of its traditional social contract of upholding the public good and providing crucial social provisions and minimal guarantees for those who are in need of such services; it also embraces a notion of color-blind racelessness. State racelessness is built on the right-wing logic of "rational racists" such as D'Souza, who argues that "[w]hat we need is a separation of race and state."[62] As Goldberg points out, this means that the state is now held

> to a standard of justice protective of individual rights and not group results.... [T]his in turn makes possible the devaluation of any individuals considered not white, or white-like, the trashing or trampling of their rights and possibilities, for the sake of preserving the right to *private* "rational discrimination" of whites.... [Thus] racist discrimination becomes privatized, and in terms of liberal legality state protected in its privacy.[63]

Defined through the ideology of racelessness, the state removes itself from either addressing or correcting the effects of racial discrimination, reducing matters of racism to individual concerns to be largely solved through private negotiations between individuals, and adopting an entirely uncritical role in the way in which the racial state shapes racial policies and their effects throughout the economic, social, and cultural landscape. Lost here is any critical engagement with state power and how it imposes immigration policies, decides who gets resources and access to a quality education, defines what constitutes a crime, how people are punished, how and whether social problems are criminalized, who is worthy of citizenship, and who is responsible for addressing racial injustices. As the late Pierre Bourdieu argued, there is a political and pedagogical need, not only to protect the social gains, embodied in state policies, that have been the outcome of important collective struggles, but also "to invent another kind of state."[64] This means challenging the political irresponsibility and moral indifference that are the organizing principles at the heart of the neoliberal vision. As Bourdieu suggests, it is necessary to restore the sense of utopian possibility rooted in the struggle for a democratic state. The racial state and its neoliberal ideology need to be challenged as part of a viable anti-racist pedagogy and politics.

Anti-racist pedagogy also needs to move beyond the conundrums of a limited identity politics and begin to include in its analysis what it would mean to imagine the state as a vehicle for democratic values and a strong proponent of social and racial justice. In part, reclaiming the democratic and public responsibility of the state would mean arguing for a state in which tax cuts for the rich, rather than social spending, are seen as the problem; using the state to protect the public good rather than waging a war on all things public; engaging and resisting the use of state power to both protect and define the public sphere as utterly white; redefining the power and role of the state so as to minimize its policing functions and strengthen its accountability to the public interests of all citizens rather than to the wealthy and corporations. Removing the state from its subordination to market values means reclaiming the importance of social needs over commercial interests and democratic politics over corporate power; it also means addressing a host of urgent social problems that include but are not limited to the escalating costs of health care, housing, the schooling crisis, the growing gap between rich and poor, the environmental crisis, the rebuilding of the nation's cities and impoverished rural areas, the economic crisis facing most of the states, and the increasing assault on people of color. The struggle over the state must be linked to a struggle for a racially just, inclusive democracy. Crucial to any viable politics of anti-racism is the role the state will play as a guardian of the public interest and as a force in creating a multiracial democracy.

Third, it is crucial for any anti-racist pedagogy and politics to recognize that power does not just inhabit the realm of economics or state power, but is also intellectual, residing in the educational force of the culture and its enormous powers of persuasion. This means that any viable anti-racist pedagogy must make the political more pedagogical by recognizing how public pedagogy works to determine and secure the ways that racial identity, issues, and relations are produced in a wide variety of sites including schools, cable and television networks, newspapers and magazines, the Internet, advertising, churches, trade unions, and a host of other public spheres in which ideas are produced and distributed. This, in turn, means becoming mindful of how racial meanings and practices are created, mediated, reproduced, and challenged through a wide variety of "discourses, institutions, audiences, markets, and constituencies which help determine the forms and meaning of publicness in American society."[65] The crucial role that pedagogy plays in shaping racial issues reaffirms the centrality of a cultural politics that recognizes the relationship between issues of representation and the operations of power, the important role that intellectuals might play as engaged, public intellectuals, and the importance of critical knowledge in challenging neoliberalism's illusion of unanimity. But an anti-racist cultural pedagogy also suggests the need to develop a language of both critique and possibility and to wage individual and collective struggles in a wide variety of dominant public spheres and alternative counter-publics. Public pedagogy as a tool of anti-racist struggles understands racial politics, not only as a signifying activity through which subject positions are produced, identities inhabited, and desires mobilized, but also as the mobilization of material relations of power as a way of securing, enforcing, and challenging racial injustices. While cultural politics offers an opportunity to understand how race matters and racist practices take hold in everyday life, such a pedagogical and cultural politics must avoid collapsing into a romanticization of the symbolic, popular, or discursive. Culture matters as a rhetorical tool and mode of persuasion, especially in the realm of visual culture, which has to be taken seriously as a pedagogical force, but changing consciousness is only a precondition to changing society and should not be confused with what it means to actually transform institutional relations of power. In part, this means contesting the control of the media by a handful of transnational corporations.[66] The social gravity of racism as it works through the modalities of everyday language, relations, and cultural expressions has to be taken seriously in any anti-racist politics, but such a concern and mode of theorizing must also be accompanied by an equally serious interest in the rise of corporate power and "the role of state institutions and agencies in shaping contemporary forms of racial subjugation and inequality."[67] Racist ideologies, practices, state formations, and institutional relations can be exposed pedagogically and linguistically, but they cannot be resolved merely in the realm of the discursive. Hence, any viable anti-racist pedagogy needs to draw attention to the distinction between critique and social transformation, to critical modes of analysis, and to the responsibility of acting individually and collectively on one's beliefs.

Another important consideration that has to be included in any notion of anti-racist pedagogy and politics is the issue of connecting matters of racial justice to broader and more comprehensive political, cultural, and social agendas. Neoliberalism exerts a powerful force in American life because its influence and power are spread across a diverse range of political, economic, social, and cultural spheres. Its ubiquity is matched by its aggressive pedagogical attempts to reshape the totality of social life in the image of the market, reaching into and connecting a wide range of seemingly disparate factors that bear down on everyday life in the United States. Neoliberalism is persuasive because its language of commercialism, consumerism, privatization, freedom, and self-interest resonates with and saturates so many aspects of public life. Differences in this discourse are removed from matters of equity and power and reduced to market niches. Agency is privatized and social values are reduced to market-based interests. And, of course, a democracy of citizens is replaced by a democracy of consumers. Progressives, citizens, and other groups who are concerned about matters of race and difference need to maintain their concerns with particular forms of oppression and subordination; yet, at the same time, the limits of various approaches to identity politics must be recognized so as not to allow them to become either fixed or incapable of making alliances with other social movements as part of a broader struggle over not just particular freedoms but also the more generalized freedoms associated with an inclusive and radical democracy.

I have not attempted to be exhaustive in suggesting what it might mean to recognize and challenge the new racism that now reproduces more subtle forms of racial subordination, oppression, and exclusion, though I have tried to point to some pedagogical and political concerns that connect racism and neoliberal politics. The color line in America is neither fixed nor static. Racism as an expression of power and exclusion takes many meanings and forms under different historical conditions. The emphasis on its socially and historically constructed nature offers hope because it suggests that what can be produced by dominant relations of power can also be challenged and transformed by those who imagine a more utopian and just world. The challenge of the color line is still with us today and needs to be recognized not only as a shameful example of racial injustice but also as a reprehensible attack on the very nature of democracy itself.

3
Class Casualties: Disappearing Youth in the Age of Market Fundamentalism

ᘒ

Ironically, children are unsafe in public schools today not because of exposure to drugs and violence, but because they have lost their constitutional protections under the Fourth Amendment.[1]

A major consequence of the tidal wave of fear, violence, and terror associated with children has been adult legislative and policy decisions to criminalize vast sectors of youth behavior.... Schools have become military fortresses. Hanging out becomes illegal. Fewer systems want to work with adolescents in need. Youngsters who have themselves been neglected or abused by adults pose too many challenges and have too many problems to be addressed. Health care and mental health services are rarely organized for adolescents. Schools want to get rid of the troublemakers and the kids who bring down the test scores. Minor offenses are no longer dealt with by retail stores, school disciplinarians, parents, or youth workers, but rather the police are called, arrests are made, petitions are filed.[2]

There is a war being waged in the United States. It is a war being waged on the domestic front that feeds off the general decay of democratic politics and reinforces what neoliberals are more than pleased to celebrate as the death of the social. The enemy for conservative forces is "big government." And yet, as Kevin Baker pointed out in *Harper's Magazine,* "since the advent of Reagan and the current Republican hegemony the federal government has by almost all objective measures become larger, more intrusive, more coercive, less accountable, and more deeply indebted than ever before."[3] But given that the current administration has such a massive government when it comes to the military, law enforcement, deficit spending, control over public schooling, and so on, this is really a war against the welfare state and the social contract itself—this is a war against the notion that everyone should have access to decent education, health care, employment, and other public services. The following two quotes signal the presence of what is at stake in this unprecedented attack on the nature of the democratic social contract. The first comes from Texas state representative Debbie Riddle; the second comes from Grover Norquist, president of the Americans for Tax Reform and arguably Washington's leading right-wing strategist:

> Where did this idea come from that everybody deserves free education? Free medical care? Free whatever? It comes from Moscow. From Russia. It comes straight out of the pit of hell.[4]

> My goal is to cut government in half in twenty-five years, to get it down to the size where we can drown it in the bathtub.[5]

As these quotes suggest, Grover Norquist and his neoliberal ilk target some parts of government for downsizing a little more energetically than other parts. They are most concerned with dismantling the segments of the public sector that serve the social and democratic needs of the nonaffluent majority of the American populace. Those, however, that provide "free" service and welfare to the privileged and opulent minority and dole out punishment to the poor are preserved from that great domestic war tool, the budgetary axe. Norquist and his cronies are really at war with any vestige of social democracy, which he equates with "creeping socialism." Commenting on Norquist's political program, John Stauber and Sheldon Rampton assert the following:

> Norquist's coalition advocates abolishing taxes, especialy estate taxes and capital-gains taxes. Regulations they want abolished include minimum-wage laws, affirmative action, health and safety regulations for workers, environmental laws and gun controls. They also support cutting or eliminating a variety of government programs including student loans, state pension funds, welfare, Americorps, the National Endowment for the Arts, farm subsidies, and popular programs such as Medicare, Social Security and education are targeted for rollbacks, beginning with privatization."[6]

For Norquist and his ilk in the Bush administration, politics is simply another form of brutalizing warfare, and those who either disagree with Bush theology or do not wholeheartedly support the authoritarian vision of Norquist, Cheney, Rumsfeld, and other neoconservatives are viewed as either unpatriotic or as enemies. Norquist makes this quite clear in his strong dismissal of the need for dialogue, doubt, or civic exchange. He writes: "We are trying to change the tones in the state capitals—and turn them toward bitter nastiness and partisanship. Bipartisanship is another name for date rape."[7] Democracy has never appeared more fragile and endangered in the United States than during the current civic and political crisis. This is especially true for young people. While a great deal has been written about the budget-busting costs of the invasion of Iraq and the passing of new anti-terrorist laws in the name of "homeland security" that make it easier to undermine the basic civil liberties that protect individuals against invasive and potentially repressive government actions, there is a disturbing silence on the part of many critics and academics regarding the ongoing insecurity and injustice suffered by young people in this country. As a result, the state is increasingly resorting to repression and punitive social policies at home and war abroad. The "war" on working-class youth and young people of color is evident in the disproportionate numbers of such individuals who provide the fodder for Bush's preventive war policy; in the silent war at home, especially since the Iraqi war and the war against terrorism are being financed from cuts in domestic funding for health care, children's education, and other public services; and, above all, in the militarization of schools through the addition of armed guards, barbed-wired security fences, and "lock-down drills." As educators turn over their responsibility for school safety to the police, the new security culture in public schools has turned them into "learning prisons."[8] Minor infractions that were once handled by teachers or guidance counselors are viewed as criminal violations and are now handled by the police. Young people are now treated like inmates or prisoners of war, stripped of their rights and subject to indignities that historically were reserved for war zones. It would be a tragic mistake for those of us concerned about democracy either to separate the war in Iraq from the many problems Americans (especially young people) face at home or to fail to recognize how war is being waged by this government on multiple fronts.

Slavoj Žižek claims that the "true target of the 'war on terror' is American society itself—the disciplining of its emancipatory excesses."[9] He is partly right. The Bush "permanent war doctrine" is aimed not just against alleged terrorists or the excesses of democracy but also against disposable populations in the homeland, whether they be young black men who inhabit our nation's jails or unemployed workers who have been abandoned both by the flight of capital and by government agencies that provide the working poor, disabled, elderly, and youth with basic social services and provisions. The financing of the war in Iraq, buttressed by what Dick Cheney calls the concept of "never-ending war," results not only in a bloated and obscene military budget but also in economic and tax policies that are financially bankrupting the states, destroying public education, and plundering public services. These multiple attacks on the poor and much-needed public services must be connected to an expanded political and social vision that refuses the cynicism and sense of powerlessness that accompanies the destruction of social goods, the corporatization of the media, the dismantling of workers' rights, and the incorporation of intellectuals. Against this totalitarian onslaught, concerned citizens, activists, and educators need a language of critique, possibility, and action—one that connects diverse struggles, uses theory as a resource, and defines politics as a critical intervention into public life. We need a language that relates the discourse of war to an attack on democracy at home and abroad—waged largely under the auspices of neoliberalism and the politics of empire—and we need to use that language in a way that captures the needs, desires, histories, and experiences that shape people's daily lives. Similarly, as democratic institutions are downsized and public goods are offered up for corporate plunder, those of us who take seriously the related issues of equality, human rights, justice, and freedom face the crucial challenge of formulating a notion of the political suitable for addressing the urgent problems facing the twenty-first century—a politics that, as Zygmunt Bauman argues, "never stops criticizing the level of justice already achieved [while] seeking more justice and better justice."[10]

The interrelationship between wars abroad and those at home suggests that the concept of war has taken a distinctly different turn in the new millennium. These days, war is rarely waged between nations. Much more frequently it is waged against drugs, terrorists, crime, immigrants, labor rights, and a host of other open-ended referents that have become synonymous with public disorder. War no longer needs to be ratified by Congress since it is now waged at various levels of government in diverse forms that escape the need for official approval or, when waged abroad, for congressional approval. War has become a permanent condition adopted by a nation-state that is largely defined by its repressive functions in the face of its refusal and increasing political powerlessness to regulate corporate power, provide social investments for the populace, and guarantee a measure of social freedom. As a permanent state of politics, informed largely by a culture of fear and insecurity, war is now, in part, a response to the impotence of public institutions to improve conditions of radical insecurity and an uncertain threat to the future.

Wars are almost always legitimated in order to make the world safe for "our children's future," but such rhetoric belies the denial of their future by the acts of aggression put into place by a range of state agencies and institutions that operate on a war footing. Such acts of aggression include the horrible effects of the militarization of schools, the use of the criminal justice system to redefine social issues such as poverty and homelessness as criminal violations, and the subsequent rise of the prison-industrial complex as a way to contain disposable populations such as youth of color who are poor and marginalized. Under the rubric of war, security, and anti-terrorism, children are "disappeared" from basic social spheres that once provided the conditions for a sense of agency and possibility, just as they are rhetorically excised from any discourse about the future. What is so troubling about the current historical moment is that youth no longer even symbolize the future. And yet, any discourse about the future has to begin with the issue of youth because more than any other group they embody the projected dreams, desires, and commitment of a society's obligations to the future. This point echoes a classical principle of modern democracy in which youth both symbolized society's responsibility to the future and offered a measure of its progress. For most of the twentieth century, Americans embraced as a defining feature of politics the idea that all levels of government should assume a large measure of responsibility for providing the resources, social provisions, security, and modes of education that simultaneously offer young people a future and the possibility of expanding the meaning and depth of a substantive democracy. In many respects, youth not only registered symbolically the importance of modernity's claim to progress; they also affirmed the centrality of the liberal, democratic tradition of the social contract in which adult responsibility was mediated through a willingness to fight for the rights of children, enact reforms that invested in their future, and provide the educational conditions necessary for them to make use of the freedoms they possessed while learning how to be critical citizens. Within such a political project, democracy was linked to the well-being of youth, and the status of how a society imagined democracy and its future was contingent on how it viewed its responsibility toward following generations.

Yet, at the dawn of the new millennium, it is not at all clear that we believe any longer in youth, the future, or the social contract, even in its minimalist version. Since the Reagan/Thatcher revolution of the 1980s, we have been told that there is no such thing as society—and, indeed, following that nefarious pronouncement, institutions committed to public welfare have been disappearing ever since. Rather than being cherished as a symbol of the future, youth are now seen as a threat to be feared and a problem to be contained. A seismic change has taken place in which youth are currently being framed as both a generation of suspects and a threat to public life. If youth once symbolized the moral necessity to address a range of social and economic ills, they are now largely portrayed as the source of most of society's problems. Hence, youth today constitute a crisis that has less to do with improving the future than with denying it. A concern for children is the defining absence in most dominant discourses about the future and the obligations this implies for adult society. To witness the abdication of adult responsibility to children we need look no further than the current state of children in America.

Waging War on Youth

A veritable Kindergulag has been erected around schoolchildren, making them subject to arbitrary curfews, physical searchers, arbitrarily applied profiling schemes, and ... random, suspicionless, warrantless drug testing.... If you're a kid in the U.S. today, martial law isn't a civics class lecture unit. It is a fact of life as the war on drugs, the war on violence and a nearly hysterical emphasis on safety have come to excuse the infliction of every kind of humiliation upon the young.[11]

Instead of providing a decent education to poor young people, American society offers them the growing potential of being incarcerated, buttressed by the fact that the United States is now the only country in the world that sentences minors to death and spends "three times more on each incarcerated citizen than on each public school pupil."[12] Instead of guaranteeing them food, decent health care, and shelter, we serve them more standardized tests; instead of providing them with vibrant public spheres, we offer them a commercialized culture in which consumerism is the only measure of citizenship. They pay a heavy price, indeed, in the burdensome currency of human suffering in the richest democracy in the world: 12.2 million children live below the poverty line; more than 16 million are at the low end of the income scale; and 9.2 million, nearly 90 percent of whom belong to working families, lack health insurance.[13] On top of that, millions lack affordable child care and decent early childhood education; in many states more money is being spent on prison construction than on education, and the infant mortality rate in the United States is the highest of any industrialized nation. *New York Times* op-ed columnist Bob Herbert reports that in Chicago "there are nearly 100,000 young people, ages 16 to 24, who are out of work, out of school and all but out of hope. Nationwide, the figure is a staggering 5.5 million and growing."[14] The magnitude of this crisis is evidenced by the fact that in some cities, such as the District of Columbia, the child poverty rate is as high as 45 percent.[15] When regrouped into racial categories, the figures become even more despairing. For example: "In 2000, the poverty rate for African Americans was 22 percent, basically double the rate for the entire nation. In Chicago the poverty rate for blacks is 29.4 percent and only 8.2 for whites. The poverty rate for black children is 40 percent, compared to 8 percent for white kids."[16]

While the United States ranks first in military technology, military exports, defense expenditures and the number of millionaires and billionaires, it ranks eighteenth among the advanced industrial nations in the gap between rich and poor children, twelfth in the percentage of children in poverty, seventeenth in efforts to lift children out of poverty, and twenty-third in infant mortality.[17] Economically, politically, and culturally, the situation of youth in the United States is intolerable and obscene. In his 2003 budget, George W. Bush did something no other president has done. He pushed through an immense tax cut—estimated at $3 trillion—in the midst of a war whose cost down the road for future generations will be staggering.

At the time of this writing, in 2004, the U.S. budget deficit is already $290 billion; the national debt is $6.84 quadrillion, estimated to reach $9.3 quadrillion by 2008.[18] The war on Iraq is costing about $4 billion a month and the Republican-controlled Congress has just passed a bill authorizing an additional $87 billion to support the "war against terrorism" being waged in Iraq and Afghanistan. At the same time that the Bush administration is giving huge tax cuts to the rich, it is cutting veterans' programs by $6 billion, including money for disabilities caused by war and for education and health care for their kids. He is also cutting $93 billion from Medicaid, making huge environmental cuts, and whittling away a vast array of domestic programs that directly benefit children. One of the most shameful cuts enacted in the federal budget took place in December 2002. Bush eliminated $300 million from a "federal program that provides subsidies to poor families so they can heat their homes in the winter."[19]

Under this insufferable climate of increased repression and misplaced priorities, young people have become the new casualties in an ongoing war against justice, freedom, citizenship, and democracy—as clearly reflected in the images we see of children in trouble. In a society that appears to have turned its back on the young, what we are increasingly witnessing in the media are images of children handcuffed, sitting in adult courts before stern judges, facing murder charges. These images are matched by endless films, videos, ads, documentaries, television programs, and journalistic accounts in which urban youth are depicted largely as gang-bangers, drug dealers, and rapists—in short, as violent, dangerous, and pathological. On the other side of the coin are images of ruling-class youth in programs such as *Born Rich, Rich Girls,* and *The Simple Life* that suggest *they* are the group with the real problems, such as having to cope with envy management and to figure out ways to "dispel the voodoo of inherited wealth."[20] Such images invoke ruling-class youth as an unapologetic paean to class power. In a society where 59 percent of college students say they will eventually be millionaires, the dominant press provides enormous coverage of celebrities such as Paris Hilton, a famous New York debutante who, as reported in the media, "has stood for the proposition that wealth comes with no obligations of tact, taste or civic responsibility. For people who dream of someday putting unearned wealth to poor use, Ms. Hilton has been a beacon."[21] In the age of Bush, class becomes less a metaphor for marking the unjust inequities of class privilege than a way of celebrating wealth and power and rubbing it in the face of the poor. This is the popular-culture version of the neoliberal view of the world now so fashionable among neoconservatives and the ultra-Right whose policies reproduce and legitimize a growing appeal to "tough love," which in reality is marked by a contempt for those who are impoverished, disenfranchised, or powerless. This is class politics waged vengefully in the realm of popular culture.

No longer seen as a crucial social investment for the future of a democratic society, young people are now demonized by the popular media and derided by politicians looking for quick-fix solutions to crime. In recent times, a whole generation of youth has been depicted as superpredators, spiraling out of control. In a society deeply troubled by their presence, they prompt in the public imagination a rhetoric of fear, control, and surveillance. The impact of such rhetoric was made all the more visible with the 2002 Supreme Court decision upholding the widespread use of random drug testing of all junior and senior high school students who desire to participate in extracurricular activities. Such impromptu drug testing registers a deep distrust of students and furthers the notion that youth should be viewed with suspicion and treated as potential criminals. In addition, school officials are increasingly subjecting students to impromptu vehicle searches, unannounced weapons inspections, and preemptive police-controlled canine searches. In some schools, students have even been "strip-searched by police officers to locate money missing from a classroom."[22] The appeal to safety in the post-Columbine, 9/11 era has become a rationale for imposing strict regimes of surveillance and security on public schools, a policy that resonates both with the larger militarization of public space and with a "largely neoconservative and neoliberal agenda that is bent on retracting civil liberties and expanding the disciplinary mechanisms of a police state."[23]

Police and drug-sniffing dogs are now common fixtures in public schools as schools increasingly resemble prisons and students are treated like suspects who need to be searched, tested, and observed under the watchful eye of administrators who appear to have less interest in education than in policing and incarceration. Trust and respect have given way to fear, disdain, and suspicion, which, in turn, are increasingly being translated into social policies that signal the shrinking of the democratic public sphere, the hijacking of civic culture, the increasing militarization of public space, and the shredding of students' Fourth Amendment rights. In Toledo, Ohio, a 14-year old student who refused to wear a bowling shirt over her low-cut midriff top was handcuffed, put in a police car, and placed in the "detention center at the Lucas County juvenile courthouse. She was booked on a misdemeanor charge and placed in a holding cell for several hours, until her mother, a 34-year old vending machine technician, got off work and picked her up."[24] More recently, in an elementary school in Pennsylvania, "an 8-year old boy in a special-education class was charged with disorderly conduct ... for his behavior in a time-out room: urinating on the floor, throwing his shoes at the ceiling and telling a teacher, 'Kids rule.'"[25] Schools are increasingly resorting to the juvenile justice system to deal with behavior problems that in the past would have been handled by school officials. This particularly loathsome shift in "school reform" toward penalizing children rather than attempting to listen to them and help them with their problems resonates with the shift in the larger culture toward criminalization of social problems, implying through punitive, militaristic models of control that educators are provided institutional legitimation to no longer view children as a worthy social investment. Instead, they see children as a problem—and the solution lies in punishing and containing them. What are we to make of a school policy that allows the arrest of "two middle-school boys whose crime was turning off the lights in the girls' bathroom" or, through zero tolerance, allows an 11-year old girl to be arrested, handcuffed, and put in the back of a police cruiser "for hiding out in the school and not going to class"?[26] Not only do children's services suffer under such a policy, but increasingly children's rights are being trampled and fewer institutions are willing to protect these rights. Consequently, their voices are almost completely absent from the debates, policies, and legislative practices that are developed in order to meet their needs.

In many suburban malls, working-class white youth as well as youth of color cannot even shop or walk around without either carrying appropriate identification cards or being accompanied by their parents. Excluded from public spaces outside of schools that once offered them the opportunity to hang out with relative security, work with mentors in youth centers, and develop their own talents and sense of self-worth, young people are forced to hang out in the streets. They are increasingly subject to police surveillance, anti-gang statutes, and curfew laws, especially in poor, urban neighborhoods. In increasingly short supply are the youth centers, city public parks, outdoor basketball courts, or empty lots where kids can play stick ball. Play areas are now rented out to the highest bidder and then "caged in by steel fences, wrought iron gates, padlocks and razor ribbon wire."[27]

Liberals, conservatives, corporate elites, and religious fundamentalists are waging a war against public spaces and laws that view children and youth as an important social investment. As discussed earlier, this includes a full-scale attack on social services, the welfare state, and the public schools. For instance, Bernadine Dohrn asserts:

> As youth service systems (schools, foster care, probation, mental health) are scaling back, shutting down, or transforming their purpose, one system has been expanding its outreach to youth at an accelerated rate: the adult criminal justice system. All across the nation, states have been expanding the jurisdiction of adult criminal court to include younger children by lowering the minimum age of criminal jurisdiction and expanding the types of offenses and mechanisms for transfer or waiver of juveniles into adult criminal court. Barriers between adult criminals and children are being removed in police stations, courthouses, holding cells, and correctional institutions. Simultaneously, juvenile jurisdiction has expanded to include both younger children and delinquency sentencing beyond the age of childhood, giving law enforcement multiple options for convicting and incarcerating youngsters.[28]

Youth have become one of the primary sites onto which class and racial anxieties are projected. Their very presence represents both the broken promises of capitalism in the age of deregulation and downsizing *and* a collective fear of the consequences wrought by systemic class inequalities and a culture of rapacious greed that has produced a generation of unskilled and displaced youth expelled from shrinking markets, blue-collar jobs, and any viable hope for the future. It is against this growing threat to basic freedom, democracy, and youth that I want to address the related issues of democracy, zero-tolerance policies, and public schools.

Class/Race and the Politics of Punishment in Schools

When the "War on Poverty" ran out of steam with the social and economic crisis that emerged in the 1970s, there was a growing shift at all levels of government from an emphasis on social investments to an emphasis on public control, social containment, and the criminalization of social problems. The latter—starting with President Ronald Reagan's war on drugs[29] and the privatization of the prison industry in the 1980s, escalating to the war on immigrants in the early 1990s, and culminating in the rise of the prison-industrial complex by the close of the decade—has now become a part of everyday culture, providing a common reference point that extends from governing prisons and regulating urban culture to running schools. This is most evident in the emergence of zero-tolerance laws that have swept the nation since the 1980s, gaining full legislative strength with the passage of the Violent Crime Control and Law Enforcement Act of 1994. Following the mandatory sentencing legislation and get-tough policies associated with the "war on drugs," this bill calls for a "three strikes and you're out" policy that puts repeat offenders, including nonviolent offenders, in jail for life, regardless of the seriousness of the crime. As I mentioned in Chapter 1, the United States is now the biggest jailer in the world, with more than 2.1 million people behind bars.

A Justice Department report points out that on any given day in this country "more than a third of the young African-American men aged 18–34 in some of our major cities are either in prison or under some form of criminal justice supervision."[30] The same department reported in April 2000 that "black youth are forty-eight times more likely than whites to be sentenced to juvenile prison for drug offenses."[31] There is a cruel irony in the fact that when poor youth of color are not being warehoused in dilapidated schools or incarcerated, they are being recruited by the Army to fight the war in Iraq. For example, as Carl Chery recently reported: "With help from *The Source* magazine, the U.S. military is targeting hip-hop fans with custom-made Hummers, throwback jerseys and trucker hats. The yellow Hummer, spray-painted with two black men in military uniform, is the vehicle of choice for the U.S. Army's 'Take It to the Streets campaign'—a sponsored mission aimed at recruiting young African Americans into the military ranks." It seems that the Army has discovered hip-hop and urban culture, and that recruiters, rather than listening to the searing indictments of poverty, joblessness, and despair that is one of its central messages, are now appealing to its most commodified elements by letting the "potential recruits hang out in the Hummer, where they can pep the sound system or watch recruitment videos."[32] Of course, they won't view any videos of Hummers being blown up in the war-torn streets of Baghdad.

Domestic militarization in the form of zero-tolerance laws, in this instance, not only functions to contain "minority populations," deprive them of their elector rights (13 percent of all black men in the United States have lost their right to vote),[33] and provide new sources of revenue for a system that "evokes the convict leasing system of the Old South";[34] it also actively promotes and legitimates retrograde and repressive social policies. For example, an increasing number of states, including California and New York, are now spending more on prison construction than on higher education.[35] In addition, School Resource Officers—armed and unarmed enforcement officials who implement safety and security measures in schools—are one of the fastest-growing segments of law enforcement in the United States.[36]

What are we to make of social policies that portray youth, especially poor youth of color, as a generation of suspects? What are we to make of a social order—headed by a pro-gun, pro-capital punishment, and pro-big business conservative such as George W. Bush—whose priorities suggest to urban youth that American society is willing to invest more in sending them to jail or the frontlines of a dubious war than in providing them with high-quality schools and a decent education? How does a society justify housing poor students in schools that are unsafe, decaying, and with few, if any, extracurricular activities while at the same time spending five times more annually—as high as $20,000 in many suburban schools—on each middle-class student, housing them in schools with Olympic swimming pools, the latest computer technology, and well-groomed buildings and grounds? What message is being sent to young people when in a state such as New York "more Blacks entered prison just for drug offenses than graduated from the state's massive university system with undergraduate, masters, and doctoral degrees combined in the 1990s"?[37] What message is being sent to youth when, as federal deficits are soaring, the Bush administration provides tax cuts for the rich—in one instance $114 billion in corporate tax concessions—while at the same time children face drastic cuts in education and health aid, as well as other massive cuts in domestic programs such as job training and summer employment opportunities? Such circumstances indicate that the culture of domestic militarization, with its policies of containment, brutalization, and punishment, has become more valued to the dominant social order than any consideration of what it means for a society to expand and strengthen the mechanisms and freedoms of a fully realized democracy.

With the current, highly charged culture of fear, children have become both a population at-risk and one of the most serious casualties. Innocence has given way to fear and distrust as children are increasingly viewed as either criminals or consumers. One consequence is that the criminalization of childhood, which now takes place in multiple spheres has become a permanent feature of the social landscape under the Bush administration. As Dohrn points out,

> The criminalizing of adolescent behavior takes place in multiple ways. Major social institutions for youth have constricted eligibility and eased methods for expulsion. Schools, child welfare systems, probation, and health services have all made it easier to violate, terminate, exclude, and expel youngsters. Where these youth go for survival, help, socialization development, care, and attention is unclear. One door that always remains open is the gateway to juvenile and criminal justice. Overcrowded juvenile correctional institutions, deficient youth facilities, and disproportionate minority confinement are among the consequences.[38]

Zero-tolerance policies have been especially cruel in terms of expanding the criminalization of youth behavior.[39] Rather than attempting to work with youth and make an investment in their psychological, economic, and social well-being, a growing number of cities are passing sweep laws—curfews and bans against loitering and cruising—designed not only to keep youth off the streets but also to make it easier to criminalize their behavior. For example, within the last decade "45 states ... have passed or amended legislation making it easier to prosecute juveniles as adults," and in some states "prosecutors can bump a juvenile case into adult court at their own discretion."[40] In Kansas and Vermont, in fact, a 10-year-old child can be tried in adult court. A particularly harsh example of the draconian measures being used against young people can be seen in the passing of Proposition 21 in California. This law makes it easier for prosecutors to try teens 14 and older in adult court if they are accused of felonies. These youth would automatically be put in adult prison and be given lengthy mandated sentences. The overall goal of the law is to largely eliminate intervention programs, increase the number of youth in prisons (especially minority youth), and keep them there for longer periods of time. Yet, the law is at odds with a number of studies indicating that putting youth in jail with adults both increases recidivism and poses a grave danger to the young offenders themselves, who, as a Columbia University study suggests, are "five times as likely to be raped, twice as likely to be beaten and eight times as likely to commit suicide than adults in the adult prison system."[41]

Paradoxically, the moral panic against crime and now terrorism that increasingly feeds the calls for punishment and revenge rather than rehabilitation programs for young people exists in conjunction with the disturbing fact that the United States is now one of only seven countries in the world that permits the death penalty for juveniles.[42] In many states, youth cannot join the military, get their ears pierced, or get a marriage license until they are 18, but youth as young as 10 can be jailed as adults and condemned to death in some states. The prize-winning novelist Ann Patchett suggested in the *New York Times* that perhaps the problem is that "as Americans, we no longer have any idea what constitutes a child."[43] This statement strikes me as ludicrous. The ongoing attacks on children's rights, the endless commercialization of youth, the downsizing of children's services, and the increasing incarceration of young people suggest more than confusion. In actuality, such policies imply that, at best, adult society no longer cares about children and, at worse, views them as an object of scorn and fear.

As the state itself is downsized and stripped of its financial resources, and as basic social services dry up, containment policies become the principal means to discipline working-class youth and restrict their ability to think critically and engage in oppositional practices. At the academic level this translates into imposing accountability schemes on schools that are really about enforcing high-stakes testing policies, enlarging school choice, and disinvesting in underprivileged rural and urban schools. Such approaches de-skill teachers, reduce learning to the lowest common denominator, undermine the possibility of critical learning, and prepare young people to be docile. Schools increasingly resemble other weakened public spheres as they are forced to cut back on trained psychologists; school nurses; programs such as music, art, and athletics; and valuable after-school activities. Jesse Jackson argues that, under such circumstances, schools not only fail to provide students with a well-rounded education, they often "bring in the police, [and] the school gets turned into a feeder system for the penal system."[44] Marginalized students learn quickly that they are surplus populations and that the journey from home to school no longer means they will next move into a job; on the contrary, school has now become a training ground for their "graduation" into containment centers such as prisons and jails that keep them out of sight, patrolled, and monitored so as to prevent them from becoming a social canker or political liability to white and middle-class populations concerned about their own safety.

Schools Emulating Prison Policies

Emulating state and federal laws passed in the 1990s that were based on mandatory sentencing and "three strikes and you're out" policies (e.g., the federal Gun-Free Schools Act of 1994), many educators first invoked zero-tolerance rules against kids who brought guns to schools. Under this law, any school receiving federal funds for education has to impose a one-year mandatory expulsion for any public school student who brings to school a firearm, such as a gun, bomb grenade, missile, or rocket. Schools have broadened these rules, which now include a gamut of student misbehavior ranging from using or circulating drugs, cigarette smoking, and sexual harassment to merely *threatening* other students. Under zero-tolerance policies, forms of punishment that were once applied to adults now apply to first-graders. Originally aimed at "students who misbehave intentionally, the law now applies to those who misbehave as a result of emotional problems or other disabilities" as well.[45] Across the nation, school districts have been lining up to embrace zero-tolerance policies. But the turning point came after the shootings at Columbine High School in 1999, when such policies increased rapidly in public schools across the United States. According to the U.S. Department of Education, about 90 percent of school systems nationwide have implemented these policies in order to deal with either violence or threats.[46] In the post-Columbine era a manufactured culture of fear cultivates a view of educational reform in which students appear to be a threat to public safety and schools increasingly begin to resemble minimum security prisons. As Tyson Lewis argues,

> Columbine has become a watershed even in the history of school security, further intensifying the connections between penitentiaries and schools. In the aftermath of the school shooting, districts across the country began to implement a plethora of new surveillance measures, [which] include the use of cameras in halls and night-vision cameras in parking lots, bomb-sniffing dogs, random locker checks, armed police guards, crime analysts, metal detectors, transparent backpacks, and computerized student ID cards. Fifteen to thirty percent of post-Columbine high schools now have metal detectors, and there are security cameras in half of all primary and secondary schools. It is an understatement to argue that schools now represent a subsector of the larger prison-industrial complex.[47]

In the face of such measures, all sense of perspective or guarantee of rights seems lost. Zero-tolerance policies have even been legitimated by the federal government: According to the renewed No Child Left Behind Act, public schools must have zero tolerance in place in order to receive federal funds. Not surprisingly, some school systems are investing in new software in order to "profile" students who might exhibit criminal behavior.[48] Overzealous laws relieve educators of exercising deliberation and critical judgment as more and more young people are either suspended or expelled from school, often for ludicrous reasons. For example, in October 2003 in Lee County, Florida, as reported in *USA Today*, a "boy was kicked out of school for a doodle that showed one stick figure shooting another. And in September, a teen in Montgomery County, Texas, was suspended and arrested for violating his school's drug policy by loaning his inhaler to a classmate who was having a severe asthmatic attack.[49] Virginia fifth-graders who allegedly put soap in their teacher's drinking water were charged with a felony.[50] A 12-year-old boy in Louisiana who was diagnosed with a hyperactive disorder was suspended for two days after telling his friends in a food line "I'm gonna get you" if they ate all the potatoes! The police then charged the boy with making "terroristic threats" and he was incarcerated for two weeks while awaiting trial. A 14-year-old disabled student in Palm Beach, Florida, was referred to the police by the school principal for allegedly stealing $2.00 from another student. He was then charged with strong-armed robbery and held for six weeks in an adult jail, even though this was his first arrest.[51] There is the absurd case of five students in Mississippi being suspended and criminally charged for throwing peanuts at each other on a school bus.[52] There is also the equally revealing example of a student brought up on a drug charge because he gave another youth two lemon cough drops.

Zero tolerance does more than offer a simple solution to a complex problem; it has become a code word for a "quick and dirty way of kicking kids out" of school.[53] Instead of creating a culture of caring and compassion mediated by deliberation and critical judgment, school officials who rely upon zero-tolerance laws are reduced to adjuncts of the local police department, largely responsible for apprehending, punishing, and turning students over to the police. As child advocate Steven Drizin asserts, zero-tolerance policies largely "rob school principals and educators of the discretion to take into account the individual circumstances of each case in deciding how to appropriately sanction school misconduct."[54] Rather than trying to figure out what causes student misbehavior, educators now simply abdicate responsibility and punish students who violate the rules, often with unjust consequences. For example, the *Denver Rocky Mountain News* reported in June 1999 that "partly as a result of such rigor in enforcing Colorado's zero-tolerance law, the number of kids kicked out of public schools has skyrocketed since 1993—from 437 before the law to nearly 2,000 in the 1996–1997 school year."[55] In Chicago, the widespread adoption of zero-tolerance policies in 1994 resulted in a 51 percent increase in student suspensions for the next four years, and a 3,000 percent increase in expulsions, jumping "from 21 in 1994–'95 to 668" the following year.[56] And in Connecticut, students are being pushed out of schools like never before: "The number of suspensions jumped about 90 percent from 1998–1999 to 2000–2001. In the 2000–2001 school year, 90,559 children were suspended from schools around the state, up from 57,626 two years earlier."[57] Annette Fuentes claims that "every year, more than 3 million students ... are suspended and nearly 100,000 more are expelled, from kindergarten through twelfth."[58] At the same time there is a growing body of evidence to suggest that zero-tolerance policies simply exacerbate the very problems they are attempting to address. For instance, Harvard University's Civil Rights Project has reported that states with "higher rates of suspension also have higher school-dropout and juvenile-crime rates."[59] Within such a climate of disdain and intolerance, expelling students does more than pose a threat to innocent kids; it also suggests that local school boards are refusing to do the hard work of exercising critical judgment, trying to understand what conditions undermine school safety, and providing reasonable support services for all students as well as viable alternatives for the troubled ones. Moreover, it is hard to understand how any school board can justify suspending or expelling kindergarten children. As Shelley Geballe, co-president of Connecticut Voices for Children, argues:

> It is inexcusable to expel a kindergarten child. The goal of a kindergarten program should be to provide the skills of not only academics but behavior. Zero tolerance that results in pushing out kids is wrongheaded, and I get concerned particularly now that we have a reduction in access to mental-health services, we have teachers who may not be well trained in understanding the emotional and developmental needs of young kids, and you have the No Child Left Behind pressures that provide further incentives to push kids out to get those standardized test scores up.[60]

As Geballe further points out, the No Child Left Behind program implemented by the Bush administration, with its investment in high-stakes testing, puts even more pressure on schools either to push underachieving students out or to do nothing to prevent them from leaving school. Raising test scores is now the major goal of educational reformers and principals, who are expected to reach district goals. Such pressure played an important role in the Houston School System, held up as a model by President George W. Bush; this system not only did nothing to prevent students from leaving school but also falsified drop-out data in order for principals to get financial bonuses and meet district demands. Similarly, Tamar Lewin and Jennifer Medina reported in the *New York Times* that a large number of students who are struggling academically are being pushed out of New York City schools in order to not "tarnish the schools' statistics by failing to graduate on time."[61] As the criminalization of young people enters into the classroom, it becomes easier for school administrators to punish students rather than to listen to them or, for that matter, to work with parents, community programs, religious organizations, and social service agencies.[62] Even though zero-tolerance policies clog up the courts and put additional pressure on an already overburdened juvenile justice system, educators appear to have few qualms about implementing them. And, as we have seen, the results are far from inconsequential for the students themselves.

Most insidiously, zero-tolerance laws—while a threat to all youth and to any viable notion of equal opportunity through education—reinforce in the public imagination the notion of students of color as a source of public fears and a threat to public school safety. Indeed, zero-tolerance policies and laws appear to be well-tailored for mobilizing racialized codes and race-based moral panics that portray black and brown urban youth as a frightening and violent threat to the safety of "decent" Americans. As I mentioned previously, not only do most of the high-profile zero-tolerance cases involve African-American students, but such policies also reinforce the racial inequities that plague school systems across the country. For example, the *New York Times* has reported on a number of studies illustrating "that black students in public schools across the country are far more likely than whites to be suspended or expelled, and far less likely to be in gifted or advanced placement classes."[63] Even in San Francisco, considered a bastion of liberalism, African-American students pay a far greater price for zero-tolerance policies. As Libero Della Piana reports: "According to data collected by Justice Matters, a San Francisco agency advocating equity in education, African Americans make up 52 percent of all suspended students in the district—far in excess of the 16 percent of [African-American youth in] the general population."[64] And as Marilyn Elias reported in an issue of *USA Today:* "In 1998, the first year national expulsion figures were gathered, 31 percent of kids expelled were black, but blacks made up only 17 percent of the students in public schools."[65] A more recent study by the U.S. Department of Education covering the 2000–2001 school year also showed that zero-tolerance laws bear down more drastically on black youth, with one in eight blacks being suspended compared to only one in fifteen whites.[66]

Feeding on moral panic and popular fear, zero-tolerance policies not only turn schools into an adjunct of the criminal justice system, they also further rationalize misplaced legislative priorities and provide profits for the security industries. And that has profound social costs. Instead of investing in early-childhood programs, repairing deteriorating school buildings, or hiring more qualified teachers, schools now spend millions of dollars to upgrade security, even when such a fortress mentality defies the simplest test of common sense. For instance, school administrators in Biloxi, Mississippi, decided to invest $2 million to install 800 cameras in 11 schools rather than use that money to hire more teachers to reduce class size, provide more books for the library, or fund extracurricular programs or a host of other useful school improvements.[67] In Tewksbury Memorial High School, Massachusetts, the new security camera system feeds into the local police station and the cost exceeds $30,000. It gets worse. In the Cleveland Municipal School District, the cost of the safety and security budget increased after Columbine from $12.5 million to $21.3 million.[68] The culture of fear and surveillance has also resulted in big profits for corporations. More metal detectors are now produced for schools than for airports and prisons. And all sorts of electronic equipment and products including security cameras, student ID cards, and see-through backpacks mean big profits for the security industry.

Young people are quickly realizing that schools have more in common with military boot camps and prisons than with other institutions in American society. In addition, as schools abandon their role as democratic public spheres and are literally "fenced off" from the communities that surround them, they lose their ability to become anything other than spaces of containment and control. In this environment, discipline and training replace education for all but the privileged as schools increasingly take on an uncanny resemblance to oversized police precincts, tragically disconnected both from the students who inhabit them and the communities that give meaning to their historical experiences and daily lives. Indeed, as schools become militarized, they lose their ability to provide students with the skills to cope with human differences, uncertainty, and the various symbolic and institutional forces that undermine political agency and democratic public life itself.

Schooling and the Crisis of Public Life

Zero-tolerance policies suggest a dangerous imbalance between democratic values and the culture of fear. Instead of security, such policies in the schools contribute to a growing climate of bigotry, hypocrisy, and intolerance that turns a generation of youth into criminal suspects. In spite of what we are told by the current Bush administration, conservative educators, the religious Right, and the cheerleaders of corporate culture, the greatest threat to education in this country does not come from disruptive students or insufficient lock-down safety measures and get-tough school policies. Nor are young people threatened by the alleged decline of academic standards, the absence of privatized choice schemes, or the lack of rigid testing measures. On the contrary, the greatest threat to young people comes from a society that refuses to view them as a social investment, consigns millions of them to live in poverty, reduces critical learning to massive testing programs, refuses to pay teachers an adequate salary, promotes policies that eliminate most crucial health and public services, and defines masculinity through the degrading celebration of a gun culture, extreme sports, and the spectacles of violence that permeate corporate-controlled media industries. It is a society that values a hollow notion of security more than basic rights, wages an assault on all nonmarket values and public goods, and engages in a ruthless transfer of wealth from the poor and middle class to the rich and privileged.

This is the culture in which we live—a culture in which punishment, greed, and intolerance have replaced social responsibility and compassion, in which issues regarding persistent poverty, inadequate health care, racial apartheid in the inner cities, and growing inequalities between rich and poor have been either removed from the inventory of public discourse and progressive social policy or factored into talk-show spectacles. This is evident in ongoing attempts by many liberals and conservatives to turn commercial-free public education over to market forces, dismantle traditional social provisions of the welfare state, relegate all vestiges of the health-care system to private interests, and mortgage social security to the whims of the stock market. Emptied of any substantial content, democracy appears imperiled as individuals are unable to translate their privately suffered misery into public concerns and collective action. The result is not only silence and indifference, but the elimination of those public spaces that reveal the rough edges of social order, disrupt consensus, and point to the need for modes of education and knowledge that link learning to the conditions necessary for developing democratic forms of political agency and civic struggle. This is a society in which biographical solutions are substituted for systemic contradictions and, as Ulrich Beck points out, institutions "for overcoming problems" are converted into "institutions for causing problems."[69]

Within such a climate of harsh discipline and moral indifference, it is easier to put young people in jail than to provide the education, services, and care they need to cope with the problems of a complex and demanding society.[70] Conservative critics such as Abigail Thernstrom actually reinforce the ongoing criminalization of school policy, the expansion of police power in the schools, and the vanishing rights of children by arguing that zero-tolerance policies are especially useful for minority and poor children. Thernstrom's comments on educational reform not only expand such policies to include the most trivial forms of transgression; they also suggest a barely concealed, racially coded standard for punishing students. She writes: "They need schools where there is zero tolerance for violence, erratic or tardy attendance, inappropriate dress, late or incomplete homework, incivility toward staff and other students, messy desks and halls, trash on the floor and other signs of disorder."[71] The notion that children should be viewed as a crucial social resource who present for any healthy society important ethical and political considerations about the quality of public life, the allocation of social provisions, and the role of the state as a guardian of public interests appears to be lost in a culture that refuses to invest in its youth as part of a broader commitment to a fully realized democracy. As the social order becomes more privatized and militarized, we increasingly face the problem of losing a generation of young people to a system of escalating intolerance, repression, and moral indifference.

The growing attack on working-class youth, youth of color, and public education in American society may say less about the reputed apathy of the populace than about the bankruptcy of the old political language and the need for a new language and vision for expanding and deepening the meaning of democracy and making the education of youth central to such a project. Made over in the image of corporate culture, schools are now valued not as a public good but as a private interest; hence, the appeal of such schools is less their capacity to educate students according to the demands of critical citizenship than their capacity to enable students to master the requirements of a market-driven economy. This is not education but training. Under these circumstances, increasing numbers of students find themselves in schools that lack any language for relating the self to public life, social responsibility, or the imperatives of democratic life. In short, democratic education with its emphasis on social justice, respect for others, critical inquiry, equality, freedom, civic courage, and concern for the collective good is suppressed and replaced by an excessive emphasis on the language of privatization, individualism, self-interest, and brutal competitiveness. Lost in this commercial and privatizing discourse of schooling is any notion of democratic community or any model of leadership capable of raising questions about what public schools should accomplish in a democracy and why under certain circumstances they fail or, for that matter, why public schools have increasingly adopted policies that bear a close resemblance to those of prisons.

I want to conclude by arguing that the growth and popularity of zero-tolerance policies within the public schools have to be understood as part of a broader crisis of democracy in which the market is now seen as the master design for all pedagogical encounters and the state is increasingly geared to measures of militarization, containment, and surveillance rather than to expansion of democratic freedoms and social investments. In this sense, the corporatizing of public schooling and the war against youth cannot be disassociated from the assault on those public spheres and public goods that provide the conditions for greater democratic participation in shaping society. Questions of safety mobilized largely by a culture of fear and legitimated through the ongoing demonization of young people in the wider society have transformed schools into what sociologist Loic Wacquant has called an extension of "a single carceral continuum"[72] that operates through the registers of surveillance, control, punishment, and exclusion. In this context, zero-tolerance legislation within the schools simply extends to young people elements of harsh control and administration implemented in other public spheres where inequalities breed dissent and resistance.

Zero tolerance has become a metaphor for hollowing out the state and expanding the forces of domestic militarization, reducing democracy to consumerism, and replacing an ethic of mutual aid with an appeal to excessive individualism and social indifference.[73] According to this logic, the notion of the political increasingly equates power with domination, and citizenship with consumerism and passivity. In this insufferable climate of manufactured indifference, increased repression, unabated exploitation, and a war on Iraq that Senator Robert Byrd believes is rooted in the arrogance of unbridled power, young people have become the new casualties in an ongoing battle against justice, freedom, social citizenship, and democracy. As despairing as these conditions appear at the present moment, they increasingly have become the basis for a surge of political resistance on the part of many youth, intellectuals, labor unions, educators, and social movements.[74] Educators, young people, parents, religious organizations, community activists, and other cultural workers need to rethink what it would mean to both interrogate and break away from the dangerous and destructive ideologies, values, and social relations of zero-tolerance policies as they work in a variety of powerful institutional spheres to reinforce modes of authoritarian control and turn a generation of youth into a generation of suspects. This suggests a struggle both for public space and for conditions supportive of public dialogue about how to imagine reappropriating a notion of politics that is linked to the creation of a strong participatory democracy while simultaneously articulating a new vocabulary, a new set of theoretical tools, and social possibilities for re-visioning civic engagement and social transformation. We have entered a period in which class warfare offers no apologies because it is too arrogant and ruthless to imagine any resistance. But the collective need and potential struggle for justice should never be underestimated even in the darkest of times.

4
Neoliberalism as Public Pedagogy

⟐

Neoliberalism as Public Pedagogy

Our age is the time of "individual utopias," of utopias privatized, and so it comes naturally (as well as being a fashionable thing to do) to deride and ridicule such projects which imply a revision of the options which are collectively put at the disposal of individuals.[1]

The ascendancy of neoliberal corporate culture into every aspect of American life both consolidates economic power in the hands of the few and aggressively attempts to break the power of unions, decouple income from productivity, subordinate the needs of society to the market, and deem public services and goods an unconscionable luxury. But it does more. It thrives on a culture of cynicism, insecurity, and despair. Conscripts in a relentless campaign for personal responsibility, Americans are now convinced that they have little to hope for—and gain from—the government, nonprofit public spheres, democratic associations, public and higher education, and other nongovernmental social forces. With few exceptions, the project of democratizing public goods has fallen into disrepute in the popular imagination as the logic of the market undermines the most basic social solidarities. The consequences include not only a weakened social state but a growing sense of insecurity, cynicism, and political retreat on the part of the general public. The incessant calls for self-reliance that now dominate public discourse betray a hollowed-out and refigured state that neither provides adequate safety nets for its populace, especially those who are young, poor, or marginalized, nor gives any indication that it will serve the interests of its citizens in spite of constitutional guarantees. As Stanley Aronowitz and Peter Bratis argue, "The nation-state lives chiefly as a repressive power [though it] also has some purchase on maintaining a degree of ideological hegemony over ...'the multitude.'"[2] In short, private interests trump social needs, and economic growth becomes more important than social justice. The capitulation of labor unions and traditional working-class parties to neoliberal policies is matched by the ongoing dismantling of the welfare state. Within neoliberalism's market-driven discourse, corporate power marks the space of a new kind of public pedagogy, one in which the production, dissemination, and circulation of ideas emerges from the educational force of the larger culture. Public pedagogy in this sense refers to a powerful ensemble of ideological and institutional forces whose aim is to produce competitive, self-interested individuals vying for their own material and ideological gain. The culture of corporate public pedagogy largely cancels out or devalues gender, class-specific, and racial injustices of the existing social order by absorbing the democratic impulses and practices of civil society within narrow economic relations. Corporate public pedagogy has become an all-encompassing cultural horizon for producing market identities, values, and practices.

Under neoliberalism, dominant public pedagogy with its narrow and imposed schemes of classification and limited modes of identification use the educational force of the culture to negate the basic conditions for critical agency. As Pierre Bourdieu has pointed out, political action is only "possible because agents, who are part of the social world, have knowledge of this world and because one can act on the social world by acting on their knowledge of this world."[3] Politics often begins when it becomes possible to make power visible, to challenge the ideological circuitry of hegemonic knowledge, and to recognize that "political subversion presupposes cognitive subversion, a conversion of the vision of the world."[4] But another element of politics focuses on where politics happens, how proliferating sites of pedagogy bring into being new forms of resistance, raise new questions, and necessitate alternative visions regarding autonomy and the possibility of democracy itself.

What is crucial to recognize in the work of theorists such as Raymond Williams, Stuart Hall, Pierre Bourdieu, Noam Chomsky, Robert McChesney, and others is that neoliberalism is more than an economic theory: It also constitutes the conditions for a radically refigured cultural politics. That is, it provides, to use Raymond Williams' term, a new mode of "permanent education" in which dominant sites of pedagogy engage in diverse forms of pedagogical address to put into play a limited range of identities, ideologies, and subject positions that both reinforce neoliberal social relations and undermine the possibility for democratic politics.[5] The economist William Greider goes so far as to argue that the diverse advocates of neoliberalism currently in control of the American government want to "roll back the twentieth century literally"[6] by establishing the priority of private institutions and market identities, values, and relationships as the organizing principles of public life. This is a discourse that wants to squeeze out ambiguity from public space, to dismantle the social provisions and guarantees provided by the welfare state, and to eliminate democratic politics by making the notion of the social impossible to imagine beyond the isolated consumer and the logic of the market.[7] The ideological essence of this new public pedagogy is well expressed by Grover Norquist, the president of the Americans for Tax Reform and arguably Washington's leading right-wing strategist, who is quoted in Chapter 3 as saying: "My goal is to cut government in half in twenty-five years, to get it down to the size where we can drown it in the bathtub."[8]

These new sites of public pedagogy that have become the organizing force of neoliberal ideology are not restricted to schools, blackboards, and test taking. Nor do they incorporate the limited forms of address found in schools. Such sites operate within a wide variety of social institutions and formats including sports and entertainment media, cable television networks, churches, and channels of elite and popular culture such as advertising. Profound transformations have taken place in the public sphere, producing new sites of pedagogy marked by a distinctive confluence of new digital and media technologies, growing concentrations of corporate power, and unparalleled meaning-producing capacities. Unlike traditional forms of pedagogy, knowledge and desire are inextricably connected to modes of pedagogical address mediated through unprecedented electronic technologies that include high-speed computers, new types of digitized film, and CD-ROMs. The result is a public pedagogy that plays a decisive role in producing a diverse cultural sphere that gives new meaning to education as a political force. What is surprising about the cultural politics of neoliberalism is that cultural studies theorists have either ignored or largely underestimated the symbolic and pedagogical dimensions of the struggle that neoliberal corporate power has put into place for the last thirty years, particularly under the ruthless administration of George W. Bush.

Making the Pedagogical More Political

The need for permanent education, in our changing society, will be met in one way or another. It is now on the whole being met, though with many valuable exceptions and efforts against the tide, by an integration of this teaching with the priorities and interests of a capitalist society, and of a capitalist society, moreover, which necessarily retains as its central principle the idea of a few governing, communicating with and teaching the many.[9]

At this point in American history, neoliberal capitalism is not simply too overpowering; on the contrary, "democracy is too weak."[10] Hence the increasing influence of money over politics, the increasing domination of public concerns by corporate interests, and the growing tyranny of unchecked corporate power and avarice. Culture combines with politics to turn struggles over power into entertainment, as occurred in California when Governor Davis was recalled and Arnold Schwarzenegger emerged as the new occupant in the governor's office. But more importantly, under neoliberalism, pedagogy has become thoroughly politicized in reactionary terms as it constructs knowledge, values, and identities through a dominant media that has become a handmaiden of corporate power. For instance, soon after the invasion of Iraq, the *New York Times* released a survey indicating that 42 percent of the American public believed that Saddam Hussein was directly responsible for the September 11 attacks on the World Trade Center and the Pentagon. CBS, too, released a news poll indicating that 55 percent of the public believed that Saddam Hussein directly supported the terrorist organization Al Qaeda. A majority of Americans also believed that Saddam Hussein had weapons of mass destruction, was about to build a nuclear bomb, and would unleash it eventually on an unsuspecting American public. None of these claims had any basis in fact, since no evidence existed even to remotely confirm their validity. Of course, the aforementioned opinions held by a substantial number of Americans did not simply fall from the sky; they were ardently legitimated by President Bush, Vice President Cheney, Colin Powell, and Condoleezza

Rice, while daily reproduced uncritically in all of the dominant media. These misrepresentations and strategic distortions circulated in the dominant press either with uncritical, jingoistic enthusiasm, as in the case of the Fox News Channel, or through the dominant media's refusal to challenge such claims—both positions, of course, in opposition to foreign news sources, such as the BBC, that repeatedly challenged such assertions. Such deceptions are never innocent and in this case appear to have been shamelessly used by the Bush administration to muster support both for the Iraqi invasion and for an ideologically driven agenda "that overwhelmingly favors the president's wealthy supporters and is driving the federal government toward a long-term fiscal catastrophe."[11]

While not downplaying the seriousness of government deception, I believe there is another issue underlying these events in which the most important casualty is not simply the integrity of the Bush administration but democracy itself. One of the central legacies of modern democracy—with its roots in the Enlightenment classical liberal tradition, and most evident in the twentieth century in works as diverse as those of W.E.B. Du Bois, Raymond Williams, Cornelius Castoriadis, John Dewey, and Paulo Freire, among others—is the important recognition that a substantive democracy cannot exist without educated citizens. For some, the fear of democracy itself translated into an attack on a truly public and accessible education for all citizens. For others such as the progressive Walter Lippman, who wrote extensively on democracy in the 1920s, it meant creating two modes of education: one for the elite who would rule the country and be the true participants in the democratic process, and the other for the masses whose education would train them to be spectators rather than participants in shaping democratic public life. Du Bois recognized that such a bifurcation of educational opportunity was increasingly becoming a matter of common sense, but he rejected it outright.[12] Similarly in opposition to the enemies of democracy and the elitists, radical social critics such as Cornelius Castoriadis, Paulo Freire, and Stuart Hall believed that education for a democratic citizenry was an essential condition of equality and social justice and had to be provided through public, higher, popular, and adult education.

While Castoriadis and others were right about linking education and democracy, they had no way, in their time, of recognizing that the larger culture would extend, if not supersede, institutionalized education as the most important educational force in the developed societies. In fact, education and pedagogy have been synonymous with schooling in the public mind. Challenging such a recognition does not invalidate the importance of formal education to democracy, but it does require a critical understanding of how the work of education takes place in a range of other spheres such as advertising, television, film, the Internet, video games, and the popular press. Rather than invalidate the importance of schooling, it extends the sites of pedagogy and in doing so broadens and deepens the meaning of cultural pedagogy. The concept of public pedagogy also underscores the central importance of formal spheres of learning that unlike their popular counterparts—driven largely by commercial interests that more often miseducate the public—must provide citizens with the critical capacities, modes of literacies, knowledge, and skills that enable them both to read the world critically and to participate in shaping and governing it. Pedagogy at the popular level must now be a central concern of formal schooling itself. My point is not that public and higher education are free from corporate influence and dominant ideologies but, rather, that such models of education, at best, provide the spaces and conditions for prioritizing civic values over commercial interests (i.e., they self-consciously educate future citizens capable of participating in and reproducing a democratic society). In spite of these models' present embattled status and contradictory roles, institutional schooling remains uniquely placed to prepare students to both understand and influence the larger educational forces that shape their lives. Such institutions, along with their cultural studies advocates by virtue of their privileged position and dedication to freedom and democracy, also have an obligation to draw upon those traditions and resources capable of providing a critical and humanistic education to all students in order to prepare them for a world in which information and power have taken on new and influential dimensions. One entry into this challenge is to address the contributions to such issues that cultural studies and critical pedagogy have made in the last few decades, particularly with respect to how the relationship between culture and power constitute a new site of both politics and pedagogy.

Cultural Studies and the Question of Pedagogy

City walls, books, spectacles, events educate—yet now they mostly *miseducate* their residents. Compare the lessons, taken by the citizens of Athens (women and slaves included), during the performances of Greek trage-

dies with the kind of knowledge which is today consumed by the specta-
tor of *Dynasty* or *Perdue de vue*.[13]

My own interest in cultural studies emerges out of an ongoing project
to theorize the regulatory and emancipatory relationship among
culture, power, and politics as expressed through the dynamics of
what can be called public pedagogy. This project concerns, in part,
the diverse ways in which culture functions as a contested sphere in
the production, distribution, and regulation of power and how and
where it operates both symbolically and institutionally as an educational, political, and economic force. Drawing upon a long tradition
in cultural studies work, culture is viewed as constitutive and political, not only reflecting larger forces, but also constructing them; in
short, culture not only mediates history, it shapes it. In this formulation, power is a central element of culture just as culture is a crucial
element of power.[14] As Bauman observes, "Culture is a permanent
revolution of sorts. To say 'culture' is to make another attempt to
account for the fact that the human world (the world moulded
by the humans and the world which moulds humans) is perpetually, unavoidably—and unremediably *noch nicht geworden* (not-
yet-accomplished), as Ernst Bloch beautifully put it."[15]

I am suggesting that culture is a crucial terrain for theorizing and
realizing the political as an articulation and intervention into the
social, a space in which politics is pluralized, recognized as contingent, and open to many formations.[16] But culture is also a crucial
sphere for articulating the dialectical and mutually constitutive dynamics between the global political circuits that now frame material
relations of power and a cultural politics in which matters of representation and meaning shape and offer concrete examples of how
politics is expressed, lived, and experienced through the modalities
of daily existence. Culture, in this instance, is the ground of both
contestation and accommodation, and it is increasingly characterized by the rise of mega-corporations and new technologies that are
transforming radically the traditional spheres of economy, industry,
society, and everyday life. I am referring not only to the development of new information technologies but also to the enormous
concentration of ownership and power among a limited number of
corporations that now control diverse media technologies and markets.[17] Culture plays a central role in producing narratives, meta-
phors, images, and desiring maps that exercise a powerful pedagogical
force over how people think about themselves and their relationship

to others. From this perspective, culture is the primary sphere in which individuals, groups, and institutions engage in the art of translating the diverse and multiple relations that mediate between private life and public concerns. It is also the sphere in which the translating and pedagogical possibilities of culture are under assault, particularly as the forces of neoliberalism dissolve public issues into utterly privatized and individualistic concerns.[18]

Against the neoliberal attack on all things social, culture must be defended as the site where exchange and dialogue become crucial affirmations of a democratically configured space of the social in which the political is actually taken up and lived out through a variety of intimate relations and social formations. Far from being exclusively about matters of representation and texts, culture becomes a site, event, and performance in which identities and modes of agency are configured through the mutually determined forces of thought and action, body and mind, and time and space. Culture is the public space where common matters, shared solidarities, and public engagements provide the fundamental elements of democracy. Culture is also the pedagogical and political ground on which communities of struggle and a global public sphere can be imagined as a condition of democratic possibilities. Culture offers a common space in which to address the radical demands of a pedagogy that allows critical discourse to confront the inequities of power and promote the possibilities of shared dialogue and democratic transformation. Culture affirms the social as a fundamentally political space just as it attempts within the current historical moment to deny its relevance and its centrality as a political necessity. And culture's urgency, as Nick Couldry observes, resides in its possibilities for linking politics to matters of individual and social agency as they are lived out in particular democratic spheres, institutional forms, and communities in process. He writes:

> For what is urgent now is not defending the full range of cultural production and consumption from elitist judgement but defending the possibility of any shared site for an emergent democratic politics. The contemporary mission of cultural studies, if it has one, lies not with the study of "culture" (already a cliché of management and marketing manuals), but with the fate of a "*common* culture," and its contemporary deformations.[19]

Central to any feasible notion of cultural studies is the primacy of culture and power, organized through an understanding of how the political becomes pedagogical, particularly in terms of how private issues are connected to larger social conditions and collective forces—that is, how the very processes of learning constitute the political mechanisms through which identities are shaped, desires mobilized, and experiences take on form and meaning within those collective conditions and larger forces that constitute the realm of the social. In this context, pedagogy is no longer restricted to what goes on in schools, but becomes a defining principle of a wide-ranging set of cultural apparatuses engaged in what Raymond Williams has called "permanent education." Williams rightfully believed that education in the broadest sense plays a central role in any viable form of cultural politics. He writes:

> What [permanent education] valuably stresses is the educational force of our whole social and cultural experience. It is therefore concerned, not only with continuing education, of a formal or informal kind, but with what the whole environment, its institutions and relationships, actively and profoundly teaches.... [Permanent education also refers to] the field in which our ideas of the world, of ourselves and of our possibilities, are most widely and often most powerfully formed and disseminated. To work for the recovery of control in this field is then, under any pressures, a priority.[20]

Williams argued that any workable notion of critical politics would have to pay closer "attention to the complex ways in which individuals are formed by the institutions to which they belong, and in which, by reaction, the institutions took on the color of individuals thus formed."[21] Williams also foregrounded the crucial political question of how agency unfolds within a variety of cultural spaces structured within unequal relations of power.[22] He was particularly concerned about the connections between pedagogy and political agency, especially in light of the emergence of a range of new technologies that greatly proliferated the amount of information available to people while at the same time constricting the substance and ways in which such meanings entered the public domain. The realm of culture for Williams took on a new role in the latter part of the twentieth century, inasmuch as the actuality of economic power and its attendant networks of pedagogical control now exercised more influence than ever before in shaping how identities are produced and desires mobilized, as well as how everyday life acquired the force of common sense.[23] Williams clearly understood that making the political more pedagogical meant recognizing that where and how the psyche locates itself in public discourse, visions, and passions provides the groundwork for agents to enunciate, act, and reflect on themselves and their relations to others and the wider social order.

Unfortunately, Williams's emphasis on making the pedagogical more political has not occupied a central place in the work of most cultural studies theorists. Pedagogy in most cultural studies accounts is either limited to the realm of schooling, dismissed as a discipline with very little academic cultural capital, or rendered reactionary through the claim that it simply accommodates the paralyzing grip of governmental institutions that normalize all pedagogical practices. Within this discourse, pedagogy largely functions to both normalize relations of power and overemphasize agency at the expense of institutional pressures, embracing what Tony Bennett calls "all agency and no structure."[24] Such criticism, however, does little to explore or highlight the complicated, contradictory, and determining ways in which the institutional pressures of schools [and other pedagogical sites] and the social capacities of educators are mediated within unequal relations of power. Instead, Bennett simply reverses the formula and buttresses his own notion of governmentality as a theory of structures without agents. Of course, this position also ignores the role of various sites of pedagogy and the operational work they perform in producing knowledge, values, identities, and subject positions. But more importantly, it reflects the more general refusal on the part of many cultural studies theorists to take up the relationship between pedagogy and agency, on the one hand, and the relationship among the crises of culture, education, and democracy, on the other. Given such a myopic vision, left-leaning intellectuals who are dismissive of formal education sites have no doubt made it easier for the more corporate and entrepreneurial interests to dominate colleges and universities.

Unfortunately, many cultural studies theorists have failed to take seriously Antonio Gramsci's insight that "[e]very relationship of 'hegemony' is necessarily an educational relationship"—with its implication that education as a cultural pedagogical practice takes place across multiple sites as it signals how, within diverse contexts, education makes us both subjects of and subject to relations of power.[25] I want to build on Gramsci's insight by exploring in greater detail the connection among democracy, political agency, and pedagogy described in the work of the late French philosopher Cornelius Castoriadis. Castoriadis has made seminal, and often overlooked, contributions to the role of pedagogy and its centrality to a substantive democracy. I focus on this radical tradition in order to reclaim a legacy of critical thinking that refuses to decouple education from democracy, politics from pedagogy, and understanding from public intervention. This tradition of critical thought signals for educators and cultural studies advocates the importance of investing in the political as part of a broader effort to revitalize notions of democratic citizenship, social justice, and the public good. But it also signals the importance of cultural politics as a pedagogical force for understanding how people buy into neoliberal ideology, how certain forms of agency are both suppressed and produced, how neoliberals work pedagogically to convince the public that consumer rights are more important than the rights people have as citizens and workers, and how pedagogy as a force for democratic change enables understanding, action, and resistance.

Education and Radical Democracy

> Let us suppose that a democracy, as complete, perfect, etc., as one might wish, might fall upon us from the heavens: this sort of democracy will not be able to endure for more than a few years if it does not engender individuals that correspond to it, ones that, first and foremost, are capable of making it function and reproducing it. There can be no democratic society without democratic *paideia*.[26]

Castoriadis was deeply concerned about what it meant to think about politics and agency in light of the new conditions of capitalism that threatened to undermine the promise of democracy at the end of the twentieth century. Moreover, he argues, like Raymond Williams, that education, in the broadest sense, is a principal feature of politics because it provides the capacities, knowledge, skills, and social relations through which individuals recognize themselves as social and political agents. Linking such a broad-based definition of education to issues of power and agency also raises a fundamental question that goes to the heart of any substantive notion of democracy: How do issues of history, language, culture, and identity work to articulate and legitimate particular exclusions? If culture in this sense becomes the constituting terrain for producing identities and constituting social subjects, education becomes the strategic and positional mechanism through which such subjects are addressed, positioned within social spaces, located within particular histories and experiences, and always arbitrarily displaced and decentered as part of a pedagogical process that is increasingly multiple, fractured, and never homogenous.

Over the last thirty years Castoriadis has provided an enormous theoretical service in analyzing the space of education as a constitutive site for democratic struggle. He pursues the primacy of education as a political force by focusing on democracy both as the realized power of the people and as a mode of autonomy. In the first instance, he insists that "democracy means power of the people ... a regime aspiring to social and personal" freedom.[27] Democracy in this view suggests more than a simply negative notion of freedom in which the individual is defended against power. On the contrary, Castoriadis argues that any viable notion of democracy must reject this passive attitude toward freedom with its view of power as a necessary evil. In its place, he calls for a productive notion of power, one that is central to embracing a notion of political agency and freedom that affirms the equal opportunity of all to exercise political power in order to participate in shaping the most important decisions affecting their lives.[28] He ardently rejects the increasing "abandonment of the public sphere to specialists, to professional politicians,"[29] just as he rejects any conception of democracy that does not create the means for "unlimited interrogation in all domains" that closed off in "advance not only every political question as well as every philosophical one, but equally every ethical or aesthetic question."[30] Castoriadis refuses a notion of democracy restricted to the formalistic processes of voting while at the same time arguing that the notion of participatory democracy cannot remain narrowly confined to the political sphere.

Democracy, for Castoriadis, must also concern itself with the issue of cultural politics. He rightly argues that progressives are required to address the ways in which every society creates what he calls its "social imaginary significations," which provide the structures of representations that offer individuals selected modes of identification, provide the standards for both the ends of action and the criteria for what is considered acceptable or unacceptable behavior, and establish the affective measures for mobilizing desire and human action.[31] The fate of democracy for Castoriadis was inextricably linked to the profound crisis of contemporary knowledge, characterized by increasing commodification, fragmentation, privatization, and a turn toward racial and patriotic conceits. As knowledge becomes abstracted from the demands of civic culture and is reduced to questions of style, ritual, and image, it undermines the political, ethical, and gov-

erning conditions for individuals and social groups to either participate in politics or construct those viable public spheres necessary
for debate, collective action, and solving urgent social problems. As
Castoriadis suggests, the crisis of contemporary knowledge provides
one of the central challenges to any viable notion of politics. He
writes:

> Also in question is the relation of ... knowledge to the society that pro-
> duces it, nourishes it, is nourished by it, and risks dying of it, as well as
> the issues concerning for whom and for what this knowledge exists. Al-
> ready at present these problems demand a radical transformation of so-
> ciety, and of the human being, at the same time that they contain its
> premises. If this monstrous tree of knowledge that modern humanity is
> cultivating more and more feverishly every day is not to collapse under its
> own weight and crush its gardener as it falls, the necessary transforma-
> tions of man and society must go infinitely further than the wildest uto-
> pias have ever dared to imagine.[32]

Castoriadis is particularly concerned about how progressives might
address the crisis of democracy in light of how social and political
agents are being produced through dominant public pedagogies in
a society driven by the glut of specialized knowledge, consumerism,
and a privatized notion of citizenship that no longer supports noncommercial values and increasingly dismisses as a constraint any view
of society that emphasizes public goods and social responsibility.
What is crucial to acknowledge in Castoriadis' view of democracy is
that the crisis of democracy cannot be separated from the dual crisis
of representation and political agency. In a social order in which the
production of knowledge, meaning, and debate is highly restricted,
not only are the conditions for producing critical social agents limited, but also lost is the democratic imperative of affirming the primacy of ethics as a way of recognizing a social order's obligation to
future generations. Ethics in this sense recognizes that the extension
of power assumes a comparable extension in the field of ethical
responsibility, a willingness to acknowledge that ethics means being able to answer in the present for actions that will be borne by
generations in the future.[33]

Central to Castoriadis' work is the crucial acknowledgment that
society creates itself through a multiplicity of organized pedagogical
forms that provide the "instituting social imaginary" or field of cultural and ideological representations through which social practices
and institutional forms are endowed with meaning, generating certain

ways of seeing the self and its possibilities in the world. Not only is the social individual constituted, in part, by internalizing such meanings, but he or she acts upon such meanings in order to also participate and, where possible, to change society. According to Castoriadis, politics within this framework becomes "the collective activity whose object" is to put into question the explicit institutions of society while simultaneously creating the conditions for individual and social autonomy.[34] Castoriadis's unique contribution to democratic political theory lies in his keen understanding that autonomy is inextricably linked to forms of civic education that provide the conditions for bringing to light how explicit and implicit power can be used to open up or close down those public spaces that are essential for individuals to meet, address public interests, engage pressing social issues, and participate collectively in shaping public policy. In this view, civic education brings to light "society's instituting power by rendering it explicit.... [I]t reabsorbs the political into politics as the lucid and deliberate activity whose object is the explicit [production] of society."[35] According to Castoriadis, political agency involves learning how to deliberate, make judgments, and exercise choices, particularly as the latter are brought to bear as critical activities that offer the possibility of change. Civic education as it is experienced and produced throughout a vast array of institutions provides individuals with the opportunity to see themselves as more than they simply are within the existing configurations of power of any given society. Every society has an obligation to provide citizens with the capacities, knowledge, and skills necessary for them to be, as Aristotle claimed, "capable of governing and being governed."[36] A democracy cannot work if citizens are not autonomous, self-judging, and independent, qualities that are indispensable for making vital judgments and choices about participating in and shaping decisions that affect everyday life, institutional reform, and governmental policy. Hence, civic education becomes the cornerstone of democracy in that the very foundation of self-government is based on people not just having the "typical right to participate; they should also be educated [in the fullest possible way] in order to be *able* to participate."[37]

From a Pedagogy of Understanding to a Pedagogy of Intervention

It is not the knowledge of good and evil that we are missing; it is the skill and zeal to act on that knowledge which is conspicuously absent in this world of ours, in which dependencies, political responsibility and cultural values part ways and no longer hold each other in check.[38]

Williams and Castoriadis were clear that pedagogy and the active process of learning were central to any viable notion of citizenship and inclusive democracy. Pedagogy looms large for both of these theorists not as a technique or *a priori* set of methods but as a political and moral practice. As a political practice, pedagogy illuminates the relationship among power, knowledge, and ideology, while self-consciously, if not self-critically, recognizing the role it plays as a deliberate attempt to influence how and what knowledge and identities are produced within particular sets of social relations. As a moral practice, pedagogy recognizes that what cultural workers, artists, activists, media workers, and others teach cannot be abstracted from what it means to invest in public life, presuppose some notion of the future, or locate oneself in a public discourse.

The moral implications of pedagogy also suggest that our responsibility as public intellectuals cannot be separated from the consequences of the knowledge we produce, the social relations we legitimate, and the ideologies and identities we offer up to students. Refusing to decouple politics from pedagogy means, in part, that teaching in classrooms or in any other public sphere should not only simply honor the experiences students bring to such sites, including the classroom, but also connect their experiences to specific problems that emanate from the material contexts of their everyday life. Pedagogy in this sense becomes performative in that it is not merely about deconstructing texts but about situating politics itself within a broader set of relations that addresses what it might mean to create modes of individual and social agency that enable rather than shut down democratic values, practices, and social relations. Such a project not only recognizes the political nature of pedagogy but also situates it within a call for intellectuals to assume responsibility for their actions—to link their teaching to those moral principles that allow them to do something about human suffering, as Susan Sontag has recently suggested.[39] Part of this task necessitates that cultural studies theorists and educators anchor their own work, however diverse, in a radical project that seriously engages the promise of an unrealized democracy against its really existing and radically incomplete forms. Of crucial importance to such a project is rejecting the assumption that theory can understand social problems without contesting their appearance in public life. Yet, any viable cultural politics needs a socially committed notion of injustice if we are to take seriously what it means to fight for the idea of the good society. I think Zygmunt Bauman is right in arguing that "[i]f there is no room for the idea of *wrong* society, there is hardly much chance for the idea of good society to be born, let alone make waves."[40]

Cultural studies theorists need to be more forcefully committed to linking their overall politics to modes of critique and collective action that address the presupposition that democratic societies are never too just or just enough, and such a recognition means that a society must constantly nurture the possibilities for self-critique, collective agency, and forms of citizenship in which people play a fundamental role in critically discussing, administrating, and shaping the material relations of power and ideological forces that bear down on their everyday lives. At stake here is the task, as Jacques Derrida insists, of viewing the project of democracy as a promise, a possibility rooted in an ongoing struggle for economic, cultural, and social justice.[41] Democracy in this instance is not a sutured or formalistic regime; it is the site of struggle itself. The struggle over creating an inclusive and just democracy can take many forms, offers no political guarantees, and provides an important normative dimension to politics as an ongoing process of democratization that never ends. Such a project is based on the realization that a democracy that is open to exchange, question, and self-criticism never reaches the limits of justice. As Bauman observes:

> Democracy is not an institution, but essentially an anti-institutional force, a "rupture" in the otherwise relentless trend of the powers-that-be to arrest change, to silence and to eliminate from the political process all those who have not been "born" into power.... Democracy expresses itself in a continuous and relentless critique of institutions; democracy is an anarchic, disruptive element inside the political system; essentially, a force for *dissent* and change. One can best recognize a democratic society by its constant complaints that it is *not* democratic enough.[42]

By linking education to the project of an unrealized democracy, cultural studies theorists who work in higher education can move beyond those approaches to pedagogy that reduce it to a methodology like "teaching of the conflicts" or relatedly opening up a culture of questioning. In the most immediate sense, these positions fail to make clear the larger political, normative, and ideological considerations that inform such views of education, teaching, and visions of the future, assuming that education is predicated upon a particular view of the future that students should inhabit. Furthermore, both positions collapse the purpose and meaning of higher education, the role of educators as engaged scholars, and the possibility of pedagogy itself into a rather short-sighted and sometimes insular notion of method, specifically one that emphasizes argumentation and dialogue. There is a disquieting refusal in such discourses to raise broader questions about the social, economic, and political forces shaping the very terrain of higher education—particularly unbridled market forces, or racist and sexist forces that unequally value diverse groups of students within relations of academic power—or about what it might mean to engage pedagogy as a basis not merely for understanding but also for participating in the larger world. There is also a general misunderstanding of how teacher authority can be used to create the conditions for an education in democracy without necessarily falling into the trap of simply indoctrinating students.[43] For instance, liberal educator Gerald Graff believes that any notion of critical pedagogy that is self-conscious about its politics and engages students in ways that offer them the possibility for becoming critical—or what Lani Guinier calls the need to educate students "to participate in civic life, and to encourage graduates to give back to the community, which, through taxes, made their education possible"[44]—either leaves students out of the conversation or presupposes too much and simply represents a form of pedagogical tyranny. While Graff is a strong advocate of creating educational practices that open up the possibility of questioning among students, he refuses to connect pedagogical conditions that challenge how they think at the moment to the next step of prompting them to think about changing the world around them so as to expand and deepen its democratic possibilities. George Lipsitz criticizes academics such as Graff who believe that connecting academic work to social change is at best a burden and at worst a collapse into a crude form of propagandizing, suggesting that they are subconsciously educated to accept cynicism about the ability of ordinary people to change the conditions under which they live.[45] Teaching students how to argue, draw on their own experiences, or engage in rigorous dialogue says nothing about why they should engage in these actions in the first place. The issue of how the culture of argumentation and questioning relates to giving students the tools they need to fight oppressive forms of power, make the world a more meaningful and just place, and develop a sense of social responsibility is missing in work like Graff's because this is part of the discourse of political education, which Graff simply equates to indoctrination or speaking to the converted.[46] Here propaganda and critical pedagogy collapse into each other. Propaganda is generally used to misrepresent knowledge, promote biased knowledge, or produce a view of politics that appears beyond question and critical engagement. While no pedagogical intervention should fall to the level of propaganda, a pedagogy that attempts to empower critical citizens can't and shouldn't avoid politics. Pedagogy must address the relationship between politics and agency, knowledge and power, subject positions and values, and learning and social change while always being open to debate, resistance, and a culture of questioning. Liberal educators committed to simply raising questions have no language for linking learning to forms of public scholarship that would enable students to consider the important relationship between democratic public life and education, politics and learning. Disabled by the depoliticizing, if not slavish, allegiance to a teaching methodology, they have little idea of how to encourage students pedagogically to enter the sphere of the political, enabling them to think about how they might participate in a democracy by taking what they learn "into new locations—a third-grade classroom, a public library, a legislator's office, a park"[47]—or, for that matter, taking on collaborative projects that address the myriad problems citizens face in a diminishing democracy.

In spite of the professional pretense to neutrality, academics need to do more pedagogically than simply teach students how to be adept at forms of argumentation. Students need to argue and question, but they need much more from their educational experience. The pedagogy of argumentation in and of itself guarantees nothing, but it is an essential step toward opening up the space of resistance against authority, teaching students to think critically about the world around them, and recognizing interpretation and dialogue as conditions for social intervention and transformation in the service of an unrealized democratic order. As Amy Gutmann brilliantly argues, education is always political because it is connected to the acquisition of agency, to the ability to struggle with ongoing relations of power, and is a precondition for creating informed and critical citizens. Educators, she believes, need to link education to democracy and recognize pedagogy as an ethical and political practice tied to modes of authority in which the "democratic state recognizes the value of political education in predisposing [students] to accept those ways of life that are consistent with sharing the rights and responsibilities of citizenship in a democratic society."[48] This notion of education is tied not to the alleged neutrality of teaching methods but to a vision of pedagogy that is directive and interventionist on the side of reproducing a democratic society. Democratic societies need educated citizens who are steeped in more than just the skills of argumentation. And it is precisely this democratic project that affirms the critical function of education and refuses to narrow its goals and aspirations to methodological considerations. This is what makes critical pedagogy different from training. Indeed, it is precisely the failure to connect learning to its democratic functions and goals that provides rationales for pedagogical approaches that strip the meaning of what it means to be educated from its critical and democratic possibilities.

Raymond Williams and Castoriadis recognize that the crisis of democracy is not only about the crisis of culture but also about the crisis of pedagogy and education. Cultural studies theorists would do well to take account of the profound transformations occurring in the public sphere and reclaim pedagogy as a central category of cultural politics. The time has come for such theorists to distinguish professional caution from political cowardice and recognize that their obligations extend beyond deconstructing texts or promoting a culture of questioning. These are important pedagogical interventions, but they do not go far enough. We need to link knowing with action, and learning with social engagement, and this requires addressing the responsibilities that come with teaching students and others to fight for an inclusive and radical democracy by recognizing that education in the broadest sense is not just about understanding, however critical, but also provides the conditions for assuming the responsibilities we have as citizens to expose human misery and to eliminate the conditions that produce it. I think Bauman is quite right in suggesting that as engaged cultural workers, we need to take up our work as part of a broader democratic project in which the good society

is a society which thinks it is not just enough, which questions the sufficiency of any achieved level of justice and considers justice always to be a step or more ahead. Above all, it is a society which reacts angrily to any case of injustice and promptly sets about correcting it.[49]

Matters of responsibility, social action, and political intervention develop not simply out of social critique but also out of forms of self-critique. The relationship between knowledge and power, on the one hand, and scholarship and politics, on the other, should always be self-reflexive about what its effects are, how it relates to the larger world, whether or not it is open to new understandings, and what it might mean pedagogically to take seriously matters of individual and social responsibility. In short, this project points to the need for educators to articulate cultural studies, not only as a resource for theoretical competency and critical understanding, but also as a pedagogical practice that addresses the possibility of interpretation as intervention in the world. Cultural studies practitioners have performed an important theoretical task in emphasizing how meaning and value are constituted in language, representations, and social relations. They have been purposely attentive to a careful and thorough reading of a diverse number of cultural texts. They have rightly addressed in great detail and complexity how power makes demands on knowledge within various cultures of circulation and transformation and how knowledge functions as a form of power. But such a critical understanding, reading, and engagement with meaning is not enough. Politics demands more than understanding; it demands that understanding be coupled with a responsibility to others. This is central to the most basic requirement of taking seriously our role as moral and political agents who can both read the world and transform it.

Neoliberalism not only places capital and market relations in a no-man's-land beyond the reach of compassion, ethics, and decency; it also undermines those basic elements of the social contract and the political and pedagogical relations it presupposes in which self-reliance, confidence in others, and a trust in the longevity of democratic institutions provide the basis for modes of individual autonomy, social agency, and critical citizenship. One of the most serious challenges faced by cultural studies, then, is the need to develop a new language and the necessary theoretical tools for contesting a variety of forms of domination put into play by neoliberalism in the twenty-first century. Part of this challenge demands recognizing that the struggles over cultural politics cannot be divorced from the contestations and conflicts put into play through the forces of dominant economic and cultural institutions and their respective modes of education. In short, cultural studies advocates must address the challenge of how to problematize and pluralize the political, engage new sites of pedagogy as crucial, strategic public spheres, and situate cultural studies within an ongoing project that recognizes that the crisis of democracy is about the interrelated crises of politics, culture, education, and public pedagogy.

5
The Politics of Hope in Dangerous Times

⤶

There is a time and place in the ceaseless human endeavor to change the world, when alternative visions, no matter how fantastic, provide the grist for shaping powerful political forces for change. I believe we are precisely at such a moment. Utopian dreams in any case never entirely fade away. They are omnipresent as the hidden signifiers of our desires. Extracting them from the dark recesses of our minds and turning them into a political force for change may court the danger of the ultimate frustration of those desires. But better that, surely, than giving in to the degenerate utopianism of neoliberalism (and all those interests that give possibility such a bad press) and living in craven and supine fear of expressing and pursuing alternative desires at all.

—David Harvey[1]

Under the prevailing reign of neoliberalism in the United States, hope appears foreclosed and progressive social change a distant memory. Imagining a life beyond capitalism or the prevailing culture of fear appears impossible at a time when the distinction between capitalism and democracy seems to have been erased. As market relations now become synonymous with a market society, freedom is reduced to a market strategy and citizenship either is narrowed to the demands of the marketplace or becomes utterly privatized. The upshot is that it has become easier to imagine the end of the world than the end of capitalism.[2] Within this dystopian universe, the public realm is increasingly reduced to an instrumental space in which individuality reduces self-development to the relentless pursuit of personal interests, and the realm of autonomy is reduced to a domain of activity "in which … private goals of diverse kinds may be pursued."[3] This is evident in ongoing attempts by many liberals and conservatives to turn commercial-free public education over to market forces, dismantle traditional social provisions of the welfare state, transform all vestiges of the health-care system to private interests, and mortgage social security to the whims of the stock market. There is a growing sense in the American popular imagination that citizen involvement, social planning, and civic engagement are becoming irrelevant in a society where the welfare state is being aggressively dismantled.[4] Those traditional, if not imagined, public spheres in which people could exchange ideas, debate, and shape the conditions that structure their everyday lives increasingly appear to have little relevance or political significance in spite of the expressions of public good that followed the tragedy that took place on September 11, 2001. In the midst of growing fears about domestic security, coupled with post-Iraqi war jingoism, dissent is now labeled as unpatriotic and is accompanied by the ongoing destruction of basic constitutional liberties and freedoms. As I have pointed out in previous chapters, under the USA PATRIOT Act, individuals can be detained by the government indefinitely without being charged, having no recourse to a lawyer, or without having the benefit of a trial. The military has been given the right to engage in domestic surveillance, and the FBI can now gain access to library records in order to peruse an individual's reading habits. In the face of such assaults upon civil liberties, leading political figures such as former Secretary of Education William Bennett have taken out ads in the *New York Times* claiming that internal dissent both aids terrorists and poses an equally serious threat to the security of the United States. Increasingly, the appeal to patriotic fervor feeds a commercial frenzy that turns collective grief into profits and political responsibility into demagoguery. If the tragedy of the events of 9/11 served to resurrect noble concepts like public service and civic courage, the all-encompassing power of the market quickly converted them into forms of civic vacuity that spawned an endless array of consumer products including everything from shoes to flag pins. But the hijacking of the grief resulting from such egregious terroristic acts did more than serve as grist for expanding markets; it also provided a pretext for using the discourse of anti-terrorism to dismantle basic civil liberties, imprison the American public within a culture of fear and repression, provide huge revenues to major corporations supporting the Bush administration, and spend billions on military weaponry designed to give legitimacy to a foreign policy based on the dangerous threat of preemptive strikes against alleged enemies of the United States.

While the role of big government and public services made a brief comeback on behalf of the common good, especially in providing crucial services related to public health and safety, President Bush and his supporters remain wedded to the "same reactionary agenda he pushed before the attack."[5] Instead of addressing the gaps in both public health needs and the safety net for workers, young people, and the poor, the Bush administration pushed through both houses of Congress a stimulus plan based primarily on tax breaks for the wealthy and major corporations, while at the same time "pressing for an energy plan that features subsidies and tax breaks for energy companies and drilling in the arctic wilderness."[6] Investing in children, the environment, crucial public services, and those most in need, once again, gives way to investing in the rich and repaying corporate contributors. Such practices suggest that little has changed with respect to economic policy, regardless of all the talk about the past being irrevocably repudiated in light of the events of September 11. Where is the public outrage over a tax "stimulus" package that gives the wealthiest 1 percent of the population 50 percent of the total tax cut while it simultaneously refuses to enact legislation lessening the financial burden for older Americans on Medicare? Where is the outrage over the Bush administration's willingness to give billions in tax breaks to the wealthy while at the same time "student loans, child-care, food stamps, school lunches, job training, veterans programs, and cash assistance for the elderly and disabled poor are all being cut"?[7] Where is the outrage over a government that will spend up to $900 billion dollars on the cost of waging a war and maintaining postwar control of Iraq at the same time that it cuts veterans' benefits and gives the rich an exorbitant tax cut? Where is the outrage over the passing of legislation such as the USA PATRIOT Act and the Homeland Security Act that gives the government unprecedented power to spy on its citizens, suspend due process, and jail people for thirty days or more without filing any criminal charges? Where is the outrage over the Bush administration's ongoing assault on the environment, scornfully evident in the government's refusal to ratify the Kyoto treaty to reduce global warming (an example now being followed by Russia)? Where is the collective anger over a government bent on ingratiating corporate interests while gutting environmental protection laws such as the Clean Air Act, evident in its attempt to eliminate federal regulations that force power plants to reduce mercury emissions, its refusal to regulate enforcement cases against coal-burning power plants, and its unwillingness to put any restraints on auto companies that continue polluting the air with high levels of auto emissions?[8] Even more serious is the government's shameful refusal to address the plight of the 30 million people in the United States who live below the poverty line, the 74 million adults and children who have no health insurance, and the 1.4 million children who are homeless.[9]

Emptied of any substantial content, "democracy" even in its current deracinated state appears imperiled as individuals are unable to translate their privately suffered misery into public concerns and collective action. Civic engagement and political agency now appear impotent, and public values are rendered invisible in light of the growing power of multinational corporations to commercialize public space and disconnect power from issues of equity, social justice, and civic responsibility.[10] As the vast majority of citizens become detached from public forums that nourish social critique, political agency not only becomes a mockery of itself but is upended by market-based choices in which private satisfactions replace social responsibilities or, as Ulrich Beck puts it, biographic solutions become a substitute for systemic change.[11] As Cornelius Castoriadis argues, under such conditions, it becomes impossible to imagine politics as the autonomy of the collective, "which can be achieved only through explicit self-institution and self-governance."[12] From this perspective, contemporary notions of freedom—legitimated as an absence of restraint and a narrow form of self-interest—have nothing to do with real autonomy and effective freedom in which individuals function as critical thinkers capable of "putting existing institutions into questions ... [so that] democracy again becomes society's movement of self-institution—that is to say, a new type of regime in the full sense of the term."[13] As the space of criticism is undercut by the absence of public spheres that encourage the exchange of information, opinion, and criticism, the horizons of a substantive democracy in which the promise of autonomous individuals and an autonomous society disappear against the growing isolation and depoliticization that marks the loss of politically guaranteed public realms—realms where the realized power of people, political participation, and engaged citizenship would otherwise make their appearance. Also rapidly disappearing are those public spaces and unmarketed cultural spaces in which people neither confuse the language of brand names with the language of autonomy and social engagement nor communicate through a commodified discourse incapable of defending vital institutions as a public good. One consequence is that political exhaustion and impoverished intellectual visions are fed by the increasingly popular assumption that there are no alternatives to the present state of affairs. As I have said in Chapter 1, neoliberalism violates the first rule of democratic politics by denying its own historical and contemporary relationship to power and ideology, largely shrouded in a discourse of objectivity and historical inevitability.

At the same time, as Manuel Castells observes, economic power is removed from politics to the degree that it has become global and extraterritorial; power now flows beyond national boundaries, largely escaping from and defying the reach of traditional centers of politics that are nation based and local.[14] The space of power appears increasingly beyond the reach of governments and, as a result, nations and citizens are increasingly removed as political agents with regard to the impact that multinational corporations have on their daily lives. This does not mean that the state has lost all of its power. On the contrary, it now works almost exclusively to deregulate business, eliminate corporate taxes, dismantle the welfare state, and incarcerate so-called disposable populations. Once again, the result is not only general indifference but the elimination of those public spaces that reveal the rough edges of social order, disrupt consensus, and point to the need for modes of education that link learning to the conditions necessary for developing democratic forms of political agency and civic struggle.

As the promise of what Takis Fotopoulos calls an "inclusive democracy"[15]—with its emphasis on the abolishment of iniquitous power relations in all economic, political, and social spheres—recedes from public memory, unfettered brutal self-interests combine with retrograde social policies to make security a top domestic priority. One consequence is that all levels of government are being hollowed out as their policing functions increasingly overpower and mediate their diminishing social functions. Reduced to dismantling the gains of the welfare state and constructing policies that criminalize social problems such as homelessness and prioritize penal methods over social investments, government is now discounted as a means of addressing basic, economic, educational, environmental, and social problems. As I mentioned earlier in the book, zero-tolerance policies link the public schools to the prison system as a substitute for education. One consequence is that the distinction between prison and school has become blurred.

The police, courts, and other disciplinary agencies have increasingly become the main forces used to address social problems and implement public policies that are largely aimed at minorities of race and color. Moreover, the increasing concerns for national security fueled by a hyped-up jingoism, especially in a post-Iraqi war climate, have amplified the forces of domestic militarization in the United States, and the American people appear increasingly drawn together "through shared fears rather than shared responsibilities."[16] Misfortune breeds contempt, and poverty is confused with personal neglect. Across the social sphere, neoliberalism's dismissal of public goods, coupled with an ecology of fear, rewrites the meaning of community through the logic of government threats, anti-terror campaigns waged against minorities, the squelching of dissent, and a highly coordinated government and media blitz in support of the invasion and occupation of Iraq.

Labeled by neoliberals and right-wing politicians as the enemy of freedom (except when it aids big business), government is discounted as a guardian of the public interest. As a result, government bears no responsibility either for the poor and dispossessed or for the collective future of young people. The disappearance of those non-commodified public spaces such as libraries, independent bookstores, union halls, adult clubs, and other sites necessary for reactivating our political sensibilities as critical citizens, engaged public intellectuals, and social agents is happening at a time when public goods are being disparaged in the name of privatization and critical public forums are ceasing to resonate as sites of utopian possibility. The lack of justice and equity in American society increases proportionately to the lack of political imagination and collective hope.

Politics devoid of a radical vision often either degenerates into cynicism or appropriates a view of power that appears to be equated only with domination. It is therefore crucial that progressives, educators, concerned citizens, and other activists respond with a renewed effort to merge politics, pedagogy, and ethics with a revitalized sense of the importance of providing the conditions for constructing critical forms of individual and social agency rather than believing the fraudulent, self-serving hegemonic assumption that democracy and capitalism are the same or, indeed, that politics as a site of contestation, critical exchange, and engagement is in a state of terminal arrest. In part, this would demand engaging the alleged argument for the death of politics as symptomatic not only of the crisis of democracy but also of the more specific crisis of vision, education, agency, and meaning that disconnects public values and ethics from the very sphere of politics.

Some social theorists such as Todd Gitlin make the plunge into forms of political cynicism easier by suggesting that any attempt to change society through a cultural politics that links the pedagogical and the political will simply augment the power of the dominant social order.[17] Lost from such accounts is the recognition that democracy has to be struggled over, even in the face of a most appalling crisis of political agency. Within this discourse, little attention is paid to the fact that struggles over politics, power, and democracy are inextricably linked to creating democratic public spheres where individuals can be educated as political agents equipped with the skills, capacities, and knowledge they need not only to actually perform as autonomous social agents but also to believe that such struggles *are worth taking up*. Neither homogeneous nor nostalgic, *the public sphere* points to a plurality of institutions, sites, and spaces; it is a sphere in which people not only talk, debate, and reassess the political, moral, and cultural dimensions of publicness but also develop processes of learning and persuasion as a way of enacting new social identities and altering "the very structure of participation and the ... horizon of discussion and debate."[18]

The struggle over politics, in this instance, is linked to pedagogical interventions aimed at subverting dominant forms of meaning in order to generate both a renewed sense of agency and a critical subversion of dominant power itself. Agency now becomes the site through which, as Judith Butler has pointed out in another context, power is not transcended but reworked, replayed, and restaged in productive ways.[19] Central to my argument is the assumption that politics is not simply about power but also, as Cornelius Castoriadis points out, "has to do with political judgments and value choices,"[20] indicating that questions of civic education and critical pedagogy (learning how to become a skilled activist) are central to the struggle over political agency and democracy. Civic education and critical pedagogy emphasize critical reflexivity, bridge the gap between learning and everyday life, make visible the connection between power and knowledge, and provide the conditions for extending democratic rights, values, and identities while drawing upon the resources of history. However, among many educators and social theorists, there is a widespread refusal to address education as a crucial means either for expanding and enabling political agency or for recognizing that such education takes place, not only within schools but across a wide variety of public spheres mediated through the very mechanisms of culture itself.

Democracy has now been reduced to a metaphor for the alleged "free" market and has nothing to do with a more substantive rendering of the term, such as what Noam Chomsky calls "involving opportunities for people to manage their own collective and individual affairs."[21] It is not that a genuine democratic public space once existed in some ideal form and has now been corrupted by the values of the market; rather, these democratic public spheres, even in limited forms, seem no longer to be animating concepts for making visible the contradiction and tension between the reality of existing democracy and the promise of a more fully realized democracy. While liberal democracy offers an important discourse around issues of "rights, freedoms, participation, self-rule, and citizenship," it has been mediated historically, as John Brenkman observes, through the "damaged and burdened tradition" of racial and gender exclusions, economic injustice, and a formalistic, ritualized democracy which substituted the swindle for the promise of democratic participation.[22] Part of the challenge of creating a substantive and inclusive democracy lies in constructing new locations of struggle, vocabularies, and subject positions that allow people in a wide variety of public spheres to become more than they are now, to question what it is they have become within existing institutional and social formations, and, as Chantal Mouffe points out, "to give some thought to their experiences so that they can transform their relations of subordination and oppression."[23]

Despite the urgency of the current historical moment, educators should avoid crude anti-theoretical calls to action. More than ever, they can appropriate scholarly and popular sources and use theory as a critical resource to name particular problems and make connections between the political and the cultural, to break what Homi Bhabha has called "the continuity and the consensus of common sense."[24] As a resource, theory becomes an important way of critically engaging and mapping the crucial relations among language, texts, everyday life, and structures of power as part of a broader effort to understand the conditions, contexts, and strategies of struggle that will lead to social transformation. I am suggesting that the tools of theory emerge out of the intersection of the past and present and respond to and are shaped by the conditions at hand. Theory, in this instance, addresses the challenge of connecting the world of the symbolic, discursive, and representational to the social gravity and force of everyday issues rooted in material relations of power.

The overriding political project at issue here calls for educators and others to produce new theoretical tools (a new vocabulary and set of conceptual resources) for linking theory, critique, education, and the discourse of possibility to the creation of the social conditions for the collective production of what Pierre Bourdieu calls realist utopias.[25] Such a project points to constructing both a new vocabulary for connecting what we read to how we engage in movements for social change, while recognizing that simply invoking the relationship between theory and practice, critique and social action, is not enough. For as John Brenkman points out, "theory becomes [a] closed circuit when it supposes it can understand social problems without contesting their manifestation in public life."[26] It is also symptomatic of a kind of retreat from the uneven battles over values and beliefs characteristic of some versions of postmodern conceptions of the political. Any attempt to give new life to a substantive democratic politics must, in part, produce alternative narratives to those employed by the producers of official memory, and address what it means to make the pedagogical more political. This means engaging the issue of what kind of educational work is necessary within different types of public spaces to enable people to use their full intellectual resources and skills both to provide a profound critique of existing institutions and to enter into the public sphere in order to interrupt the operations of dominant power and fully address what Zygmunt Bauman calls the "hard currency of human suffering."[27]

If emancipatory politics is to meet the challenge of neoliberal capitalism, politics needs to be theorized not as a science or set of objective conditions but as a point of departure in specific and concrete situations. This means rethinking the very meaning of the political so that it can provide a sense of direction but no longer be used to provide complete answers. In short, such a politics entails that we ask why and how particular social formations have a specific shape and come into being, and what it might mean to rethink such formations in terms of opening up new sites of struggles and movements. Politics in this sense offers a notion of the social that is open and provisional, providing a conception of democracy that is never complete but constantly amenable to different understandings of the contingency of its decisions, mechanisms of exclusions, and operations of power.[28] In this formulation, the struggle for justice and against injustice never ends. In the absence of such languages and the public spheres that make them operative, politics becomes narcissistic, reductionist, and it caters to the mood of widespread pessimism and the cathartic allure of spectacle or the seductions of consumerism. Emptied of its political content, public space increasingly becomes either a site of self-display—a favorite space for the public relations intellectual, speaking ever so softly on National Public Radio—or a site for the reclaiming of a form of social Darwinism represented most explicitly in reality-based television with its endless instinct for the weaknesses of others and its masochistic affirmation of ruthlessness and steroidal power. Or, it becomes a site where citizenship is stripped of its civic responsibilities and is reduced to the narrow obligations and needs of an unfettered individualism. Escape, avoidance, and narcissism are now coupled with the public display, if not celebration, of those individuals who define agency in terms of their survival skills rather than their commitment to dialogue, critical reflection, solidarity, and relations that open up the promise of public engagement with important social issues. Indeed, reality TV now embraces the arrogance of neoliberal power as it smiles back at us, while simultaneously legitimating downsizing and the ubiquity of the political economy of fear.

Educated Hope[29]

Against an increasingly oppressive corporate-based globalism, educators and other cultural workers need to resurrect a language of resistance and possibility, a language that embraces a militant utopianism while constantly being attentive to those forces that seek to turn such hope into a new slogan or punish and dismiss those who dare look beyond the horizon of the given. Central to any viable notion of politics is the recognition that hope must be part of a broader question creating the pedagogical conditions for producing individual and social agents who are willing to "make use of the freedom they have and to acquire the freedom they are told they have but have not."[30] Hope, in this instance, is one of the preconditions for individual and social struggle, for the ongoing practice of critical education in a wide variety of sites, and for courage on the part of intellectuals inside and outside of the academy who use the resources of theory to address pressing social problems. But hope is also a referent for civic courage and its ability to mediate the memory of loss and the experience of injustice as part of a broader attempt to open up new locations of struggle, contest the workings of oppressive power, and undermine various forms of domination. For hope to be more than an empty abstraction, it must be firmly anchored in the realities and contradictions of everyday life and have some hold on the present. This suggests a notion of hope that, as Derrida describes it, is willing to take up the "necessity to rethink the concepts of the possible and the impossible" in the face of the current attacks on public life and democracy worldwide.[31]

As I have argued elsewhere, the philosopher Ernst Bloch provides important theoretical insights on the importance of hope.[32] He argues that hope must be concrete, a spark that not only reaches out beyond the surrounding emptiness of privatization but anticipates a better world in the future, a world that speaks to us by presenting tasks based on the challenges of the present time. For Bloch, utopianism becomes concrete when it links the possibility of the "*not yet*" with forms of political agency animated by a determined effort to engage critically with the past and present in order to address pressing social problems and realizable tasks.[33] Bloch believes that utopianism cannot be removed from the world and is not "something like nonsense or absolute fancy; rather it is *not yet* in the sense of a possibility; that it could be there if we could only do something for it."[34] As a discourse of critique and social transformation, utopianism in Bloch's view is characterized by a "militant optimism," one that foregrounds the crucial relationship between critical education and political agency, on the one hand, and the concrete struggles needed, on the other hand, to give substance to the recognition that every present is incomplete. For theorists such as Bloch, utopian thinking is anticipatory rather than messianic, mobilizing rather than therapeutic. At best, such thinking, as Anson Rabinach argues, "points beyond the given while remaining within it."[35] The longing for a more human society in this instance does not collapse into a retreat from the world but emerges out of critical and practical engagements with present behaviors, institutional formations, and everyday practices. Hope in this context does not ignore the worst dimensions of human suffering, exploitation, and social relations; on the contrary, it acknowledges the need to sustain the "capacity to see the worst and offer more than that for our consideration."[36] The great challenge to militant utopianism, with its hope of keeping critical thought alive, rests in the emerging consensus among a wide range of political factions that neoliberal democracy is the best we can do. The impoverishment of intellectuals—with their growing refusal to speak of addressing, if not ending, human suffering and social injustices—is now matched by the poverty of a social order that cannot conceive of any alternative to itself.

Feeding into the increasingly dominant view that society cannot be fundamentally improved outside of market forces, neoliberalism strips utopianism of its possibilities for social critique and democratic engagement. By doing so it undermines the need to reclaim utopian thinking as both a discourse of human rights and a moral referent for dismantling and transforming dominant structures of wealth and power.[37] At the same time, neoliberalism undermines both the language of solidarity and those public spaces in which it is nourished, acted upon, and translated into a vibrant social movement and political force.

The loss of hope and the collapse into cynicism can be found all across the ideological spectrum extending from the Left to the Right. What is shared among these groups is the presupposition that utopian thinking is synonymous with state terrorism and that progressive visionaries are nothing less than unrealistic, if not dangerous, ideologues. The alternative offered here is what Russell Jacoby calls a "convenient cynicism,"[38] the belief that human suffering, hardship, and massive inequalities in all areas of life are simply inherent in human nature and an irreversible part of the social condition. Or, in its liberal version, the belief that "America's best defense against utopianism as terrorism is preserving democracy as it currently exist[s] in the world"[39]—a view largely shared by ultra-conservatives such as Lynne Cheney, John Ashcroft, and Norman Podhoretz. Within this discourse, hope is foreclosed, politics becomes militarized, and resistance is privatized, aestheticized, or reduced to some form of hyper-commercialized escapism. Against a militant and radically democratic utopianism, the equation of terrorism and utopianism appears deeply cynical. Neoliberalism not only appears flat, it also offers up an artificially conditioned optimism—operating at full capacity in the pages of *Fast Company*, *Wired Magazine*, the *Wall Street Journal*, and *Forbes* as well as in the relentless entrepreneurial hype of figures such as George Gilder and the Nike and Microsoft revolutionaries—in which it becomes increasingly difficult to imagine a life beyond the existing parameters of market pleasures, mail-order catalogues, shopping malls, and Disneyland.[40] The profound anti-utopianism that is spurred on by neoliberalism and its myth of the citizen as consumer and markets as sovereign entities, and its collapse of the distinction between both market liberties and civic liberties, on the one hand, and a market economy and a market society, on the other, not only commodifies a critical notion of political agency, it also undermines the importance of multiple democratic public spheres.

Against the dystopian hope of neoliberalism, I want to argue for the necessity of educated hope as a crucial component of a radically charged politics "grounded in broad-based civic participation and popular decision making."[41] Educated hope as a form of oppositional utopianism makes visible the necessity for progressives and other critical intellectuals to be attentive to the ways in which institutional and symbolic power are tangled up with everyday experience. Any politics of hope must tap into individual experiences while at the same time linking individual responsibility with a progressive sense of social agency. Politics and pedagogy alike spring "from real situations and from what we can say and do in these situations."[42] At its best, hope translates into civic courage as a political and pedagogical practice that begins when one's life can no longer be taken for granted. In doing so, it makes concrete the possibility for transforming politics into an ethical space and public act that confronts the flow of everyday experience and the weight of social suffering with the force of individual and collective resistance and the unending project of democratic social transformation. Emphasizing politics as a pedagogical practice and performative act, educated hope accentuates the notion that politics is not only played out on the terrain of imagination and desire but is also grounded in relations of power mediated through the outcome of situated struggles dedicated to creating the conditions and capacities for people to become critically engaged political agents.

Combining the discourse of critique and hope is crucial to affirming that critical activity offers the possibility for social change, one that views democracy as a project and a task, as an ideal type that is never finalized and has a powerful adversary in the social realities it is meant to change. Postcolonial theorist Samir Amin echoes this call by arguing that educators should consider addressing the project of a more realized democracy as part of an ongoing process of democratization. According to Amin, democratization "stresses the dynamic aspect of a still-unfinished process" while rejecting notions of democracy that are given a definitive formula.[43] An oppositional cultural politics can take many forms, but given the current assault on democratic public spheres, it seems imperative that progressives revitalize the struggles over social citizenship, particularly those aimed at expanding liberal freedoms, ensuring the downward distribution of resources, and creating forms of collective insurance that provide a safety net for individual incapacities and misfortunes. Simultaneously, any viable cultural politics must address the necessity to develop collective movements that can challenge the subordination of social needs to the dictates of commercialism and capital.

Central to such a politics would be a critical public pedagogy that attempts to make visible alternative models of radical democratic relations in a wide variety of sites. These spaces can make the pedagogical more political by raising fundamental questions such as: What is the relationship between social justice and the distribution of public resources and goods? What conditions, knowledge, and skills are prerequisites for political agency and social change? At the very least, such a project involves understanding and critically engaging dominant public transcripts and values within a broader set of historical and institutional contexts. It means moving beyond the often paralyzing language of critique or refusing to relate the discourse of politics to the everyday relations through which people experience their lives. It also means refusing to offer scripted narratives that fix people in a particular notion of identity, agency, or future. As I have stressed before, many educators have failed to take seriously Antonio Gramsci's insight that "[e]very relationship of 'hegemony' is necessarily an educational relationship"—with its implication that education as a cultural pedagogical practice takes place across multiple sites as it signals how, within diverse contexts, education makes us both subjects of and subject to relations of power.[44] Education in this sense assigns critical meaning to action, connects understanding with engagement, and links engagement with the hope of democratic transformation. In other words, it is a precondition for producing subjects capable of making their own histories within diverse economies of power and politics. As Edward Said has insisted, education mediated through the politics of hope is not about "appropriating power and then using it to create new forms of orthodoxy and antidemocratic authority ... but [about] the employment of the simpler, and indeed more elegant, spur of trying right now to alleviate human suffering, reducing the wakefulness of corporate profligacy and redirecting resources back to communities and individuals."[45] In what follows, I comment on what it would mean to make the pedagogical more political as part of a broader effort to reclaim the radically democratic role of public and higher education, as well as on the implication of addressing educators as critical public intellectuals.

Public Intellectuals and Higher Education

In opposition to the corporatizing of schooling, educators need to define public and higher education as a resource vital to the promise and realization of democratic life. Such a task points, in part, to the need for academics, students, parents, social activists, labor organizers, and artists to join together and oppose the transformation of higher education into commercial spheres, to resist what Bill Readings has called a consumer-oriented, corporate university more concerned about accounting than accountability.[46] As Zygmunt Bauman reminds us, schools are among the few public spaces left where students can learn the "skills for citizen participation and effective political action. And where there are no [such] institutions, there is no 'citizenship' either."[47] Likewise, higher education may be one of the few remaining sites in which students can learn about the limits of commercial values, address what it means to learn the skills of social citizenship, and work to deepen and expand the possibilities of collective agency and democratic life. I think Toni Morrison is right in arguing that "[i]f the university does not take seriously and rigorously its role as a guardian of wider civic freedoms, as interrogator of more and more complex ethical problems, as servant and preserver of deeper democratic practices, then some other regime or menage of regimes will do it for us, in spite of us, and without us."[48]

Defending higher education as a vital public sphere is necessary to develop and nourish the proper mediation between civil society and corporate power, between identities founded on democratic principles and identities steeped in forms of competitive, self-interested individualism that celebrate selfishness, profit-making, and greed. This view suggests that higher education should be defended through intellectual work that self-consciously recalls the tension between the democratic imperatives or possibilities of public institutions and their everyday realization within a society dominated by market principles. Education is not training, and learning at its best is connected to the imperatives of social responsibility—though we must recognize that political agency does not reduce the citizen to a mere consumer.

I believe that academics and others bear an enormous responsibility in opposing neoliberalism by bringing democratic political culture back to life. As part of this challenge, educators, students, and others must begin to organize individually and collectively against those corporate forces that increasingly define the university less as a social institution than a business, less as a public good than a private benefit. As higher education is reduced to the sovereignty of the market, academic labor is being reconfigured in ways that not only remove faculty from issues of governance but increasingly replace faculty with part-time workers and full-time careers with fixed term appointments. For example, in "2001 only about one-quarter of new faculty appointments were to full-tenure track positions (i.e., half were part-time, and more than half of the remaining full-time positions were 'off' the tenure track."[49] Resisting this ongoing assault on higher education demands that educators take seriously the importance of sustained political education and critical pedagogy as a necessary step in redefining the meaning and purpose of higher education as a public sphere essential to creating a democratic society. Radical pedagogy as a form of resistance might be premised on the assumption that educators vigorously oppose any attempt on the part of liberals and conservatives in conjunction with corporate forces to reduce them to the role of either technicians or multinational operatives. But equally important, such questions need to be addressed as part of a broader concern for renewing the struggle for social justice and democracy. Such a struggle, as the writer Arundhati Roy points out, demands that as intellectuals we ask ourselves some very "uncomfortable questions about our values and traditions, our vision for the future, our responsibilities as citizens, the legitimacy of our 'democratic institutions,' the role of the state, the police, the army, the judiciary, and the intellectual community."[50]

Edward Said argued that the public intellectual must function within institutions, in part, as an exile, as someone whose "place it is publicly to raise embarrassing questions, to confront orthodoxy and dogma, to be someone who cannot easily be co-opted by governments or corporations."[51] From this perspective, the educator as public intellectual becomes responsible for linking the diverse experiences that produce knowledge, identities, and social values in the university to the quality of moral and political life in the wider society; and he or she does so by entering into public conversations unafraid of controversy or of taking a critical stand.

The issue is not whether public or higher education has become contaminated with politics; it is more importantly about recognizing that education is already a space of politics, power, and authority. The crucial matter at stake is how to appropriate, invent, direct, and control the multiple layers of power and politics that constitute both the institutional formation of education and the pedagogies that are often an outcome of deliberate struggles to put into place particular notions of knowledge, values, and identity. As committed educators, we cannot eliminate politics, but we can work against a politics of certainty, a pedagogy of censorship, and an institutional formation that closes down rather than opens up democratic relations. This requires that we work diligently to construct a politics without guarantees, one that perpetually questions itself as well as all those forms of knowledge, values, and practices that appear beyond the process of interrogation, debate, and deliberation. Against a pedagogy and politics of certainty, it is crucial for educators to develop pedagogical practices that problematize considerations of institutional location, mechanisms of transmission, and effects.

Public intellectuals need to approach social issues mindful of the multiple connections and issues that tie humanity together; but they need to do so as border intellectuals moving within and across diverse sites of learning as part of an engaged and practical politics that recognizes the importance of "asking questions, making distinctions, restoring to memory all those things that tend to be overlooked or walked past in the rush to collective judgment and action."[52]

If educators are to function as public intellectuals, they need to provide the opportunities for students to learn that the relationship between knowledge and power can be emancipatory, that their histories and experiences matter, and that what students say and do counts in their struggle to unlearn privileges, productively reconstruct their relations with others, and transform, when necessary, the world around them. More specifically, such educators need to argue for forms of pedagogy that close the gap between the university and everyday life.

At one level, this suggests pedagogical practices that affirm and critically enrich the meaning, language, and knowledge that students actually use to negotiate and inform their lives. Unfortunately, however, the political, ethical, and social significance of the role that popular culture plays as the primary pedagogical medium for young people remains largely unexamined. Educators need to challenge the assumption that popular cultural texts cannot be as profoundly important as traditional sources of learning in teaching about important issues framed through, for example, the social lens of poverty, racial conflict, and gender discrimination. This is not a matter of pitting popular culture against traditional curricular sources. More importantly, it is a matter of using both in a mutually informative way, always mindful of how these spheres of knowledge might be employed to teach students how to be skilled citizens, whether that means learning how to use the Freedom of Information Act, know constitutional rights, build coalitions, write policy papers, learn the tools of democracy, analyze social problems, or learn how to make a difference in one's life through individual and social engagements.

As I have said throughout this book, intellectuals bear a special ethical and political responsibility at a time when the forces of mass persuasion and power assault all things democratic and noncommercial on this planet. The urgency of the current historical moment demands that intellectuals discard the professionalism, careerism, and isolation that make them largely irrelevant. Intellectuals inside and outside the university have an important obligation to offer alternative critical analyses, dismantle the illusory discourse of power, and work with others in creating an international social movement for social justice and radical change. In short, educators need to become provocateurs; they need to take a stand while refusing to be involved in either a cynical relativism or doctrinaire politics. Central to intellectual life is the pedagogical and political imperative that academics engage in rigorous social criticism while becoming a stubborn force for challenging false prophets, deflating the claims of triumphalism, and critically engaging all those social relations that promote material and symbolic violence.

At the same time, intellectuals must be deeply critical of their own authority and understand how it structures classroom relations and cultural practices. In this way, the authority they legitimate in the classroom (as well as in other public spheres) would become both an object of self-critique and a critical referent for expressing a more "fundamental dispute with authority itself."[53] This is not to say that teachers should abandon authority or simply equate all forms of authority with the practice of domination, as some radical educators have suggested. On the contrary, authority in the sense I am describing here follows Gramsci in calling upon educators to assert authority in the service of encouraging students to think beyond the conventions of common sense, to expand the horizons of what they know, and to discover their own sense of political agency and what it means to appropriate education as a critical function. Crucial here is the recognition that while the teacher "is an actor on the social and political stage, the educator's task is to encourage human agency, not mold it in the manner of Pygmalion."[54] As Said mentions in a different context, "the role of the intellectual is not to consolidate authority, but to understand, interpret, and question it: this is another version of speaking truth to power."[55]

Conclusion

There is a lot of talk among academics in the United States and elsewhere about the death of politics and the inability of human beings to imagine a more equitable and just world in order to make it better. I would hope that of all groups, educators would be the most vocal and militant in challenging this assumption by reclaiming the university's subversive role—specifically, by combining critiques of dominant discourses and the institutional formations that support and reproduce them with the goal of limiting human suffering while at the same time attempting to create the concrete economic, political, social, and pedagogical conditions necessary for an inclusive and substantive democracy. Critical scholarship is crucial to such a task, but it is not enough. Individual and social agency becomes meaningful as part of the willingness to imagine otherwise in order to act otherwise. Scholarship has a civic and public function, and it is precisely the connection between knowledge and the larger society that makes visible its ethical and political function. Knowledge can and should be used for amplifying human freedom and promoting social justice, and not simply for creating profits or future careers. Intellectuals need to take a position, and, as Said argues, they have an obligation to "remind audiences of the moral questions that may be hidden in the clamour of public debates ... and deflate the claims of [neoliberal] triumphalism."[56] Combining theoretical rigour with social relevance may be risky politically and pedagogically, but the promise of a substantive democracy far outweighs the security and benefits that accompany a retreat into academic irrelevance and the safe haven of a no-risk professionalism that requires, as Paul Sabin observes, "an isolation from society and vows of political chastity."[57]

To think beyond the given is a central demand of politics, but it is also a condition for individual and collective agency. At the heart of such a task is both the possibility inherent in hope and the knowledge and skills available in a critical education. At this particular moment in the United States, cynicism has become a major tool in the war against democracy. But rather than make despair convincing, I think it is all the more crucial to take seriously Derrida's provocation that "[w]e must do and think the impossible. If only the possible happened, nothing more would happen. If I only did what I can do, I wouldn't do anything."[58] In the next chapter, I want to present more than a theoretical discourse for engaging hope as a central element in any viable form of democratic politics. In effect, I want to engage the importance of this discourse through the work of the late Edward Said for whom hope offered the basis for a lived relationship with the world, a relationship in which politics and agency were inextricably connected to the modalities of social responsibility, critical engagement, and collective action. Said in this instance provides an existential and social model for working through the complex relationship among theory and practice, hope and agency, and commitment and civic courage.

6
Edward Said and the Politics of Worldliness

⤙⤚

The violence of neoliberalism can be explained through the existential narratives of those who experience its lived relations as well as through conceptual analyses provided by intellectuals. As I have mentioned in Chapter 1, the power of neoliberalism resides not merely in the force of material relations of power and in the realm of the economic but also in the realm of knowledge, ideas, and beliefs. Such a recognition points to the role that intellectuals might play in order to restore a sense of utopian possibility and collective resistance and struggle. But it also suggests that the struggle against neoliberalism demands a new understanding of what it means to be a public intellectual, which, in turn, requires a new language of politics itself. This chapter attempts to address both the nature of what it means to be a public intellectual and the politics such an understanding would entail by selectively examining the work of the late Edward Said. Said embodied both a particular kind of politics and a specific notion of how intellectuals should engage public life. It is crucial that we critically examine his work and legacy as part of a broader pedagogical and political struggle against neoliberalism's universal pretensions and the force of its allegedly conventional wisdom.

Crisis and criticism are two concepts that are pivotal to defining both the nature of domination and the forms of opposition that often emerge in response to it. Within the last decade, the urgency associated with the notion of crisis and its implied call to connect matters of knowledge and scholarship to the worldly space of politics has largely given way to a concept of criticism among many academics, suggesting a narrowing of the definition of politics and an inattentiveness to the public spaces of struggle, politics, and power. As Sheldon Wolin points out, crisis invokes a particular notion of worldliness in which politics embodies a connection between theory and public life.[1] In contrast, criticism signifies a more disembodied, less tactical version of politics. Such a politics downplays or disregards worldliness and is generally more contemplative, spectatorial, and in "search of distance rather than intervention driven by urgency."[2]

Those in the academy who support the professional act of criticism often argue that the close reading of texts has important educational value, especially for students learning how to read critically.[3] But Wolin's notion of criticism as "unworldly" does not deny the pedagogical value of a critical attentiveness to texts; it argues, instead, against the insularity of such a pedagogical task, one that has a tendency to ignore questions of intervention and degenerate into either scholasticism, formalism, or career opportunism. Alternately, a politics of crisis often links knowledge and learning to the performative and worldly space of action and engagement, energizing people not only to think critically about the world around them but also to use their capacities as social agents to intervene in public life and confront the myriad forms of symbolic, institutional, and material relations of power that shape their lives. It is this connection between pedagogy and agency, knowledge and power, thought and action that must be mobilized in order to confront the current crisis of authoritarianism looming so large in the United States today.

Within the last four decades, few intellectuals have done more than Edward Said to offer a politics of worldliness designed to confront the crisis of democracy under the reign of neoliberalism and the emerging authoritarianism in the United States, Israel, and other nations throughout the world. Said is indeed one of the most widely known, influential, and controversial public intellectuals of the latter part of the twentieth century. While acknowledged primarily as a critic of Western imperialism and a fierce advocate for the liberation of the Palestinian people, he is also widely recognized for his important contributions as a scholar whose work has had an enormous impact on a variety of individuals, groups, and social movements. His importance as a cultural theorist and engaged intellectual is evident in his path-breaking work on culture, power, history, literary theory, and imperialism. Not only is Said responsible for the founding of such academic genres as postcolonial studies and colonial discourse analysis, but his work has had an enormous influence on a wide range of disciplines as well as on an array of academics and cultural workers, including visual artists, museum curators, film-makers, anthropologists, and historians. He is one of the few academics whose voice and work addressed with equal ease a variety of specialized and general audiences within a global public sphere. While always clear, he was never simplistic, and he managed throughout the course of his forty-year career to provide theoretical discourses and critical vocabularies that enabled a range of academics and activists within a variety of disciplines and public spaces not only to speak truth to power and write against the historical narratives fashioned by ruling classes and groups, but also to reclaim a politics in which matters of power, agency, resistance, and collective struggle became paramount.

A controversial and courageous public intellectual, Said provided a model for what it means to combine scholarship and commitment. And yet he did not shy away from the difficult theoretical and political task of trying to understand how the current elements of authoritarianism in changing historical contexts could be addressed and resisted. Said recognized that the newer models of authoritarianism, with their drive toward absolute power and relentless repression of dissent, were taking different forms from those twentieth-century regimes of terror that marked the former Soviet Union, Nazi Germany, and fascist Italy. Proto-fascism in the new millennium was now emerging under the banner of democracy, though it manifested a reckless unilateralism in foreign affairs, an embrace of religious fundamentalism, a neoliberal assault on the welfare state, and the corporate control of a mass media reduced largely to a cranky, if not sometimes cowardly, adjunct of corporate and government interests. The war on terrorism, Said rightly recognized, has become a rationale for a war on democracy, unleashing both material and symbolic violence at home and abroad against any movement fighting for justice, liberty, and equality, but especially for the rights of the Palestinians.

Attentive to how the university and other dominant sites of power construct historical narratives, Said urged generations of students to take seriously the narrativizing of political culture as a central feature of modern politics. His now-legendary works *Orientalism* and *Culture and Imperialism* probe deeply into questions concerning who controls the conditions for telling historical narratives, which agents produce such stories, how such stories become part of the fabric of common sense, and what it might mean for scholars and activists to seriously engage the fact that struggles over culture are also struggles over meaning, identity, power, inclusion, and the future.[4] As expected, such interventions reaped no rewards from established powers, and his own work was constantly policed and dismissed as either anti-American or anti-Semitic. Of course, Said's work *should* be taken up critically, but I want to challenge the frequent denigration of his public interventions in terms which often implied that the real object of such attacks was the existence of any form of influential criticism emerging from the academy that called American power into question. One recent example of such a hostile dismissal can be found in the way that one of the most powerful newspapers in the world, the *New York Times,* framed his obituary. Richard Bernstein, the author and a noted conservative, constantly invoked Said's critics who claimed that his work was "drenched in jargon," that it "ignored vast bodies of scholarship," and that his critiques of Israel were tantamount to "supporting terrorism."[5] Bernstein even went so far as to bring up a story, written in 2000, about a photograph that pictured Said at the Lebanese border allegedly about to throw a rock at an Israeli guardhouse. What makes Bernstein's commentary all the more shocking is its juxtaposition to the *New York Times'* obituary of Leni Riefenstahl, the filmmaker for the Third Reich who had died a few weeks before Said.[6] Considered one of Hitler's most brilliant propagandists, Riefenstahl was treated to a memorial far more generous and forgiving than the one accorded later to Said. This display of crassly distorted reporting may say less about Bernstein's own ideological prejudices than about the mainstream media's general propensity to be more supportive and comfortable with authoritarian ideologies than with intellectuals who critique and resist what they perceive as both the escalation of human suffering and the increasing slide of the United States into a new and dangerous form of authoritarianism.[7]

While it is a daunting task to try to assess the contributions of Edward Said's overall work in these dire times in order to resist the increasing move toward what Sheldon Wolin calls an "inverted totalitarianism"[8] and what I call, in this book, a proto-fascism, I think it might be useful to commence such a project by providing a critical commentary on the relevance of Said's notion of wakefulness, and how it shapes both his important consideration of academics as oppositional public intellectuals and his related emphasis on cultural pedagogy and cultural politics. I want to begin with a passage that I believe offers a key to the ethical and political force of much of his writing. This selection is taken from his 1999 memoir *Out of Place,* which describes the last few months of his mother's life in a New York hospital and the difficult time she had falling asleep because of the cancer that was ravaging her body. Recalling this traumatic and pivotal life experience, Said's meditation moves between the existential and the insurgent, between private suffering and worldly commitment, between the seductions of a "solid self" and the reality of a contradictory, questioning, restless, and, at times, uneasy sense of self. He writes:

> "Help me to sleep, Edward," she once said to me with a piteous trembling in her voice that I can still hear as I write. But then the disease spread into her brain, and for the last six weeks she slept all the time. ... [M]y own inability to sleep may be her last legacy to me, a counter to her struggle for sleep. For me sleep is something to be gotten over as quickly as possible. I can only go to bed very late, but I am literally up at dawn. Like her I don't possess the secret of long sleep, though unlike her I have reached the point where I do not want it. For me, sleep is death, as is any diminishment in awareness. ... Sleeplessness for me is a cherished state to be desired at almost any cost; there is nothing for me as invigorating as immediately shedding the shadowy half-consciousness of a night's loss, than the early morning, reacquainting myself with or resuming what I might have lost completely a few hours earlier. I occasionally experience myself as a cluster of flowing currents. I prefer this to the idea of a solid self, the identity to which so many attach so much significance. These currents, like the themes of one's life, flow along during the waking hours, and at their best, they require no reconciling, no harmonizing. They are "off" and may be out of place, but at least they are always in motion, in time, in place, in the form of all kinds of strange combinations moving about, not necessarily forward, sometimes against each other, contrapuntally yet without one central theme. A form of freedom, I like to think, even if I am far from being totally convinced that it is. That skepticism too is one of the themes I particularly want to hold on to. With so many dissonances in my life I have learned actually to prefer being not quite right and out of place.[9]

It is this sense of being awake, displaced, caught in a combination of diverse circumstances that suggests a particular notion of worldliness—a critical and engaged interaction with the world we live in mediated by a responsibility for challenging structures of domination and for alleviating human suffering. As an ethical and political stance, worldliness rejects modes of education removed from political or social concerns, divorced from history and matters of injury and injustice. In commenting on his own investment in worldliness, Said writes: "I guess what moves me mostly is anger at injustice, an intolerance of oppression, and some fairly unoriginal ideas about freedom and knowledge."[10] For Said, being awake becomes a central metaphor for defining the role of academics as oppositional public intellectuals, defending the university as a crucial public sphere, engaging the ways in which culture deploys power, and taking seriously the idea of human interdependence while at the same time always living on the border—one foot in and one foot out, an exile and an insider for whom home was always a form of homelessness. A relentless border crosser, Said embraced the idea of the "traveler" as an important metaphor for engaged intellectuals. As Stephen Howe, partly quoting Said, points out: "It was an image which depended not on power, but on motion, on daring to go into different worlds, use different languages, and 'understand a multiplicity of disguises, masks, and rhetorics. Travelers must suspend the claim of customary routine in order to live in new rhythms and rituals. ... [T]he traveler crosses over, traverses territory, and abandons fixed positions all the time.'"[11] And as a border intellectual and traveler, Said embodied the notion of always "being not quite right," evidenced by his principled critique of all forms of certainties and dogmas and his refusal to be silent in the face of human suffering at home and abroad.

Being awake meant accepting the demands of worldliness, which implied giving voice to complex and controversial ideas in the public sphere, recognizing human injury beyond the privileged space of the academy, and using theory as a form of criticism to redress injustice.[12] Worldliness required not being afraid of controversy, making connections that are otherwise hidden, deflating the claims of triumphalism, bridging intellectual work and the operation of politics. Worldliness meant refusing the now-popular sport of academic bashing or embracing a crude call for action at the expense of rigorous intellectual and theoretical work. On the contrary, it entailed combining rigor and clarity, on the one hand, and civic courage and political commitment, on the other. From the time of his own political awakening after the 1967 Arab-Israeli war, Said increasingly became a border crosser, moving between his Arab past and his New York present, mediating his fierce defense of Palestinian rights and the demands of a faculty position that gave him the freedom to write and teach while at the same time the university wielded institutional power to depoliticize the politics of knowledge or, to use Said's words, "impose silence and the normalized quiet of unseen power."[13]

A number of us writing in the fields of critical pedagogy and cultural studies in the early 1980s were particularly taken with Said's view of the engaged public intellectual—specifically, his admonition to intellectuals to function within institutions, in part, as exiles "whose place it is publicly to raise embarrassing questions, to confront orthodoxy and dogma (rather than to produce them), to refuse to be easily co-opted by governments or corporations." This politically charged notion of the oppositional intellectual as homeless, in exile, and living on the border, occupying an unsutured, shifting, and fractured social space in which critique, difference, and a utopian potentiality can endure, provided the conceptual framework for developing my own concept of border pedagogy—a mode of pedagogy that is oppositional, questioning, and political, and not only cuts across disciplines but also moves between different zones of theoretical and cultural differences.[14] Said's notion of the academic as an engaged intellectual traveling within and between different disciplines, locations, sites of pedagogy, and social formations provided the conceptual framework for generations of educators fighting against the deadly instrumentalism that shaped dominant educational models of the time.

Said also provided many of us in the academy with a critical vocabulary for extending the meaning of politics and critical awareness. In part, he did this by illuminating the seductions of what he called the cult of professionalism with its specialized languages, its neutralizing of ideology and politics through a bogus claim to objectivism, and its sham elitism and expertise rooted in all the obvious gendered, racial, and class-specific hierarchies. He was almost ruthless in his critique of a narrow ethic of professionalism with its tendency toward quietism and its obsessive refusal to take sociopolitical issues seriously. For Said, professionalism separated culture, language, and knowledge from power and in doing so avoided the vocabulary for understanding and questioning how dominant authority worked through and on institutions, social relations, and individuals. Rooted in narrow specialisms and thoroughly secure in their professed status as experts, many full-time academics retreated into narrow modes of scholarship that displayed little interest in how power was used in institutions and social life to include and exclude, provide the narratives of the past and present, and secure the authority to define the future.[15] Abdirahman A. Hussein captures lucidly the crux of Said's critique of the seductions of professionalism and its underlying propensity to depoliticize academics and render them either irrelevant politically or complicitous with dominant power. He writes:

> [W]hat could be called a narrow ethic of professionalism covers up the absence of any really engaged ethics of worldliness. With the exception of a tiny minority, [too many academics] have undoubtedly succumbed to the same fastidious dodginess that hamstrings the typical academic humanist—the self-inflicted amnesia about serious socio-political issues; the studied, carefully nursed, quasi-religious quietism; the stuffy self-importance and pettifoggery; the spurious myth that weightless "theoria" effortlessly wafts over the quotidian realm of "praxis." In short, what transpires under the grandiloquent rubrics of "philosophy," "literary studies," and "critical theory" in the United States and Britain constitutes a substantial part of the cloy, immunizing minutiae of hegemonic culture—that vast, multi-dimensional process of elaboration, saturation, and fine-tuning which cocoons individuals and collectivities in civil society while at the same time camouflaging projections of political, industrial, and military power.[16]

Said was especially critical of those intellectuals who slipped into a kind of professional somnambulism in which matters of theory have less to do with a conscious challenge to politics, power, and injustice than with either a deadening scholasticism or a kind of arcane cleverness—a sort of narcotic performance in fashionable irony—that neither threatens anyone or opposes anything. He was extremely disheartened by the academic turn in literary theory and cultural studies toward a depoliticized version of postmodernism in the 1980s, and he viewed such a turn as an unacceptable retreat from one of the primary obligations of politics and intellectuals: "to reduce the violence and hatred that have so often marked human social interaction."[17] But he did more than supply a language of critique; he also illustrated what it meant to link text to context, knowledge to social change, culture to power, and commitment to courage. He gave us a language for politicizing culture, theorizing politics, thinking about what it meant to lead a "nonfascist" life, and recognizing what it meant to make the pedagogical more political. Not only did his pioneering work give us a deeper understanding of how power is deployed through culture, but he laid the foundation for making culture a central notion of politics and politics a crucial feature of pedagogy, thus providing an invaluable connection between pedagogy and cultural politics. More specifically, Said made it clear that pedagogy resided not merely in schools but in the force of the wider culture, and in doing so he expanded not only the sites of pedagogy but the possible terrains of struggle within a vast number of public spheres.

Refusing to separate learning from social change, he constantly insisted that we fail theory when we do not firmly grasp what we mean by the political, and that theorizing a politics of and for the twenty-first century is one of the most challenging issues facing the academy. He urged us to enter into a dialogue with ourselves, our colleagues, and our students about politics and the knowledge we seek to produce together, and to connect such knowledge to broader public spheres and issues. He argued that the role of engaged intellectuals is not to consolidate authority but to understand, interpret, and question it.[18] According to Said, social criticism has to be coupled with a vibrant self-criticism, the rejection "of the seductive persuasions of certainty,"[19] and the willingness to take up critical positions without becoming dogmatic or intractable. What is particularly important about Said's work is his recognition that intellectuals have a special responsibility to promote a state of wakefulness by moving beyond the language of pointless denunciations. Accordingly, he refused to view the oppressed as doomed actors or power as simply a crushing form of oppression. For Said, individuals and collectivities had to be regarded as potential agents and not simply as victims or ineffectual dreamers. It is this legacy of critique and possibility, of resistance and agency, that infuses his work with concrete hope and offers a wealth of resources to people in and outside the academy who struggle on multiple fronts against the rising forces of authoritarianism both at home and abroad.

At a time when domination comes not only from the New Right and neoconservatives but also from the religious Right, Said's emphasis on secularism—"the observation that human beings make their own history"[20]—reminds us of the need to fight against all those forces that relegate reason to the dustbin of history, as well as to recognize the multiple sites in which a mindless appeal to scripture, divine authority, and other extra-social forms of dogmatism undermines the possibility of human agency. For Said, new sites of pedagogy had to be developed and old ones used to educate existing and future generations about the value of critical thought and social engagement. Said believed that criticism was always intertwined with public life and that rather than lifting the activity of the contemporary critic out of the world it firmly placed him or her in the material and political concerns of the global public sphere, one that could never be removed from the considerations of history, power, politics, and justice. And it is this linking of a healthy skepticism for what authorities say and Said's insistence on the need for human beings to make their own history that gives his notion of secular criticism such force. Of course, Said was against all fundamentalisms, religious and political, and he believed that secular criticism should always come before solidarity. Priestly acolytes occupy not only churches, mosques, and synagogues but also the university, and their quasi-religious quietism—with its appeal either to extra-social forces (such as the hidden hand of history or the market) or to complex, theoretical discourses that drown out the worldliness of the text, language, and public life—must be rejected at all costs. Said's beliefs about the public intellectual and secular criticism informed each other, as is clear in his claim that "even in the very midst of a battle in which one is unmistakably on one side against another, there should be criticism, because there must be critical consciousness if there are to be issues, problems, values, even lives to be fought for."[21]

Near the end of his life, Said argued that the U.S. government was in the hands of a cabal, a junta "dominated by a group of military-minded neoconservatives who are fanatically pro-Israel."[22] For Said, the battle over democracy was in part a struggle over the very status of politics as a critical engagement, agency as an act of intervention geared at shaping public life, and resistance as the ability to think critically and act with civic courage. He believed that any vestige of culture as a site of political struggle and courage was being erased from the American landscape. He argued that such acts of symbolic violence could be seen in Laura Bush's attempt to bring together poets in ways that gave art "a decorative rather than engaged status,"[23] in Attorney General John Ashcroft's ordering that the "Spirit of Justice" statue be covered up so as to hide the view of her naked breasts, and in the United Nation's willingness to cover up a reproduction of Picasso's famous anti-war painting *Guernica* during a visit by Secretary of Defense Colin Powell to the Security Council. Said believed such acts of censorship provided further evidence of the fact that Americans live in a culture increasingly ruled by fear and repression, a culture where the gap between rich and poor has become obscene, and where the stranglehold of the far Right on government does not bode well for the environment, youth, labor, people of color, or the reproductive rights of women.

To take back this country from the radical Right and the religious extremists, we as intellectuals need to abide by Edward Said's call to speak the truth to power, but we must do it in a vast number of sites, including education, and we must do it not just individually but also collectively. In doing so, we must be willing to untangle the complexities of global power as it creates new social divisions, social formations, and potential sites of resistance. One important social formation that must be addressed is that of youth, whose voices, experiences, and political power must not only be taken seriously but also understood as a crucial element in forming possible alliances that bring together young people, labor unions, intellectuals, educators, and religious organizations. In addition, we need a new politics marked by a serious investment in cultural pedagogy, an appropriation of new and old technologies for producing knowledge, and a propensity for combining critique with acts of refusal, including—as Joseph Hough, the current president of the faculty at Union Theological Seminary, argues—nonviolent civil disobedience.[24] The most important question facing this country is what changes need to be made in how we think and act politically to make a claim for a substantive and inclusive democracy.

So much of what Said wrote, and did with his life, offers both a model and an inspiration for what it means to take back politics, social agency, collective struggle, and the ability to define the future. Said recognized with great insight that academics, students, and other cultural workers had important roles to play in arousing and educating the public to think and act as active citizens in an inclusive democratic society. Most importantly, he called upon such groups to put aside their petty squabbling over identities and differences and to join together collectively in order to become part of what he termed, quoting C.L.R. James, a "rendezvous of victory,"[25] a fully awake, worldly coalition against those forces at home and abroad that are pushing us into the age of totalitarianism lite, without anyone much noticing, or for that matter complaining.

Notes

⟜⟞

Notes to Preface

1. Susan George, "A Short History of Neo-Liberalism: Twenty Years of Elite Economics and Emerging Opportunities for Structural Change," *Conference on Economic Sovereignty in a Globalizing World* (March 24–26, 1999). Available online at http://www.globalexchange.org/campaigns/econ101/neoliberalism.html.pf.

2. James Harding, "Globalization's Children Strike Back," *Financial Times* (September 11, 2001). Available online at http://specials.ft.com/countercap/FT33EJSLGRC.html.

3. William K. Tabb, "Race to the Bottom?" in Stanley Aronowitz and Heather Gautney, eds., *Implicating Empire: Globalization & Resistance in the 21st-Century World Order* (New York: Basic Books, 2003), p. 153.

4. Lewis Lapham, "Buffalo Dances," *Harper's Magazine* (May, 2004), pp. 9, 11.

5. Stanley Aronowitz and Heather Gautney, "The Debate About Globalization: An Introduction," in Stanley Aronowitz and Heather Gautney, eds., *Implicating Empire: Globalization & Resistance in the 21st-Century World Order* (New York: Basic Books, 2003), p. 3.

6. Stanley Aronowitz, *How Class Works* (New Haven, CT: Yale University Press, 2003), p. 30.

7. *Multinational Monitor* (September 2001), pp. 7–8. See also David Moberg, "Plunder and Profit," *In These Times* (March 29, 2004), pp. 20–21.

8. Sean Gonsalves, (April 20, 2004). How to skin a rabbit. *The Cape Cod Times*. Available [On-line]: www.commondreams.org/views04/0420-05.htm. Accessed on April 24, 2004.

9. Cheryl Woodard (2004, April 15). Who Really Pays Taxes in America? Taxes and Politics in 2004. AskQuestions.org. Available [On-line]: http://www.askquestions.org/articles/taxes/. Accessed on April 24, 2004.

10. Lisa Duggan, *The Twilight of Equality: Neoliberalism, Cultural Politics, and the Attack on Democracy* (Boston: Beacon Press, 2003), p. 16.

11. Cited in Kellie Bean, "Coulter's Right-Wing Drag," *The Free Press* (October 29, 2003). Available online at www.freepress.org/departments/display/20/2003/441.

12. Editorial, "GE Microsoft Bring Bigotry to Life: Hate Talk Host Michael Savage Hired by MSNBC," *Fairness and Accuracy in Reporting* (July/August 2003). Available online at http://www.fair.org/activisim/MSNBC-savage.html.

13. Fredric Jameson, *The Seeds of Time* (New York: Columbia University Press, 1994), p. xii.

14. Susan Buck-Morss, *Thinking Past Terror: Islamism and Critical Theory on the Left* (London: Verso, 2003), pp. 65–66.

15. George Soros, *The Bubble of American Supremacy* (New York: Public Affairs, 2004), p. 10.

16. Here I am quoting David Frum and Richard Perle, cited in Lewis H. Lapham, "Dar al-Harb," *Harper's Magazine* (March 2004), p. 8. The same fascistically inspired triumphalism can be found in a number of recent books that have been churned out to gratify the demands of a much-celebrated jingoism. See, for example, Joseph Farah, *Taking America Back* (New York: WND Books, 2003); Michelle Malkin, *Invasion: How America Still Welcomes Terrorists, Criminals, and Other Foreign Menaces to Our Shores* (New York: Regnery Publishing, 2002); William J. Bennett, *Why We Fight: Moral Clarity and the War on Terrorism* (New York: Regnery, 2003).

17. Cited in Lapham, "Dar al-Harb," p. 8. The full exposition of this position can be found in David Frum and Richard Perle, *An End to Evil: How to Win the War on Terror* (New York: Random House, 2004).

18. For a rather vivid example of how dissent is criminalized, see the transcript for "Going Undercover/Criminalizing Dissent," which was aired by *NOW with Bill Moyers* on March 5, 2004. The program documents how undercover agents from all levels of government are infiltrating and documenting peaceful protests in America.

19. Zygmunt Bauman, *Globalization: The Human Consequences* (New York: Columbia University Press, 1998), pp. 9–10.

20. George, "A Short History of Neo-Liberalism."

21. David Kotz, "Neoliberalism and the U.S. Economic Expansion of the '90s," *Monthly Review* 54:11 (April 2003), p. 16.

22. See, for instance, Friedrich Hayek, *The Road to Serfdom*, 50th ed. (Chicago: University of Chicago Press, 1994), and Milton Friedman, *Capitalism and Freedom*, 40th Anniversary Issue (Chicago: University of Chicago Press, 2002).

23. Pierre Bourdieu, *Acts of Resistance* (New York: Free Press, 1989), p. 35.

24. Colin Leys, *Market-Driven Politics* (London: Verso, 2001), p. 2.

25. Lisa Duggan, *The Twilight of Equality: Neoliberalism, Cultural Politics, and the Attack on Democracy* (Boston: Beacon Press, 2003), p. 34.

26. Ibid., p. xvi.

27. Bill Moyers, "The Media, Politics, and Censorship," Common Dreams News Center (May 10, 2004). Available on-line: www.commondreams.org/cgi-bin/print.cgi?file=/viewes04/0510-10.htm. See also Eric Alterman, "Is Koppel a Commie," *The Nation* (May 24, 2004), p. 10.

28. Buck-Morss, *Thinking Past Terror*, p. 103.

29. Imre Szeman, "Learning to Learn from Seattle," *Review of Education/Pedagogy/Cultural Studies* 24:1–2 (2002), pp. 4–5.

30. Alain Touraine, *Beyond Neoliberalism* (London: Polity Press, 2001), p. 2.

31. Alex Callinicos, "The Anti-Capitalist Movement After Genoa and New York," in Stanley Aronowitz and Heather Gautney, eds., *Implicating Empire: Globalization & Resistance in the 21st-Century World Order* (New York: Basic Books, 2003), p. 147.

32. Buck-Morss, *Thinking Past Terror*, pp. 4–5.

Notes to Chapter 1

1. Susan George, "A Short History of Neo-Liberalism: Twenty Years of Elite Economics and Emerging Opportunities for Structural Change," *Global Policy Forum* (March 24–26, 1999). Available online at http://www.globalpolicy.org/globaliz/econ/histneol.htm.

2. Manning Marable, "9/11: Racism in a Time of Terror," in Stanley Aronowitz and Heather Gautney, eds., *Implicating Empire: Globalization & Resistance in the 21st-Century World Order* (New York: Basic Books, 2003), p. 3.

3. Senator Robert C. Byrd, "Challenging 'Pre-emption,'" *The Nation* (December 15, 2003). Available online at www.common dreams.org/views03/1215-12.htm.

4. Thomas L. Friedman, "Crazier Than Thou," *New York Times* (February 13, 2002), p. A31.

5. Sheldon S. Wolin, "A Kind of Fascism Is Replacing Our Democracy," *Newsday* (Long Island, NY) (July 18, 2003). Available online at www.commondreams.org/views03/0718-07.htm.

6. Walter Cronkite, "The Trial of Saddam Hussein," *Denver Post* (December 21, 2003). Available online at www.denverpost.com/Stories0,141336~1839593,00.html. An extensive list of international agreements broken by the United States can be found in Rich Du Boff, "Mirror Mirror on the Wall, Who's the Biggest Rogue of All?" *ZNet Commentary* (August 7, 2003). Available online at Xnetupdates@smail.zmag.org.

7. Noam Chomsky, "There Is Good Reason to Fear Us," *Toronto Star* (September 7, 2003). Available online at www.commondreams.org/views03/0907-03.htm.

8. Senator Robert C. Byrd, "Challenging 'Pre-emption,'" *The Nation* (December 15, 2003). Available online at www.commondreams.org/views03/1215-12.htm.

9. This policy is spelled out in great detail in Donald Kagan, *Rebuilding America's Defenses,* in *A Report of the Project for the New American Century* (Washington, DC, September 2000).

10. See Christopher Scheer, Lakshmi Chaudhry, and Robert Scheer David, *The Five Biggest Lies Bush Told Us About Iraq* (New York: Seven Stories Press, 2003); and David Corn, *The Lies of George W. Bush* (New York: Crown Publishers, 2003).

11. Robert Jay Lifton, "American Apocalypse," *The Nation* (December 22, 2003), p. 12. These themes are developed extensively in Robert Jay Lifton, *Super Power Syndrome: America's Apocalyptic Confrontation with the World* (New York: Thunder Mouth Press, 2003).

12. Katha Pollitt, "Show and Tell in Abu Ghraim," *The Nation* (May 24, 2004), p. 9.

13. Patricia J. Williams, "In Kind," *The Nation* (May 31, 2004), p. 10.

14. Graydon Carter, "The President? Go Figure," *Vanity Fair* (December 2003), p. 69. For an extensive analysis of the budget deficit, see Richard Kogan, "Deficit Picture Even Grimmer Than New CBO Projections Suggest," *Center on Budget and Policy Priorities* (August 26, 2003). Available online at http://www.cbpp.org/8-26-03bud.htm.

15. On the tax issue, see Paul Krugman, *Fuzzy Math: The Essential Guide to the Bush Tax Plan* (New York: Norton, 2001).

16. Larry Wheeler and Robert Benincase, "State Budget Belt-Tightening Squeezes Health Care for Kids," *USA Today* (December 19, 2003), p. 15A.

17. Center on Budget and Policy Priorities, "Up to 1.6 Million Low-Income People—Including About Half a Million Children—Are Losing Health Coverage Due to State Budget Cuts" (December 22, 2003). Available online at http://www.cbpp.org/12-22-03health-pr.htm.

18. Children's Defense Fund Press Release, "White House Wages Budget War Against Poor Children" (February 3, 2003). Available online at www.cdfactioncouncil.org/FY2004_pressrelease.htm.

19. "Rep Bernie Sanders vs. Chairman Alan Greenspan," *Common Dreams News Center* (July 16, 2003). Available online at www.commondreams.org/views03/0716-13.htm.

20. Cited in Bernie Sanders, "USA: Ex-Im Bank, Corporate Welfare at Its Worst," *Corporate Watch* (May 15, 2002), p. 1. Available online at www.corpwatch.org/news/PND.jsp?articleid=2570.

21. Jackson Lears, "How a War Became a Crusade," *New York Times* (March 11, 2003), p. A29.

22. President George W. Bush, Address to Joint Session of Congress, "September 11, 2001, Terrorist Attacks on the United States."

23. Gary Wills, "With God on His Side," *New York Times Sunday Magazine* (March 30, 2003), p. 29.

24. Ann Coulter, *Treason: Liberal Treachery from the Cold War to the War on Terrorism* (New York: Crown Forum, 2003), p. 16.

25. Cited in Jay Bookman, "Ann Coulter Wants to Execute You," *Atlanta Journal-Constitution* (February 18, 2002). Available online at www.indybay.org/news/20002/02/116560.php.

26. Kathleen Parker, "Politics Are Out of Place in a Time of War," *Townhall* (November 1, 2003). Available on-line at www.townhall.com/columinists/Kathleenparker/kp20031101.shtml.

27. Cited in "Savage Nation: It's not Just Rush," *Media Matters for America* (May 13, 2004). Available on-line: http://mediamatters.org/items/200405130004

28. Both quotations are from Umberto Eco, "Eternal Fascism: Fourteen Ways of Looking at a Blackshirt," *New York Review of Books* (November-December 1995), p. 12.

29. Paul Krugman, "The Uncivil War," *New York Times* (November 25, 2003), p. A29.

30. For a brilliant analysis of the link between the Bush administration's war on terrorism and the assault on constitutional freedoms, see David Cole, *Enemy Aliens: Double Standards and Constitutional Freedoms in the War on Terrorism* (New York: The New Press, 2003).

31. Ben Bagdikian, "Beware the Geeks Bearing Lists," *ZNet Commentary* (December 24, 2002). Available online at www.Zmag.org/sustainers.content/2002-12/07bagdikian.cfm.

32. Anthony Lewis, "Un-American Activities," *New York Review of Books* (October 23, 2003), p. 18.

33. This issue is taken up in great detail in Cynthia Brown, ed., *Lost Liberties: Ashcroft and the Assault on Personal Freedom* (New York: The New Press, 2003); Nat Hentoff, *The War on the Bill of Rights and the Gathering Resistance* (New York: Seven Stories Press, 2003); and David Cole, *Enemy Aliens* (New York: The New Press, 2003).

34. Arundhati Roy, *War Talk* (Boston: South End Press, 2003), p. 34.

35. Ryan J. Foley, "Feds Win Right to War Protesters' Records," *Miami Herald* (February 7, 2003). Available online at http://www.miami.com/mld/miamiherald/news/breaking_news/7901637.htm.

36. I want to thank my wonderful colleague Sophia A. McClennen for bringing this case to my attention.

37. Juan Stam, "Bush's Religious Language," *The Nation* (December 22, 2003), p. 27.

38. There are many excellent books dealing with the rise of right-wing authoritarianism in the United States. Some examples include Charles Higham, *American Swastika* (New York: Doubleday, 1985); Susan Canedy, *America's Nazis* (Menlo Park, CA: Markgraf Publications, 1990); Russ Bellant, *Old Nazis, The New Right, and the Republican Party* (Boston: South End Press, 1991); Paul Hainsworth, ed., *The Extreme Right in Europe and North America* (London: Pinter, 1992); Chip Berlet, Matthew Lyons, and Suzanne Phar, eds., *Eyes Right: Challenging the Right-Wing Backlash* (Boston: South End Press,

1995); Sara Diamond, *Roads to Domination: Right-Wing Movements and Political Power in the United States* (New York: Guilford Press, 1995); Michael Novick, *White Lies, White Power* (Monroe, ME: Common Courage Press, 1995); Lyman Tower Sargent, ed., *Extremism in America* (New York: New York University Press, 1995); Chip Berlet and Matthew Lyons, *Right-Wing Populism in America: Too Close for Comfort* (New York: Guilford Press, 2000); and Martin A. Lee, *The Beast Reawakens: Fascism's Resurgence from Hitler's Spymasters to Today's Neo-Nazi Groups and Right-Wing Extremists* (New York: Routledge, 2000).

39. "Nelson Mandela: The U.S.A. Is a Threat to World Peace," *Newsweek Web Exclusive* (September 11, 2002). Available online at www.msnbc.com/news/806174.asp?cp1=1.

40. "European Majority Sees United States as Greatest Threat to World Security, Above Even North Korea," *Newsweek Web Exclusive* (November 7, 2003). Available online at www.intelmessages.org/messages/National_Security/www-board/messages_03/6148.

41. Nigel Morris, "Livingston Says Bush Is 'Greatest Threat to Life on Planet,'" *The Independent/UK* (November 18, 2003). Available online at http://portland.indymedia.org/en/2003/11/275040.shtml.

42. George Soros, *The Bubble of American Supremacy* (New York: Public Affairs, 2004), p. 3.

43. This issue is discussed in Harvey Wasserman and Bob Fitrakis, "Senator Byrd, Major Media Spread Coverage of Bush-Nazi Nexus," *Free Press* (Columbus, Ohio, October 22, 2003). Available online at http://www.scoop.co.nz/mason/stories/HL0310/S00193.htm. On the same day that this story broke, the Associated Press ran a national story connecting President Bush's grandfather, Prescott Bush, to Adolf Hitler. Bush's grandfather, it appears, had his bank seized by the federal government because he had helped finance Adolf Hitler's rise to power.

44. Michael Lind, *Made in Texas: George W. Bush and the Southern Takeover of American Politics* (New York: Basic Books, 2002).

45. Zbigniew Brzezinski, "To Lead, US Must Give Up Paranoid Policies," *International Herald Tribune* (November 15, 2003). Available online at www.commondreams.org/headlines03/1115-01.htm.

46. Cited in Rift Goldstein, "Cheney's Hawks 'Hijacking Policy,'" *Common-Dreams* (October 30, 2003). Available online at http://www.commondreams.org/headlines03/1030-08.htm.

47. Cited in Matthias Streitz, "US Nobel Laureate Slams Bush Gov't as 'Worst' in American History," *Der Spiegel* (July 29, 2003). Available online at www.commondreams.org/headlines03/0729-06.htm.

48. Arundhati Roy, "Instant-Mix Imperial Democracy (Buy One, Get One Free)," *Common Dreams* (May 18, 2003). Available online at http://www.commondreams.org/views03/0518-01.htm.

49. Ibid.

50. Ibid.

51. Arundhati Roy, *War Talk* (Cambridge: South End Press, 2003), pp. 36–37. On the growing right-wing politicization of the U.S. Supreme Court, see Martin Garbus, *Courting Disaster: The Supreme Court and the Unmaking of American Law* (New York: Times Book, 2002).

52. See "Testimony of Attorney General John Ashcroft to the Senate Committee on the Judiciary" (December 6, 2001). Available online at www.usdoj.gov/ag/testimony/2001/.

53. Roy has been lambasted in the conservative *Weekly Standard*, which gave her the facetious "Susan Sontag Award" for anti-war comments. *The New Republic* followed suit with its equally absurd "Idiocy Award." Roy responded to the increasing chorus of criticism with an article in *The Guardian*, in which she argued that the charge of anti-Americanism being leveled against her simply meant that "the chances are that he or she will be judged before they're heard and the argument will be lost in the welter of bruised national pride." See Arundhati Roy, "Not Again," *The Guardian* (September 27, 2002). Available online at www.ratical.org/ratville/CAH/AR092702.html.

54. Cited in Alexander Stile, "The Latest Obscenity Has Seven Letters," *New York Times* (September 13, 2003), p. B17.

55. Sheldon Wolin, "Inverted Totalitarianism: How the Bush Regime Is Effecting the Transformation to a Fascist-Like State," *The Nation* (May 19, 2003), p. 13.

56. Ibid., pp. 13–14.

57. Ibid., pp. 13–14.

58. Ibid., pp. 14–15.

59. James Traub, "Weimar Whiners," *New York Times Magazine* (June 1, 2003), p. 11.

60. David Cole, *No Equal Justice: Race and Class in the American Criminal Justice System* (New York: The New Press, 1999); Michael Parenti, *Lockdown America: Police and Prisons in the Age of Crisis* (London: Verso, 1999); Marc Mauer, *Race to Incarcerate* (New York: The New Press, 1999); Marc Mauer and Meda Chesney-Lind, *Invisible Punishment: The Collateral Consequences of Mass Imprisonment* (New York: The New Press, 2002).

61. Pierre Tristram, "One Man's Clarity in America's Totalitarian Time Warp," *Daytona Beach News Journal* (January 27, 2004). Available online at www.commondreams.org/views0401027-08.htm.

62. Bertram Gross, *Friendly Fascism: The New Face of Power in America* (Montreal: Black Rose Books, 1985). For an excellent recent analysis of fascism that equals Gross's work, see Roberto Paxton, *The Anatomy of Fascism* (New York: Alfred A. Knopf, 2004).

63. Umberto Eco, "Eternal Fascism: Fourteen Ways of Looking at a Blackshirt," *New York Review of Books* (November-December 1995), p. 15.

64. Kevin Passmore, *Fascism* (London: Oxford University Press, 2002), p. 90.

65. Ibid., p. 19.

66. Alexander Stille, "The Latest Obscenity Has Seven Letters," *New York Times* (September 13, 2003), p. 19.

67. Paxton cited in Samantha Power, "The Original Axis of Evil," The *New York Times* (Book Review) (May 2, 2004). Available online: http://query.nytimes.com/gst/fullpage.html?res= 9C0CE0DB153AF931A35756C0A9629C8B63. See also Robert O. Paxton, *The Anatomy of Fascism* (New York: Alfred A. Knopf, 2004).

68. Mark Neocleous, *Fascism* (Minneapolis: University of Minnesota Press, 1997), p. 91.

69. Bill Moyers, "This Is Your Story—The Progressive Story of America. Pass It On," text of speech to the "Take Back America" Conference (June 4, 2003). Available online at www.utoronto.ca/csus/pm/moyers.htm.

70. William Greider, "The Right's Grand Ambition: Rolling Back the 20th Century," *The Nation* (May 12, 2003), pp. 1–12. There has indeed been a drastic increase in income and wealth inequality in the last few decades. For example, Paul Krugman, using data from the Congressional Budget Office, recently pointed that "between 1973 and 2000 the average real income of the bottom 90 percent of American taxpayers actually fell by 7 percent. Meanwhile, the income of the top 1 percent rose by 148 percent, the income of the top 0.1 percent rose by 343 percent and the income of the top 0.01 percent rose 599 percent" (Krugman, "The Death of Horatio Alger," *The Nation* [January 5, 2004], p. 16).

71. Greider, "The Right's Grand Ambition: Rolling Back the 20th Century," pp. 1–12.

72. See Jürgen Habermas, *The Structural Transformation of the Public Sphere* (Cambridge, MA: MIT Press, 1991) [reprint edition]; and David Harvey, *Spaces of Capital: Towards a Critical Geography* (New York: Routledge, 2001). The literature on the politics of space is far too extensive to cite, but of special interest are Michael Keith and Steve Pile, eds., *Place and the Politics of Identity* (New York: Routledge, 1993); Doreen Massey, *Space, Place, and Gender* (Minneapolis: University of Minnesota, 1994); and Margaret Kohn, *Radical Space: Building the House of the People* (Ithaca: Cornell University Press, 2003).

73. Jo Ellen Green Kaiser, "A Politics of Time and Space," *Tikkun* 18:6 (2003), pp. 18–19.

74. Margaret Kohn, *Radical Space: Building the House of the People* (Ithaca: Cornell University Press, 2003), p. 7.

75. Kaiser, "A Politics of Time and Space," pp. 17–18.

76. Zygmunt Bauman, *Globalization: The Human Consequences* (New York: Columbia University Press, 1998), pp. 25–26; original emphasis.

77. Susan Buck-Morss, *Thinking Past Terror* (New York: Verso, 2003), p. 29.

78. Stanley Aronowitz, *The Last Good Job in America* (Lanham, MD: Rowman and Littlefield, 2001), p. 160.

79. Richard Falk, "Will the Empire Be Fascist?" *The Transnational Foundation for Peace and Future Research* (March 24, 2003). Available online at http://www.transnational.org/forum/meet/2003/Falk_FascistEmpire.html.

80. Victoria de Grazia, *The Culture of Consent: Mass Organization of Leisure in Fascist Italy* (New York: Cambridge University Press, 2002). Originally published in 1981.

81. Robert McChesney and John Nichols, *Our Media, Not Theirs: The Democratic Struggle Against Corporate Media* (New York: Seven Stories Press, 2002), pp. 48–49.

82. Jeff Sharlet, "Big World: How Clear Channel Programs America," *Harper's Magazine* (December 2003), pp. 38–39.

83. On the relationship between democracy and the media, see Robert W. McChesney, *Rich Media, Poor Democracy: Communication Politics in Dubious Times* (New York: The New Press, 1999).

84. McChesney and Nichols, *Our Media, Not Theirs,* pp. 52–53.

85. Transcript of *NOW with Bill Moyers* (February 13, 2004), p. 2.

86. Umberto Eco, "Eternal Fascism: Fourteen Ways of Looking at a Blackshirt," *The New York Review of Books* (November-December 1995), p. 15.

87. Paul O'Neill, former treasury secretary who served in the Bush administration for two years, claimed on *60 Minutes* that Bush and his advisors started talking about invading Iraq ten days after the inauguration, eight months before the tragic events of September 11. See CBS News, "Bush Sought Way to Invade Iraq," *60 Minutes Transcript* (July 11, 2004). Available online at http://www.cbsnews.com/stories/2004/01/09/60minutes/main592330.shtml. For a chronicle of lies coming out of the Bush administration, see David Corn, *The Lies of George Bush* (New York: Crown, 2003). Richard Clarke, a former top White House security chief under President Bush, asserted before a congressional committee investigating the September 11 attacks that "[b]y invading Iraq, the president of the United States has greatly undermined the war on terrorism." Available online at www.commondreams.org/headlines04/0324-09.htm. Clarke argues in his new book that the Bush administration was so intent on invading Iraq that it ignored the threat from al Qaeda months before the 9/11 attack. See Richard Clarke, *Against All Enemies* (New York: Free Press, 2004).

88. Abbott Gleason, "The Hard Road to Fascism," *Boston Review* (Summer 2003). Available online at http://www.bostonreview.net/BR28.3/gleason.html.

89. Bob Herbert, "Casualties at Home," *New York Times* (March 27, 2003), p. A27.

90. Renana Brooks, "The Language of Power, Fear, and Emptiness," *The Nation* (June 24, 2003). Available online at http://reclaimdemocracy.org/weekly-2003/bush-language-power-fear.html.

91. The relevant excerpt from this interview can be found in Platform Section, "Millions and Millions Lost," *Harper's Magazine* (January 2004), p. 16.

92. This insight comes from Juan Stam, "Bush's Religious Language," *The Nation* (December 22, 2003), p. 27.

93. Bush's use of doublespeak is so pronounced that the National Council of Teachers of English awarded him its 2003 Doublespeak Award. See http://www.govst.edu/users/ghrank/Introduction/bush2003.htm.

94. Ruth Rosen, "Bush Doublespeak," *San Francisco Chronicle* (July 14, 2003). Available online at www.commondreams.org/views03/0714-10.htm.

In January 2004, former Vice President Al Gore, in a major speech on Bush's environmental policies, said: "Indeed, they often use Orwellian language to disguise their true purposes. For example, a policy that opens national forests to destructive logging of old-growth trees is labeled Healthy Forest Initiative. A policy that vastly increases the amount of pollution that can be dumped into the air is called the Clear Skies Initiative." Gore is cited in Bob Herbert, "Masters of Deception," *New York Times* (January 16, 2004), p. A21.

95. Cited in Jennifer Lee, "U.S. Proposes Easing Rules on Emissions of Mercury," *New York Times* (December 3, 2003), p. A20.

96. Eric Pianin, "Clean Air Rules to Be Relaxed," *Washington Post* (August 23, 2003). Available online at www.washingtonpost.com/ac2/wp-dyn/A34334-2003Aug22?.

97. The *New York Times* reported that the Environmental Protection Agency actually eliminated references to any studies that "concluded that warming is at least partly caused by rising concentrations of smokestack and tail pipe emissions and could threaten health and ecosystems." Cited in Huck Gutman, "On Science, War, and the Prevalence of Lies," *The Statesman* (June 28, 2003). Available online at http://www.commondreams.org/views03/0628-04.htm.

98. For all of the direct government sources for these lies, see *One Thousand Reasons to Dump George Bush*, especially the section titled "Honesty." This is available online: http://thousandreasons.org/the_top_ten.html. Also see David Corn, *The Lies of George W. Bush* (New York: Crown Publishers, 2003).

99. See Corn, *The Lies of George W. Bush*, pp. 228–230.

100. Both quotes can be found in Paul Krugman, "Standard Operating Procedure," *New York Times* (June 3, 2004), p. A17.

101. See Lloyd Grove, "Lowdown," *New York Daily News* (January 11, 2004). The reference is Available online at www.unknownnews.net/insanity011404.html.

102. Cited in Paul Krugman, "Going for Broke," the *New York Times* (January 20, 2004), p. A21.

103. Dana Milbank, "Religious Right Finds Its Center in Oval Office," *Washington Post* (December 24, 2001), p. A02.

104. Ibid.

105. Ibid.

106. Cited in Jill Lawrence, "Bush's Agenda Walks the Church-State Line," *USA Today* (January 29, 2003). Available online at www.usatoday.com/news/washington/2003-01-29-bush-religion_x.htm.

107. See Stephen Mansfield, *The Faith of George W. Bush* (New York: Tarcher/Penguin, 2003). Cited in Sydney H. Schanberg, "The Widening Crusade," *The Village Voice* (October 15–21, 2003). Available online at www.villagevoice.com.issues/0342/schanberg.phb.

108. Robyn E. Blumner, "Religiosity as Social Policy," *St. Petersburg Times* (September 28, 2003). Available online at www.sptimes.com/2003/09/28/news_pf/Columns/religiosity_as_social.shtml.

109. Paul Harris, "Bush Says God Chose Him to Lead His Nation," *The*

Guardian (November 1, 2003). Available online at www.observer.co.uk. On the child tax credit, see Bob Herbert, "The Reverse Robin Hood," *New York Times* (June 2, 2003), p. A17.

110. Joseph L. Conn, "Faith-Based Fiat," *Americans United for Separation of Church and State* (January 2002). Available online at www.au.org/churchstate/cs01031.htm.

111. Robyn E. Blumner, "Religiosity as Social Policy," *St. Petersburg Times* (September 28, 2003). Available online at www.sptimes.com/2003/09/28/news_pf/Columns/religiosity_as_social.shtml.

112. Jonathan Turley, "Raze the Church/State Wall? Heaven Help Us!" *Los Angeles Times* (February 24, 2003). Available online at www.enrongate.com/news/index.asp?id=169632.

113. Alan Cooperman, "Paige's Remarks on Religion in Schools Decried," *Washington Post* (April 9, 2003). Available online at www.washingtonpost.com/wp-dyn/articles/A59692-2003Apr8.html.

114. Cited in Blumner, "Religiosity as Social Policy."

115. Graydon Carter, "The President? Go Figure," *Vanity Fair* (December 2003), p. 70.

116. John Ashcroft, "Remarks to National Religious Broadcasters Convention in Nashville Tennessee on February 19, 2002. Text is distributed by the Department of State and is Available online at http://usembassy-australia.state.gov/hyper/2002/0219/epf204.htm.

117. Elizabeth Amon, "Name Withheld," *Harper's Magazine* (August 2003), p. 59.

118. Cited in William M. Arkin, "The Pentagon Unleashes a Holy Warrior," *Los Angeles Times* (October 16, 2003). Available online at www.latimes.com/news/opinion/commentary/la-oe-arkin16oct16,1,2598862.

119. Ibid.

120. Cited from the transcript from *NOW with Bill Moyers* (December 26, 2003). Available online at http://www.pbs.org/now/transcript/transcript248_full.html.

121. Gary Wills, "With God On His Side," *New York Times Sunday Magazine* (March 30, 2003), p. 26.

122. Cited from an interview with Reverend James Forbes Jr., on *NOW with Bill Moyers* (December 26, 2003). Available online at http://www.pbs.org/now/transcript/transcript248_full.html.

123. "Bill Moyers Interviews Union Theological Seminary's Joseph Hough," *NOW with Bill Moyers.* (October 24, 2003). Available online at www.commondreams.org/views03/1027-01.

124. David Hager is cited in H. Wokusch, "Make War Not Love: Abstinence, Aggression, and the Bush White House," Common Dreams News Center (October 23, 2003). Available online at http://www.commondreams.org/views03/1026-01.htm.

125. John R. Gillis, ed., *The Militarization of the Western World* (New Brunswick: Rutgers University Press, 1989). On the militarization of urban space, see Mike Davis, *City of Quartz* (New York; Vintage, 1992); and

Kenneth Saltman and David Gabbard, eds., *Education as Enforcement: The Militarization and Corporatization of Schools* (New York: Routledge, 2003). For a discussion of the current neoconservative influence on militarizing American foreign policy, see Donald Kagan and Gary Schmidt, *Rebuilding America's Defenses,* which is one of many reports outlining this issue, developed under the auspices of *The Project for the New American Century.* Available online at www.newamericancentury.org.

126. Catherine Lutz, "Making war at home in the United States: Militarization and the current crisis,"*American Anthropologist* 104:723.

127. Kevin Baker, "We're in the Army Now: The G.O.P.'s Plan to Militarize Our Culture," *Harper's Magazine* (October 2003), p. 40.

128. Jorge Mariscal, "'Lethal and Compassionate': The Militarization of US Culture," *CounterPunch* (May 5, 2003). Available online at http://www.counterpunch.org/mariscal05052003.html.

129. Falk, "Will the Empire Be Fascist?"

130. George Monbiot, "States of War," *The Guardian/UK* (October 14, 2003). Available online at www.commondreams.org/views03/1014-09.htm.

131. Mariscal, "'Lethal and Compassionate.'

132. Kevin Baker, "We're in the Army Now: The G.O.P.'s Plan to Militarize Our Culture," *Harper's Magazine* (October 2003), p. 38.

133. Ibid., p. 37.

134. Ibid., p. 37.

135. Ruth Rosen, "Politics of Fear," *San Francisco Chronicle* (December 30, 2003). Available online at www.commondreams.org/views02/1230-02.htm.

136. The Iraqi war coverage by Fox News and MSNBC was named by *Time* magazine, no less, in its "The Year in Culture" section, as "the worst display of patriotism" for 2003. See *Time* (January 5, 2004), p. 151.

137. Richard H. Kohn, "Using the Military at Home: Yesterday, Today, and Tomorrow," *Chicago Journal of International Law* 94:1 (Spring 2003), pp. 174–175.

138. Ibid.

139. David Goodman, "Covertly Recruiting Kids," *Baltimore Sun* (September 29, 2003). Available online at www.commondreams.org/views03/1001-11.htm.

140. Elissa Gootman, "Metal Detectors and Pep Rallies: Spirit Helps Tame a Bronx School, *New York Times* (February 4, 2004), p. C14.

141. Gail R. Chaddock, "Safe Schools at a Price," *Christian Science Monitor* (August 25, 1999), p. 15.

142. Tamar Lewin, "Raid at High School Leads to Racial Divide, Not Drugs," *New York Times* (December 9, 2003), p. A16.

143. Sandra Rimer, "Unruly Students Facing Arrest, Not Detention," *New York Times* (January 2, 2004), p. 15.

144. Ibid.

145. Randall Beger, "Expansion of Police Power in the Public Schools and the Vanishing Rights of Students," *Social Justice* 29:1–2 (2002), p. 124.

146. Peter B. Kraska, "The Military-Criminal Justice Blur: An Introduction,"

in Peter B. Kraska, ed., *Militarizing the American Criminal Justice System* (Boston: Northeastern University Press, 2001), p. 3.

147. See, especially, Christian Parenti, *Lockdown America: Police and Prisons in the Age of Crisis* (London: Verso Press, 1999).

148. Kraska, "The Military-Criminal Justice Blur," p.10.

149. Jonathan Simon, "Sacrificing Private Ryan: The Military Model and the New Penology," in Peter B. Kraska, ed., *Militarizing the American Criminal Justice System* (Boston: Northeastern University Press, 2001), p.113.

150. These figures are taken from the following sources: Gary Delgado, "'Mo' Prisons Equals Mo' Money," *Colorlines* (Winter 1999–2000), p. 18; Fox Butterfield, "Number in Prison Grows Despite Crime Reduction," *New York Times* (August 10, 2000), p. A10; and Lewis, "Un-American Activities," p. A1.

151. Sanho Tree, "The War at Home," *Sojourner's Magazine* (May-June, 2003), p. 5.

152. For some extensive analyses of the devastating effects the criminal justice system is having on black males, see Michael Tonry, *Malign Neglect: Race, Crime, and Punishment in America* (New York: Oxford University Press, 1995); Jerome Miller, *Search and Destroy: African-American Males in the Criminal Justice System* (Cambridge: Cambridge University Press, 1996); David Cole, *No Equal Justice: Race and Class in the American Criminal Justice System* (New York: The New Press, 1999); Michael Parenti, *Lockdown America: Police and Prisons in the Age of Crisis* (London: Verso, 1999); Marc Mauer, *Race to Incarcerate* (New York: The New Press, 1999); Marc Mauer and Meda Chesney-Lind, *Invisible Punishment: The Collateral Consequences of Mass Imprisonment* (New York: The New Press, 2002).

153. Cited in David Barsamian, "Interview with Angela Davis," *The Progressive* (February 2001), p. 35.

154. Cited in "Men and Jewelry; Prison as Exile; Unifying Laughter and Darkness," in the Melange section of the *Chronicle of Higher Education* (July 6, 2001), p. B4.

155. Marsical, "Lethal and Compassionate: The Militarization of US Culture."

156. Matt Slagle, "Military Recruits Video-Game Makers," *Chicago Tribune* (October 8, 2003), p. 4.

157. Nick Turse, "The Pentagon Invades Your Xbox," *Dissident Voice* (December 15, 2003). Available online at www.dissidentvoice.org/Articles9/Turse_Pentagon-Video-Games.htm.

158. For a list of such "toys," see Nicholas Turse, "Have Yourself a Pentagon Xmas," *The Nation* (January 5, 2004), p. 8. For a more extensive list, visit www.tomdispatch.com.

159. R. Lee Sullivan, "Firefight on Floppy Disk," *Forbes Magazine* (May 20, 1996), pp. 39–40.

160. Gloria Goodale, "Video Game Offers Young Recruits a Peek at Military Life," *Christian Science Monitor* (May 31, 2003), p. 18.

161. Wayne Woolley, "From 'An Army of One' to Army of Fun; Online Video Game Helps Build Ranks," *Times-Picayune* (September 7, 2003), p. 26.

162. This description comes from "Gaming News—October 2003" and is Available online at http://www.gamerstemple.com/news/1003/100331.asp.

163. Ibid.

164. Turse, "The Pentagon Invades Your Xbox."

165. Maureen Tkacik, "Military Toys Spark Conflict on Home Front," *Wall Street Journal* (March 31, 2003), p. B1.

166. Amy C. Sims, "Just Child's Play," Fox News Channel (August 21, 2003). Available online at www.wmsa.net/news./FoxNews/fn-030822_childs_play.htm.

167. Mike Conklin, "Selling War at Retail," *Chicago Tribune* (May 1, 2003), p. 1.

168. Both quotes are from Cathy Horyn, "Macho America Storms Europe's Runways," *New York Times* (July 3, 2003), p. A1.

169. Umberto Eco, "Eternal Fascism: Fourteen Ways of Looking at a Blackshirt," *The New York Review of Books* (November-December 1995), p. 13.

170. This quote by Coulter has been cited extensively. It can be found online at http://www.coulterwatch.com/files/BW_2-003-bin_Coulter.pdf.

171. Kevin Baker, "We're in the Army Now: The G.O.P.'s Plan to Militarize Our Culture," *Harper's Magazine* (October 2003), p. 38.

172. There are a number of important works on the politics of neoliberalism. I have found the following particularly useful: Pierre Bourdieu, *Acts of Resistance: Against the Tyranny of the Market* (New York: The New Press, 1998); Pierre Bourdieu, "The Essence of Neoliberalism," *Le Monde Diplomatique* (December 1998), available online at http://www.en.monde-diplomatique.fr/1998/12/08bourdieu); Zygmunt Bauman, *Work, Consumerism and the New Poor* (London: Polity, 1998); Noam Chomsky, *Profit Over People: Neoliberalism and the Global Order* (New York: Seven Stories Press, 1999); Jean Comaroff and John L. Comaroff, *Millennial Capitalism and the Culture of Neoliberalism* (Durham: Duke University Press, 2000); Anatole Anton, Milton Fisk, and Nancy Holmstrom, eds., *Not for Sale: In Defense of Public Goods* (Boulder: Westview Press, 2000); Alain Touraine, *Beyond Neoliberalism* (London: Polity Press, 2001); Colin Leys, *Market Driven Politics* (London: Verso, 2001); Randy Martin, *Financialization of Daily Life* (Philadelphia: Temple University Press, 2002); Ulrich Beck, *Individualization* (London: Sage, 2002); Doug Henwood, *After the New Economy* (New York: The New Press, 2003); Lisa Duggan, *The Twilight of Equality: Neoliberalism, Cultural Politics, and the Attack on Democracy* (Boston: Beacon Press, 2003); and Pierre Bourdieu, *Firing Back: Against the Tyranny of the Market 2*. Translated by Loic Wacquant (New York: The New Press, 2003).

173. Professor Minqi Li provides an important summary of neoliberal policies and their effects: "A neoliberal regime typically includes monetarist policies to lower inflation and maintain fiscal balance (often achieved by reducing public expenditures and raising the interest rate), 'flexible' labor markets (meaning removing labor market regulations and cutting social welfare), trade and financial liberalization, and privatization. These policies are an attack by the global ruling elites (primarily finance capital of the leading capitalist states) on the working people of the world. Under neoliberal capitalism decades of social progress and developmental efforts have been reversed. Global inequality in income and wealth has reached unprecedented

levels. In much of the world, working people have suffered pauperization. Entire countries have been reduced to misery" (Minqi Li, "After Neoliberalism," *Monthly Review* [January 2003], p. 21).

174. For instance, a U.N. Human Development Report states that "the world's richest 1 percent receive as much income as the poorest 57 percent. The income gap between the richest 20 percent and the poorest 20 percent in the world rose from 30:1 in 1960 to 60:1 in 1990, and to 74:1 in 1999, and is projected to reach 100:1 in 2015. In 1999–2000, 2.8 billion people lived on less than $3 a day, 840 million were undernourished, 2.4 billion did not have access to any form of improved sanitation services, and one in every six children in the world of primary school age were not in school. About 50 percent of the global nonagricultural labor force is estimated to be either unemployed or underemployed." Cited in ibid.

175. George Steinmetz, "The State of Emergency and the Revival of American Imperialism: Toward an Authoritarian Post-Fordism," *Public Culture* 15:2 (Spring 2003), p. 337.

176. Steinmetz, "The State of Emergency and the Revival of American Imperialism," p. 337.

177. Barry Bluestone and Bennett Harrison, *The Deindustrialization of America: Plant Closings, Community Abandonment and the Dismantling of Basic Industry* (New York: Basic Books, 1982), p. 6

178. Aronowitz, *How Class Works*, p. 21.

179. Ibid., p. 101.

180. Stanley Aronowitz, "Introduction," in Paulo Freire, *Pedagogy of Freedom* (Lanham, MD: Rowman and Littlefield, 1998), p. 7.

181. Bourdieu, *Firing Back: Against the Tyranny of the Market 2*, p. 38.

182. Doug Henwood, *After the New Economy* (New York: The New Press, 2003); Kevin Phillips, *Wealth and Democracy: A Political History of the American Rich* (New York: Broadway, 2003); Paul Krugman, *The Great Unraveling: Losing Our Way in the New Century* (New York: W. W. Norton, 2003).

183. Aronowitz, *How Class Works*, p. 102.

184. William Greider, "The Right's Grand Ambition: Rolling Back the 20th Century," *The Nation* (May 12, 2003), p. 8

185. Edward S. Herman and Robert W. McChesney, *The Global Media: The New Missionaries of Global Capitalism* (Washington and London: Cassell, 1997), p. 3.

186. I address this issue in Henry A. Giroux, *Public Spaces, Private Lives: Democracy Beyond 9/11* (Lanham, MD: Rowman and Littlefield, 2003).

187. James Rule, "Markets, in Their Place," *Dissent* (Winter 1998), p. 31.

188. Zygmunt Bauman, *The Individualized Society* (London: Polity Press, 2001), p. 107.

189. Ibid.

190. Alan Bryman, *Disney and His Worlds* (New York: Routledge, 1995), p. 154.

191. Of course, there is widespread resistance to neoliberalism and its institutional enforcers such as the WTO and IMF among many intellectuals, students, and global justice movements, but this resistance rarely gets aired

in the dominant media—and when it does, it is often dismissed as irrelevant or tainted by Marxist ideology.

192. George Soros, *The Bubble of American Supremacy* (New York: Public Affairs, 2004), p. 10.

193. Pierre Bourdieu, "The Essence of Neoliberalism," *Le Monde Diplomatique* (December 1998), p. 4. Available online at http://www.en.monde-diplomatique.fr/1998/12/08bourdieu).

194. Paul Tolme, "Criminalizing the Homeless," *In These Times* (April 14, 2003), pp. 6–7.

195. Staff of Democracy Now, "Uncharitable Care: How Hospitals Are Gouging and Even Arresting the Uninsured," *CommonDreams* (January 8, 2004). Available online at http://www.commondreams.org/headlines04/0108-07.htm.

196. Jean and John Comaroff, "Millennial Capitalism: First Thoughts on a Second Coming," *Public Culture* 12:2 (2000), p. 305.

197. Herbert Marcuse, *Technology, War and Fascism: The Collected Papers of Herbert Marcuse*, Vol. I, edited by Douglas Kellner (New York: Routledge, 1998).

198. John and Jean Comaroff, "Millennial Capitalism: First Thoughts on a Second Coming," *Public Culture* 12:2 (2000), p. 332.

199. Ibid.

200. Pierre Bourdieu, *Acts of Resistance: Against the Tyranny of the Market* (New York: The New Press, 1998).

201. Pierre Bourdieu and Günter Grass, "The 'Progressive' Restoration: A Franco-German Dialogue," *New Left Review* 14 (March-April, 2003), p. 66.

202. Theodor Adorno, "Education After Auschwitz," in Theodor Adorno, *Critical Models: Interventions and Catchwords* (New York: Columbia University Press, 1998), p. 191.

Notes to Chapter 2

1. W.E.B. Du Bois, *The Souls of Black Folk*, in *Three Negro Classics* (New York: Avon Books, 1965), p. 221.

2. It is important to note that while such covert modes of expression may be true of anti-black racism, they certainly do not characterize the racist policies being enacted by the United States against immigrants and nationals from the Middle East. The racial profiling, harassment, and outright use of unconstitutional means to intimidate, deport, and jail members of the Arab and Muslim populations in the United States represent a most shameful period in this country's ongoing history of state-sanctioned racist practices. Thus, while the focus of this chapter is on black-white relations, I am not suggesting that racism encompasses only the latter. Obviously, any full account of racism would have to be applied to the wide range of groups who constitute diverse peoples of color and ethnic origin.

3. Howard Winant, "Race in the Twenty-First Century," *Tikkun* 17:1 (2002), p. 33.

4. Cited in David Shipler, "Reflections on Race," *Tikkun* 13:1 (1998), p. 59.

5. Dinesh D'Souza, *The End of Racism* (New York: The Free Press, 1995); Jim Sleeper, *Liberal Racism: How Fixating on Race Subverts the American Dream* (Lanham, MD: Rowman and Littlefield, 2002); Stephan and Abigail Thernstrom, *America in Black and White: One Nation, Indivisible* (New York: Simon and Schuster, 1999).

6. Cited in Tim Wise, "See No Evil: Perception and Reality in Black and White," *ZNet Commentary* (August 2, 2002). Available online at www.znet commentary@tao.ca. The Gallup Poll on Black-White Relations in the United States—2001 Update is available online at http://www.gallup.com/poll/specialReports/.

7. As Greg Winter points out, the Center for Equal Opportunity and the American Civil Rights Institute, two groups that oppose affirmative action, have launched a new offensive "against scholarships and summer programs intended to ease minority students into college life." See Winter, "Colleges See Broader Attack on Their Aid to Minorities," *New York Times* (March 30, 2003), p. A15.

8. Following is a representative sample of works that point to the pervasive racism at work in American life: Howard Winant, *The World Is a Ghetto: Race and Democracy Since World War II* (New York: Basic Books, 2001); Manning Marable, *The Great Wells of Democracy: The Meaning of Race in American Life* (New York: BasicCivitas Books, 2002); David Theo Goldberg, *The Racial State* (Malden, MA: Blackwell Books, 2002); Steve Martinot, *The Rule of Racialization: Class, Identity, Governance* (Philadelphia: Temple University Press, 2003).

9. Michael Omi, "Racialization in the Post-Civil Rights Era," in Avery Gordon and Christopher Newfield, eds., *Mapping Multiculturalism* (Minneapolis: University of Minnesota Press, 1996), p. 183.

10. Jack Geiger, "The Real World of Race," *The Nation* (December 1, 1997), p. 27.

11. See, for instance, Shelby Steele, "The Age of White Guilt," *Harper's Magazine* (November 2002), pp. 33–42.

12. This position is fully developed in Shelby Steele, *The Content of Our Character* (New York: Harper, 1990).

13. John McWhorter, "Don't Do Me Any Favors," *American Enterprise Magazine* (April/May 2003). Available on line at www.theamericanenterprise.org/taeam03d.htm.

14. Zygmunt Bauman, *The Individualized Society* (London: Polity Press, 2001), p. 205.

15. Charles Murray, *Losing Ground: American Social Policy, 1950–1980* (New York: Basic Books, 1985).

16. For excellent analyses of this shift in race relations, see Eduardo Bonilla-Silva, *White Supremacy and Racism in the Post-Civil Rights Era* (Boulder: Lynne Rienner Publishers, 2001); and Amy Elizabeth Ansell, *New Right, New*

Racism: Race and Reaction in the United States and Britain (New York: New York University Press, 1997).

17. Douglas Kellner, "Globalization and New Social Movements: Lessons for Critical Theory and Pedagogy," in Nicholas Burbules and Carlos Torres, eds., *Globalization and Education* (New York: Routledge/Falmer, 2000), p. 307.

18. Bauman, *The Individualized Society*, p. 159.

19. Lewis H. Lapham, "Res Publica," *Harper's Magazine* (December 2001), p. 8.

20. Zygmunt Bauman, *Globalization: The Human Consequences* (New York: Columbia University Press, 1998), p. 47.

21. Ansell, *New Right, New Racism*, p. 111.

22. Ibid., pp. 20–21.

23. Charles Gallagher, "Color-Blind Privilege: The Social and Political Functions of Erasing the Color Line in Post Race America," unpublished essay, p. 12.

24. Ibid., p. 11.

25. This issue is taken up brilliantly in David Theo Goldberg, *The Racial State* (Malden, MA: Blackwell Books, 2002), especially on pp. 200–238.

26. Manning Marable, "Beyond Color-Blindness," *The Nation* (December 14, 1998), p. 29.

27. For specific figures in all areas of life, see Bonilla-Silva, *White Supremacy and Racism in the Post-Civil Rights Era,* especially the chapter titled "White Supremacy in the Post–Civil Rights Era," pp. 89–120.

28. Paul Street, "A Whole Lott Missing: Rituals of Purification and Racism Denial," *Z Magazine* (December 22, 2002). Available online at www.zmag.org/content/print_article.cfm?itemID=2784&seciton.

29. I address these issues in detail in Henry A. Giroux, *Public Spaces, Private Lives: Democracy Beyond 9/11* (Lanham, MD: Rowman and Littlefield, 2002).

30. Loic Wacquant, "From Slavery to Mass Incarceration: Rethinking the 'Race Question' in the U.S.," in *New Left Review* (January–February 2002), p. 44.

31. Paul Street, "Mass Incarceration and Racist State Priorities at Home and Abroad," *DissidentVoice* (March 11, 2003), pp. 6–7. Available online at http://www.dissidentvoice.org/Articles2/Street_MassIncarceration.htm.

32. Richard J. Herrnstein and Charles Murray, *The Bell Curve: Intelligence and Class Structure in American Life* (New York: The Free Press, 1994), pp. 533–534, 551.

33. Nikhil Aziz, "Moving Right On! Fairness, Family, and Faith," *The Public Eye* 16:2 (Summer 2002), p. 5.

34. See "Civil Rights" within the Mission section of the CIR's website, at http://www.cir-usa.org/civil_rights_theme.html.

35. For an excellent summary and analysis of many of these legal cases, see Aziz, "Moving Right On!"

36. Ibid., p. 15.

37. Zsuza Ferge, "What Are the State Functions That Neoliberalism Wants to Eliminate?" in Antole Anton, Milton Fisk, and Nancy Holmstrom, eds.,

Not for Sale: In Defense of Public Goods (Boulder: Westview Press, 2000), p. 183.

38. David Theo Goldberg, *The Racial State* (Malden, MA: Blackwell, 2002), p. 217. The ideas in the sentence prior to this quote are also taken from Goldberg's text.

39. Jean Comaroff and John L. Comaroff, "Millennial Capitalism: First Thoughts on a Second Coming," *Public Culture* 12:2 (2000), pp. 305–306.

40. Aziz, "Moving Right On!" p. 6.

41. Cited in Philip Klinker, "The 'Racial Realism' Hoax," *The Nation* (December 14, 1998), p. 37.

42. Dinesh D'Souza, *The End of Racism: Principles for a Multiracial Society* (New York: The Free Press, 1995), p. 268.

43. Patricia J. Williams, *Seeing a Color-Blind Future: The Paradox of Race.* (New York: Noonday Press, 1997). pp. 18, 26.

44. John Meacham, "A Man Out of Time," *Newsweek* (December 23, 2003), p. 27.

45. Ibid.

46. On Trent Lott's voting record on matters of race, see Derrick Z. Jackson, "Brother Lott's Real Record," *Boston Globe* (December 18, 2002). Available online at www.commondreams.org/views02/1218-09.htm.

47. See Robert Kuttner, "A Candid Conversation About Race in America," *Boston Globe* (December 27, 2002). Available online at www.commondreams.org/views02/1225-02.htm.

48. David Brooks, "We Don't Talk This Way," *Newsweek* (December 23, 2002), p. 31.

49. Cited in David Roediger, *Toward the Abolition of Whiteness* (London: Verso Press, 1994), p. 8.

50. Frank Rich, "Bonfire of the Vanities," *New York Times* (Saturday, December 21, 2002), p. A35.

51. Ibid.

52. I have taken this idea from David Theo Goldberg, *Racial Subjects: Writing on Race in America* (New York: Routledge, 1997), pp. 17–26.

53. Ellis Cose, "Lessons of the Trent Lott Mess," *Newsweek* (December 23, 2002), p. 37.

54. Ibid.

55. David Theo Goldberg, "Racialized Discourse," in *Racist Culture* (Malden, MA: Blackwell, 1993), pp. 54, 55, 56.

56. Teun A. Van Dijk, "Denying Racism: Elite Discourse and Racism," in Philomena Essed and David Theo Goldberg, eds., *Race Critical Theories: Texts and Contexts* (Malden, MA: Blackwell, 2002), pp. 323–323.

57. Jean Comaroff and John L. Comaroff, "Millennial Capitalism: First Thoughts on a Second Coming," *Public Culture* 12:2, p. 322.

58. James Rule, "Markets, in Their Place," *Dissent* (Winter 1998), p. 31.

59. Bauman, *The Individualized Society,* p. 107.

60. Ibid.

61. Leerom Medovoi, "Globalization as Narrative and Its Three Critiques," *Review of Education/Pedagogy/Cultural Studies* 24:1–2 (2002), p. 66.

62. D'Souza, *The End of Racism*, p. 545.

63. David Theo Goldberg, *The Racial State* (Malden, MA: Blackwell, 2002), p. 229.

64. Pierre Bourdieu and Günter Grass, "The 'Progressive' Restoration: A Franco-German Dialogue," *New Left Review* 14 (March–April 2002), p. 71.

65. John Brenkman, "Race Publics: Civic Illiberalism, or Race After Reagan," *Transition* 5:2 (Summer 1995), p. 8.

66. On this subject, see Robert W. McChesney and John Nichols, *Our Media, Not Theirs* (New York: Seven Stories Press, 2002).

67. David Goldberg and John Solomos, "Introduction to Part III," in David Goldberg and John Solomos, eds., *A Companion to Ethnic and Racial Studies* (Malden, MA: Blackwell, 2002), p. 231.

Notes to Chapter 3

1. Randall R. Beger, "Expansion of Police Power in Public Schools and the Vanishing Rights of Students." *Social Justice* 29:1/2 (2002), p. 127.

2. Bernadine Dohrn, "Look Out, Kid, It's Something You Did," in Valerie Polakow, ed., *The Public's Assault on America's Children* (New York: Teachers College Press, 2000), p. 161.

3. Kevin Baker, "We're in the Army Now: The G.O.P.'s Plan to Militarize Our Culture," *Harper's Magazine* (October 27, 2003), pp. 38–39.

4. Cited in *NOW with Bill Moyers.*

5. Cited in Robert Dreyfus, "Grover Norquist: 'Field Marshal' of the Bush Plan," *The Nation* (May 14, 2001), p. 1. Available online at http://www.thenation.com/doc.mhtml?i=20010514&s=dreyfuss.

6. John Stauber and Sheldon Rampton, "The War at Home," Common Dreams News Center (May 17, 2004). Available on-line: www.common dreams.org/cgi-in/print.cgi?file=/views04/0517-08.htm

7. Ibid.

8. Gail Chaddock, "Safe Schools at a Price." *Christian Science Monitor* (August 24, 1999), p. 15.

9. Slavoj Žižek, "Today Iraq. Tomorrow....Democracy?" *In These Times* (May 5, 2003), p. 28.

10. Zygmunt Bauman, *Society Under Siege* (Malden, MA: Blackwell, 2002).

11. Peter Cassidy, "Last Brick in the Kindergulag" (May 12, 2003), available online at alternet.org/print.hgml?StoryId=13616.

12. Heather Wokusch, "Leaving Our Children Behind," *Common Dreams News Center* (July 8, 2002). Available online at www.commondreams.org/views02/0708-08.htm.

13. Lynette Clemetson, "More Americans in Poverty in 2002 Census Study Says," *New York Times* (September 27, 2003), pp. A1, A10.

14. Bob Herbert, "Young, Jobless, Hopeless." *New York Times* (January 6, 2003), p. A35.

15. Childhood Poverty Research Brief 2, "Child Poverty in the States: Levels and Trends from 1979 to 1998" (September 13, 2001). Available online at http://www.nccp.org.

16. Paul Street, "Race, Prison, and Poverty: The Race to Incarcerate in the Age of Correctional Keynesianism," *Z Magazine* (May 2001), p. 26.

17. These figures largely come from Children's Defense Fund, *The State of Children in America's Union: A 2002 Action Guide to Leave No Child Behind* (Washington, DC: Children's Defense Fund Publication, 2002), pp. iv–v, 13.

18. Graydon Carter, "The President? Go Figure." *Vanity Fair* (December 5, 2003), pp. 69–70.

19. Ibid., p. 69.

20. David Garland, "Men and Jewelry; Prison as Exile; Unifying Laughter and Darkness," *Chronicle of Higher Education* (July, 6 2001), p. B4.

21. John Leland, "Once You've Seen Paris, Everything Is E=mc²," *New York Times* (Sunday Styles) (November 23, 2003), p. 9.

22. Beger, "Expansion of Police Power in Public Schools and the Vanishing Rights of Students," p. 124.

23. Tyson Lewis, "The Surveillance Economy of Post-Columbine Schools," *Review of Education/Pedagogy/Cultural Studies* 25:4 (October–December 2003), pp. 335–355.

24. Sara Rimer, "Unruly Students Facing Arrests, Not Detention," *New York Times* (January 4, 2004), p. 1.

25. Ibid., p. 15.

26. Ibid.

27. Robin D.G. Kelley, *Yo' Mama's Disfunktional!: Fighting the Culture Wars in Urban America* (Boston: Beacon Press, 1997).

28. Dohrn, "Look Out, Kid, It's Something You Did," p. 175.

29. For an insightful commentary on the media and the racial nature of the war on drugs, see Jimmie L. Reeves and Richard Campbell, *Cracked Coverage: Television News, the Anti-Cocaine Crusade, and the Reagan Legacy* (Durham: Duke University Press, 1994).

30. Cited in Steven Donziger, *The Real War on Crime: The Report of the National Criminal Justice Commission* (New York: Harper Perennial, 1996), p. 101.

31. Cited in Eyall Press, "The Color Test," *Lingua Franca* (October 2000), p. 55.

32. Carl Chery, "U.S. Army Targets Black Hip-Hop Fans," *Wire/Daily Hip-Hop News* 21 (October 2003). Available online at www.sohh.com/article_print.php?content_ID=5162.

33. Street, "Race, Prison, and Poverty."

34. Lisa Featherstone, "A Common Enemy: Students Fight Private Prisons," *Dissent* (Fall 2000), p. 78.

35. Erik Lotke, "The Prison-Industrial Complex," *Multinational Monitor* (November 26, 1996). Available online at http://www.igc.org/ncia/pic.html.

36. Beger, "Expansion of Police Power in Public Schools and the Vanishing Rights of Students," p. 121

37. Street, "Race, Prison, and Poverty," p. 26. Even more shameful is the fact that such discrimination against African-Americans is often rationalized from the Olympian heights of institutions such as Harvard University by apologists like lawyer Randall Kennedy, who argues that laws, criminal policies, and police practices are necessary to protect "good" blacks from "bad" blacks who commit crimes. See Kennedy, *Race, Crime, and the Law* (New York: Pantheon, 1997).

38. Dohrn, "Look Out, Kid, It's Something You Did," p. 161.

39. For a moving narrative of the devastating effects of the juvenile justice system on teens, see Edward Humes, *No Matter How Loud I Shout: A Year in the Life of Juvenile Court* (New York: Touchstone, 1996).

40. Margaret Talbot, "The Maximum Security Adolescent," *New York Times Magazine* (September 10, 2000), p. 42.

41. Evelyn Nieves, "California Proposal Toughens Penalties for Young Criminals," *New York Times* (March 6, 2000), pp. A1, A15.

42. Sara Rimer and Raymond Bonner, "Whether to Kill Those Who Killed as Youths," *New York Times* (August 22, 2000), p. A16.

43. Ann Patchett, "The Age of Innocence," *New York Times Sunday Magazine* (September 29, 2002), p. 17.

44. Interview with Jesse Jackson, "First Class Jails, Second-Class Schools," *Rethinking Schools* (Spring 2000), p. 16.

45. American Bar Association. "Report on Zero Tolerance Laws" (May 28, 2003), p. 3. Available online at www.abanet.org/crimjust/juvius/zerotolreport.html.

46. Kate Zernike, "Crackdown on Threats in School Fails a Test," *New York Times* (May 17, 2001), p. A21.

47. Lewis, "The Surveillance Economy of Post-Columbine Schools," p. 336.

48. Brian Moore, "Letting Software Make the Call," *Chicago Reader* 29:49 (2000), p. 18.

49. Editorial, " *USA Today* (October 2003).

50. Ellen Goodman, "'Zero Tolerance' Means Zero Chance for Troubled Kids," *Centre Daily Times* (January 4, 2000), p. 8.

51. These examples are taken from a report on zero-tolerance laws by the American Bar Association dated May 28, 2003. Available online at www.abanet.org/crimjust/juvius/zerotolreport.html.

52. Beger, "Expansion of Police Power in Public Schools and the Vanishing Rights of Students," p. 123.

53. Goodman, "'Zero Tolerance' Means Zero Chance for Troubled Kids," p. 8.

54. Steven Drizin, "Arturo's Case," in William Ayers, Bernadine Dohrn, and Rick Ayers, eds., *Zero Tolerance* (New York: The New Press, 2001), p. 32.

55. Editorial, "Zero Tolerance Is the Policy," *Denver Rocky Mountain News* (June 22, 1999), p. 38A.

56. Gregory Michie, "One Strike and You're Out: Does Zero Tolerance Work? Or Does Kicking Kids Out of School Just Make Things Worse?" *Chicago Reader.* 29:49 (2000), p. 24.

57. Jane Gordon, "In Schools, Bad Behavior Is Shown the Door," *New York Times* (November 16, 2003), p. 14CN.

58. Annette Fuentes, "Discipline and Punish," *The Nation* (December 15, 2003), pp. 17–20.

59. Editorial, "Zero Tolerance Takes Student Discipline to Harsh Extremes," *USA Today* (January 2, 2004), p. 11A.

60. Cited in Gordon, "In Schools, Bad Behavior Is Shown the Door," p. 2.

61. Tamar Lewin and Jennifer Medina, "To Cut Failure Rate, Schools Shed Students," *New York Times* (July 31, 2003), p. A1.

62. It was reported in the *New York Times* that in responding to the spate of recent school shootings, the FBI has provided educators across the country with a list of behaviors that could identify "students likely to commit an act of lethal violence." One such behavior is "resentment over real or perceived injustices." The reach of domestic militarization thus becomes more evident as the FBI takes on the role of monitoring not only potentially disruptive student behavior but also the degree to which teachers are positioned to become adjuncts of the criminal justice system. The story and quotes appear in an editorial titled "F.B.I. Caution Signs for Violence in Classroom," *New York Times* (September 7, 2000), p. A18.

63. Tamar Lewin, "Study Finds Racial Bias in Public Schools," *New York Times* (March 11, 2000), p. A14.

64. Libero Della Piana, "Crime and Punishment in Schools: Students of Color Are Facing More Suspensions Because of Racially Biased Policies," *San Francisco Chronicle* (February 9, 2000), p. A21.

65. Marilyn Elias, "Disparity in Black and White?" *USA Today* (December 11, 2000), p. 9D.

66. Editorial, "Zero Tolerance Takes Student Discipline to Harsh Extremes," *USA Today* (January 2, 2004), p. 11A.

67. Sam Dillon, "Cameras Watching Students, Especially in Biloxi," *New York Times* (September 24, 2003), p. A24.

68. Lewis, "The Surveillance Economy of Post-Columbine Schools," p. 337.

69. Ulrich Beck, *The Reinvention of Politics,* translated by Mark Ritter (Cambridge: Polity Press, 1995), p. 7.

70. As has been widely reported, the prison industry has become big business, with many states spending more on prison construction than on university construction. See Anthony Lewis, "Punishing the Country," *New York Times* (December 2, 1999), p. A1.

71. Abigail Thernstrom, "Schools Are Responsible for the Main Source of Racial Inequality Today," *Los Angeles Times* (November 13, 2003), p. B17.

72. Loic Wacquant, "From Slavery to Mass Incarceration: Rethinking the

'Race Question' in the U.S.," *New Left Review* (January–February 2002), p. 52.

73. For a provocative analysis of the relationship between what Norman Geras calls "the contract of mutual indifference" and neoliberalism's refusal of the social as a condition for contemporary forms of mutual indifference, see Geras, *The Contract of Mutual Indifference* (London: Verso Press, 1998).

74. For some recent commentaries on the new student movement, see Lisa Featherstone, "The New Student Movement," *The Nation* (May 15, 2000), pp. 11–15; David Samuels, "Notes from Underground: Among the Radicals of the Pacific Northwest," *Harper's Magazine* (May 2000), pp. 35–47; Katazyna Lyson, Monique Murad, and Trevor Stordahl, "Real Reformers, Real Results," *Mother Jones* (October 2000), pp. 20–22; Alexander Cockburn, Jeffrey St. Clair, and Allan Sekula, *5 Days that Shook the World* (London: Verso Press, 2000); Mark Edelman Boren, *Student Resistance* (New York: Routledge, 2001); and Imre Szeman, "Learning from Seattle," Special Issue of *Review of Education/Pedagogy/Cultural Studies* 24:1–2 (January–June 2002).

Notes to Chapter 4

1. Zygmunt Bauman, *Work, Consumerism and the New Poor* (Philadelphia: Open University Press, 1998), pp. 97–98.

2. Stanley Aronowitz and Peter Bratsis, "State Power, Global Power," in Stanley Aronowitz and Peter Bratsis, eds., *Paradigm Lost: State Theory Reconsidered* (Minneapolis: University of Minnesota Press, 2002), p. xvii.

3. Pierre Bourdieu, *Language and Symbolic Power* (Cambridge, MA: Harvard University Press, 2001), p. 127.

4. Ibid., p. 128.

5. For some general theoretical principles for addressing the new sites of pedagogy, see Jeffrey R. DiLeo, Walter Jacobs, and Amy Lee, "The Sites of Pedagogy," *Symploke* 10:1–2 (2003), pp. 7–12.

6. William Greider, "The Right's Grand Ambition: Rolling Back the 20th Century," *The Nation* (May 12, 2003), p. 11.

7. One interesting analysis on the contingent nature of democracy and public space can be found in Rosalyn Deutsche, *Evictions: Art and Spatial Politics* (Cambridge, MA: MIT Press, 1998).

8. Cited in Robert Dreyfuss, "Grover Norquist: 'Field Marshal' of the Bush Plan," *The Nation* (May 14, 2001), p. 1. Available online at http://www.thenation.com/doc.mhtml?i=20010514&s=dreyfuss.

9. Raymond Williams, *Communications*, rev. ed. (New York: Barnes & Noble, 1966), p. 15.

10. Benjamin R. Barber, "A Failure of Democracy, Not Capitalism," *New York Times* (Monday, July 29, 2002), p. A23.

11. Bob Herbert, "The Art of False Impression," *New York Times* (August 11, 2003), p. A17.

12. W.E.B. Du Bois, *Against Racism: Unpublished Essays, Papers, Addresses,*

1887–1961," edited by Herbert Aptheker (Amherst: University of Massachusetts Press, 1985).

13. Cornelius Castoriadis, cited in Zygmunt Bauman, *The Individualized Society* (London: Polity Press, 2001), p. 127.

14. Michele Barrett, *Imagination in Theory* (New York: New York University Press, 1999), p. 161.

15. Zygmunt Bauman and Keith Tester, *Conversations with Zygmunt Bauman* (Malden, MA.: Polity Press, 2001), p. 32.

16. On the importance of problematizing and pluralizing the political, see Jodi Dean, "The Interface of Political Theory and Cultural Studies," in Jodi Dean, ed., *Cultural Studies and Political Theory* (Ithaca: Cornell University Press, 2000), pp. 1–19.

17. Robert W. McChesney and John Nichols, *Our Media, Not Theirs: The Democratic Struggle Against Corporate Media* (New York: Seven Stories Press, 2002).

18. Zygmunt Bauman, *In Search of Politics* (Stanford: Stanford University Press, 1999).

19. Nick Couldry, "In the Place of a Common Culture, What?" *Review of Education/Pedagogy/Cultural Studies* (in press), p. 6.

20. Raymond Williams, "Preface to Second Edition," *Communications* (New York: Barnes and Noble, 1967), pp. 15, 16.

21. Raymond Williams, "Preface to Second Edition," *Communications* (New York: Barnes and Noble, 1967), p. 14.

22. See, especially, Raymond Williams, *Marxism and Literature* (New York: Oxford University Press, 1977); and Raymond Williams, *The Year 2000* (New York: Pantheon, 1983).

23. Williams, *Marxism and Literature.*

24. See Tony Bennett, *Culture: A Reformer's Science* (Thousand Oaks, CA: Sage, 1998), p. 223.

25. Antonio Gramsci, *Selections from the Prison Notebooks* (New York: International Press, 1971), p. 350.

26. Cornelius Castoriadis, "Democracy as Procedure and Democracy as Regime," *Constellations* 4:1 (1997), p. 10.

27. Cornelius Castoriadis, "The Problem of Democracy Today," *Democracy and Nature* 8 (April 1996), p. 19.

28. Cornelius Castoriadis, "The Nature and Value of Equity," *Philosophy, Politics, Autonomy: Essays in Political Philosophy* (New York: Oxford University Press, 1991), pp. 124–142.

29. Cornelius Castoriadis, *The World in Fragments,* edited and translated by David Ames Curtis (Stanford: Stanford University Press, 1997), p. 91.

30. Both quotes are taken from Cornelius Castoriadis, "Culture in a Democratic Society," *The Castoriadis Reader,* edited by David Ames Curtis (Malden, MA: Blackwell, 1997), pp. 343, 341.

31. Cornelius Castoriadis, "The Crisis of the Identification Process," *Thesis Eleven* 49 (May 1997), pp. 87–88.

32. Cornelius Castoriadis, "The Anticipated Revolution," *Political and So-

cial Writings, Vol. 3 edited and translated by David Ames Curtis (Minneapolis: University of Minnesota Press, 1993), pp. 153–154.

33. John Binde, "Toward an Ethic of the Future," *Public Culture* 12:1 (2000), p. 65.

34. Cornelius Castoriadis, "The Greek Polis and the Creation of Democracy," *Philosophy, Politics, Autonomy: Essays in Political Philosophy* (New York: Oxford University Press, 1991), p. 102.

35. Cornelius Castoriadis, "Power, Politics, and Autonomy," *Philosophy, Politics, Autonomy: Essays in Political Philosophy* (New York: Oxford University Press, 1991), p. 144–145.

36. Castoriadis, "Democracy as Procedure and Democracy as Regime," p.15. It is crucial here to note that Castoriadis develops his notions of both democracy and the primacy of education in political life directly from his study of ancient Greek democracy.

37. Castoriadis, "The Problem of Democracy Today," p. 24.

38. Bauman and Tester, *Conversations with Zygmunt Bauman*, p. 131.

39. Susan Sontag, "Courage and Resistance," *The Nation* (May 5, 2003), pp. 11–14.

40. Zygmunt Bauman, *Society Under Siege* (Malden, MA: Blackwell: 2002), p. 170.

41. Jacques Derrida, "Intellectual Courage: An Interview," translated by Peter Krapp, *Culture Machine* 2 (2000), pp. 1–15.

42. Zygmunt Bauman, *The Individualized Society* (London: Polity Press, 2001), pp. 54–55.

43. Gerald Graff appears to have made a career out of this issue by either misrepresenting the work of Paulo Freire and others, citing theoretical work by critical educators that is outdated and could be corrected by reading anything they might have written in the last five years, creating caricatures of their work, or holding up extreme and ludicrous examples as characteristic of what is done by people in critical pedagogy (or, more generally, by anyone who links pedagogy and politics). For more recent representations of this position, see Gerald Graff, "Teaching Politically Without Political Correctness," *Radical Teacher* 58 (Fall 2000), pp. 26–30; and Gerald Graff, *Clueless in Academe* (New Haven: Yale University Press, 2003).

44. Lani Guinier, "Democracy Tested," *The Nation* (May 5, 2003) p. 6. Guinier's position is in direct opposition to that of Graff and his acolytes. For instance, see A Conversation Between Lani Guinier and Anna Deavere Smith, "Rethinking Power, Rethinking Theater," *Theater* 31:3 (Winter 2002), pp. 31–45.

45. George Lipsitz, "Academic Politics and Social Change," in Jodi Dean, ed., *Cultural Studies and Political Theory* (Ithaca: Cornell University Press, 2000), pp. 81–82.

46. For a more detailed response to this kind of watered-down pedagogical practice, see Stanley Aronowitz, *The Knowledge Factory* (Boston: Beacon Press, 2000); and Henry A. Giroux, *The Abandoned Generation: Democracy Beyond the Culture of Fear* (New York: Palgrave, 2003).

47. Interview with Julie Ellison, "New Public Scholarship in the Arts and Humanities," *Higher Education Exchange* (2002), p. 20.

48. Amy Gutmann, *Democratic Education* (Princeton: Princeton University Press, 1998), p. 42.

49. Bauman and Tester, *Conversations with Zygmunt Bauman*, p. 63.

Notes to Chapter 5

1. David Harvey, *Spaces of Hope* (Berkeley: University of California Press, 2000), p. 195.

2. This paraphrase is actually taken from Fredric Jameson's quotation: "It seems to be easier for us today to imagine the thoroughgoing deterioration of the earth and of nature than the breakdown of late capitalism." See Jameson, *The Seeds of Time* (New York: Columbia University Press, 1994), p. xii.

3. Perry Anderson, *A Zone of Engagement* (London: Verso, 1992), p. 335.

4. Zygmunt Bauman, *Work, Consumerism, and the New Poor* (Philadelphia: Open University Press, 1998).

5. Editorial, "Bush's Domestic War," *The Nation* (December 31, 2001), p. 3.

6. Ibid.

7. Molly Ivins, "Bush's Sneak Attack on 'Average' Taxpayers," *Chicago Tribune* (March 27, 2003). Available online at www.commondreams.org/views03/0327-04.htm.

8. Jennifer Lee, "U.S. Proposes Easing Rules on Emissions of Mercury," *New York Times* (December 3, 2003), p. A20.

9. See Jaider Rizvi, "United States: Hunger in a Wealthy Nation," *Tierramerica/Interpress Service* (March 26, 2003). Available online at www.foodfirst.org/media/news/2003/hungerwealthy.html. Also see Jennifer Egan, "To Be Young and Homeless," *New York Times Magazine* (March 24, 2002), p. 35.

10. Robert McChesney, *Rich Media, Poor Democracy: Communication Politics in Dubious Times* (New York: The New Press, 1999).

11. Ulrich Beck, *Risk Society: Towards a New Modernity* (Thousand Oaks, CA: Sage, 1992), p. 137.

12. Cornelius Castoriadis, "Democracy as Procedure and as Regime," *Constellations* 4:1 (1997), p. 5.

13. Ibid., p. 10.

14. See the work of Manual Castells, especially his *The Information Age: Economy, Society and Culture, Volume III: End of Millennium* (Malden, MA: Basil Blackwell, 1998).

15. Takis Fotopoulos, *Towards an Inclusive Democracy* (London and New York: Cassell, 1997).

16. Anatole Anton, "Public Goods as Commonstock: Notes on the Receding Commons," in Anatole Anton, Milton Fisk, and Nancy Holmstrom, eds., *Not for Sale: In Defense of Public Goods* (Boulder: Westview Press, 2000), pp. 3–4.

17. See, for example, Todd Gitlin, "The Anti-Political Populism of Cultural

Studies," in M. Ferguson and P. Golding, eds., *Cultural Studies in Question* (Thousand Oaks, CA: Sage, 1998), pp. 25–38; Tony Bennett, "Cultural Studies: A Reluctant Discipline," *Cultural Studies* 12:4, pp. 528–545; and Ian Hunter, *Rethinking the School: Subjectivity, Bureaucracy, Criticism* (New York: St. Martin's Press, 1994).

18. John Brenkman, "Race Publics: Civil Illiberalism, or Race After Reagan," *Transition* 5:2 (Summer 1995), p. 7.

19. Gary Olson and Lynn Worsham, "Changing the Subject: Judith Butler's Politics of Radical Signification," *JAC* 20:4 (2000), p. 741.

20. Cornelius Castoriadis, "Institutions and Autonomy," in Peter Osborne, ed., *A Critical Sense* (New York: Routledge, 1996), p. 8.

21. Noam Chomsky, *Profits Over People: Neoliberalism and Global Order* (New York: Seven Stories Press, 1999), p. 92.

22. Brenkman, "Race Publics," p. 123.

23. Gary Olson and Lynn Worsham, "Rethinking Political Community: Chantal Mouffe's Liberal Socialism." *JAC* 18:3 (1999), p. 178.

24. Ibid., p. 11.

25. Pierre Bourdieu, "For a Scholarship with Commitment," *Profession* (2000), p. 43.

26. John Brenkman, "Extreme Criticism," in J. Butler, J. Guillary, and K. Thomas, eds., *What's Left of Theory* (New York: Routledge, 2000), p. 130.

27. Zygmunt Bauman, *Globalization: The Human Consequences* (New York: Columbia University Press, 1998), p. 5.

28. Simon Critchley, "Ethics, Politics, and Radical Democracy—The History of a Disagreement," *Culture Machine*. Available online at www.culturemachine.tees.ac.uk/frm_f1.htm.

29. This section draws from a chapter on utopian hope in Henry A. Giroux, *Public Spaces, Private Lives* (Lanham, MD: Rowman and Littlefield, 2002).

30. Zygmunt Bauman "The Journey Never Ends: Zygmunt Bauman Talks with Peter Beilharz," in Peter Beilhurz, ed., *The Bauman Reader* (Oxford: Blackwell, 2001), p. 342.

31. Jacques Derrida, "The Future of the Profession or the Unconditional University," in *Derrida Downunder*, edited by Laurence Simmons and Heather Worth (Auckland, New Zealand: Dunmore Press, 2001), p. 7.

32. Giroux, *Public Spaces, Private Lives*.

33. Bloch's great contribution in English on the subject of utopianism can be found in his three-volume work, *The Principle of Hope*, Vols. I, II, and III, translated by Neville Plaice, Stephen Plaice, and Paul Knight (Cambridge, MA: MIT Press, 1986; originally published in 1959).

34. Ernst Block, "Something's Missing: A Discussion Between Ernst Bloch and Theodor W. Adorno on the Contradictions of Utopia Longing," in Ernst Bloch, *The Utopian Function of Art and Literature: Selected Essays* (Cambridge, MA: MIT Press, 1988), p. 3.

35. Anson Rabinach, "Ernst Bloch's *Heritage of Our Times* and the Theory of Fascism," *New German Critique* 11 (Spring 1977), p. 11.

36. Thomas L. Dunn, "Political Theory for Losers," in Jason A. Frank and John Tambornino, eds., *Vocations of Political Theory* (Minneapolis: University of Minnesota Press, 2000), p. 160.

37. Russell Jacoby, "A Brave Old World," *Harper's Magazine* (December 2000), pp. 72–80; Geras, "Minimum Utopia: Ten Theses," pp. 41–42; Leo Panitch and Sam Gindin, "Transcending Pessimism: Rekindling Socialist Imagination," in Leo Panitch and Sam Gindin, eds., *Necessary and Unnecessary Utopias* (New York: Monthly Review Press, 1999), pp. 1–29; David Harvey, *Spaces of Hope* (University of California Press, 2000); Russell Jacoby, *The End of Utopia: Politics and Culture in an Age of Apathy* (New York: Basic Books, 1999).

38. Jacoby, "A Brave Old world," p. 80.

39. Norman Podhoretz, cited in Ellen Willis, "Buy American," *Dissent* (Fall 2000), p. 110.

40. For a critique of the entrepreneurial populism of this diverse group, see Thomas Frank, *One Market Under God: Extreme Capitalism, Market Populism and the End of Economic Democracy* (New York: Doubleday, 2000).

41. Carl Boggs, *The End of Politics: Corporate Power and the Decline of the Public Sphere* (New York: Guilford Press, 2000), p. 7.

42. Alain Badiou, *Ethics: An Essay on the Understanding of Evil* (London: Verso, 2001), p. 96.

43. Samir Amin, "Imperialization and Globalization," *Monthly Review* (June 2001), p. 12.

44. Antonio Gramsci, *Selections from the Prison Notebooks* (New York: International Press, 1971), p. 350.

45. Edward Said, "Scholarship and Commitment: An Introduction," *Profession* (2000), pp. 8–9.

46. Bill Readings, *The University in Ruins* (Cambridge, MA: Harvard University Press, 1996).

47. Zygmunt Bauman, *In Search of Politics* (Stanford: Stanford University Press, 1999), p. 170.

48. Toni Morrison, "How Can Values Be Taught in the University?" *Michigan Quarterly Review* (Spring 2001), p. 278.

49. Martin Finklestein, "The Morphing of the American Academic Profession," *Liberal Education* 89:4 (2003), p. 1.

50. Arundhati Roy, *Power Politics* (Cambridge, MA: South End Press, 2001), p. 3.

51. Edward Said, *Representations of the Intellectual* (New York: Pantheon, 1994), p. 11.

52. Ibid., p. 52–53.

53. R. Radhakrishnan, "Canonicity and Theory: Toward a Poststructuralist Pedagogy," in Donald Morton and Mas'ud Zavarzadeh, eds., *Theory/Pedagogy/Politics* (Urbana: University of Illinois Press, 1991), 112–135.

54. Stanley Aronowitz, Introduction to Paulo Freire's *Pedagogy of Freedom* (Lanham, MD: Rowman and Littlefield, 1998), pp. 10–11.

55. Edward Said, *Reflections on Exile and Other Essays* (Cambridge, MA: Harvard University Press, 2001), p. 503.

56. Ibid., p. 504.

57. Paul Sabin, "Academe Subverts Young Scholars' Civic Orientation," *Chronicle of Higher Education* (February 8, 2002), p. B24.

58. Jacques Derrida, "No One Is Innocent: A Discussion with Jacques Derrida About Philosophy in the Face of Terror," *The Information Technology, War and Peace Project*. Available online at http://www.watsoninstitute.org/infopeace/911.

Notes to Chapter 6

1. Sheldon Wolin, "Inverted Totalitarianism," *The Nation* (May 19, 2003), pp. 13–15.

2. Ibid., p. 14.

3. Gerald Graff, *Beyond the Culture Wars: How Teaching the Conflicts Can Revitalize American Education* (New York: W. W. Norton and Company, 1992); Stanley Fish, *Professional Correctness: Literary Studies and Political Change* (New York: Clarendon Press, 1995).

4. Edward Said, *Orientalism* (New York: Vintage Press, 1979); Edward Said, *Culture and Imperialism* (New York: Knopf, 1992).

5. Richard Bernstein, "Edward W. Said, Literary Critic and Advocate for Palestinian Independence, Dies at 67," *New York Times* (September 26, 2003), p. C23.

6. Alan Riding, "Leni Riefenstahl, 101, Dies; Film Innovator Tied to Hitler," *New York Times* (September 10, 2003), p. C14.

7. A classic example of this can be seen in the *New York Times Sunday Magazine* dated November 2, 2003, in which Deborah Solomon interviews Noam Chomsky. Solomon ends the interview by suggesting that Chomsky is a self-hating Jew because he criticizes Israeli policies, needs to be psychoanalyzed, and is driven by ambition. At that point she asks Chomsky if he feels guilty about "living a bourgeois life and driving a nice car" and if he has "considered leaving the United States permanently?" Clearly these questions reveal much more about Solomon, her editors, and the *New York Times* than they might about Chomsky, though he answers all of her questions in ways that reveal how foolish she is. Two of the questions and answers are worth repeating verbatim: *How would you explain your large ambition?* [Chomsky:] "I am driven by many things. I know what some of them are. The misery that people suffer and the misery for which I share responsibility. That is agonizing. We live in a free society, and privilege confers responsibility." *If you feel so guilty, how can you justify living a bourgeois life and driving a nice car?* [Chomsky:] "If I gave away my car, I would feel even more guilty. When I go to visit peasants in southern Colombia, they don't want me to give up my car. They want me to help them. Suppose I gave up material things—my computer, my car and so on—and went to live on a hill in Montana where I grew my own food. Would that help anyone? No."

8. Wolin, "Inverted Totalitarianism."

9. Edward Said, *Out of Place: A Memoir* (New York: Knopf, 1999).

10. Stephen Howe, "Edward Said: The Traveller and the Exile," *Open Democracy* (October 2, 2003). Available online at www.opendemocracy.net/articles/ViewPopUpArticle.jsp?id=10&articleId=1561.

11. Ibid.

12. Elaine Scarry, "Beauty and the Scholar's Duty to Justice," *Profession 2000*, pp. 21–31.

13. Edward Said, "The Public Role of Writers and Intellectuals," *The Nation* (October 1, 2001), p. 31.

14. Henry Giroux, *Border Crossings* (New York: Routledge, 1992).

15. Stanley Aronowitz, *How Class Works* (New York: Yale University Press, 2003), p. 53.

16. Hussein, *Edward Said: Criticism and Society*, p. 302.

17. Grant Kester, *Conversation Pieces* (Berkeley: University of California Press, 2004), p. 152.

18. Edward Said, *Representations of the Intellectual: The 1993 Reith Lectures* (New York: Pantheon Books, 1994), pp. 8–9.

19. Hussein, *Edward Said: Criticism and Society*, p. 297.

20. Edward Said, "On Defiance and Taking Positions," *Reflections on Exile and Other Essays* (Cambridge: Harvard University Press, 2000), p. 501.

21. Edward Said, *The World, the Text and the Critic* (Cambridge, MA: Harvard University Press, 1983), p. 28.

22. Edward Said, "At the Rendezvous of Victory," in Edward Said, *Culture and Resistance: Interviews with David Barsamian* (Cambridge, MA: South End Press, 2003), p. 167.

23. Ibid., p. 166.

24. Bill Moyers, "'Enough Is Enough': Bill Moyers Interviews Union Theological Seminary's Joseph Hough on *NOW with Bill Moyers*" (October 24, 2003). Transcript available online at http://www.commondreams.org/views03/1027-01.htm.

25. Edward Said, "At the Rendezvous of Victory."

Index

❧

abortion, 28–29, 47
Abu Ghraib prison, xiv–xv, 3–4, 6–7, 26
ACLU. *See* American Civil Liberties Union
Adorno, Theodor, 53
affirmative action, 58, 66–68, 71, 172n7
Afghanistan, 3, 6, 30, 34, 87
African-Americans, 32, 37, 92; and
    criminal justice system, xii, 14, 39,
    57, 66, 90–91, 168n152; and poverty,
    65–66, 86–87; and zero-tolerance
    policies, 99, 101–102
AIDS education, 5
airline industry, 48
air pollution, 5, 24–25, 128, 165n94
Akerlof, George A., 10
Al Qaeda, 20, 25, 108
American Civil Liberties Union
    (ACLU), 13, 26, 30
American Civil Rights Institute, 172n7
Americans for Tax Reform, 23, 82, 107
Americorps, 82
Amin, Samir, 137
Amnesty International, 26
Anderson, Perry, 182n3
Ansell, Elizabeth, 63–64, 172n16
Antiballistic Missile Treaty, 2
Anton, Anatole, 169n172, 182n16
Argentina, viii, x
Aristotle, 118
Aronowitz, Stanley, 106, 156n6, 156n5;

on neoliberalism, 45, 47; on security
    state, 19–20, 51
Ashcroft, John, xiv, 9, 136, 154; and
    civil liberties, 12, 13, 21, 29–30; on
    Confederate legacy, 72; religious faith
    of, 29–31
authoritarianism, 1–9, 14–32, 44–53,
    160n38; *see also* fascism
"axis of evil," 2
Ayers, William, 177n52
Aziz, Nikhil, 68

Badiou, Alain, 184n42
Baker, Kevin, 34, 44, 81–82
Ball, Brian, 41
Barnett, Scott, 40
Bauman, Zygmunt, xv, 60, 133,
    169n172; on culture, 111–112; on
    democracy, 120, 139; on justice, 84,
    123; on public space, 19, 50, 62
Beck, Ulrich, 101, 128, 169n172
Beger, Randall, 38
Bellant, Russ, 160n38
Bennett, Tony, 114
Bennett, William J., 126, 157n16
Berlet, Chip, 160n38
Bernstein, Richard, 148
Bhabha, Homi, 132
Bin Laden. *See* Laden, Osama bin
Blair, Eric Arthur. *See* Orwell, George

Index

Darwinism. *See* social Darwinism
Davis, Jefferson, 72
Davis, Mike, 166n125
Dean, Jodi, 180n16
democracy, 14, 33, 43–44; Amin on,
137; Bauman on, 120; Chomsky on,
132; and consumerism, xi, xv, 62–63,
69, 103; education for, 53, 102, 109–
110, 115–118, 132–144; Mandela on,
9–10; and race, 54–58, 75–80; and
religion, ix, xiii–xiv; threats to, 44–53,
83–84, 125–134, 142–143
deregulation, 45, 47, 52
Derrida, Jacques, 120, 135, 143
Deutsche, Rosalyn, 179n7
Dewey, John, 109
Diamond, Sara, 160n38
dissent, 8–9, 20, 126; criminalization of,
xiv–xv, 6–7; in mass media, xviii–xix,
12, 22, 24, 148, 162n53, 170n191,
185n7; and pedagogy, 120–124, 140–
142
Donziger, Steven, 176n28
downsizing, ix, xiii, 48; *see also*
unemployment
Drake University, 8–9
Drizin, Steven, 97
drugs, xii, 63; and prisons, 38–39, 92–
93; and schools, 36–39, 86, 88–89,
95–97; war on, 38, 84, 91, 176n27
D'Souza, Dinesh, 55, 70, 77
Du Bois, W.E.B., 54–55, 109
Duggan, Lisa, xviii, 157n10, 169n172
Dyson, Michael, 56

Eco, Umberto, 15, 22, 43
education, 138–142; cost of, 86, 92–93;
99–100; for democracy, 53, 102, 109–
110, 115–118, 132–144; and No Child
Left Behind Act, 36, 96, 98;
"permanent," 107, 113, 131; *see also*
pedagogy
Elias, Marilyn, 99
Enron company, viii
entrepreneurialism, 58
environmentalism, vii–viii, xx, 5, 24–25,
47, 127–128, 165n94
Environmental Protection Agency
(EPA), 25, 165n97

Essed, Philomena, 174n56
ethnicity. *See* race
exclusion, xvi, 1, 129, 155; and class,
xvii, 91–95; and hiring practices, 28

faith-based initiatives, 28–29
Falk, Richard, 20–21, 34
Falwell, Jerry, 30–31
Farah, Joseph, 157n16
farm subsidies, 82
fascism, 11–16, 32, 43; defined, 15–16;
Eco on, 15, 22, 43; Falk on, 20–21;
see also proto-fascism
fashion, military, 40, 43
fear, 24, 125–126; culture of, xiv, 37, 46,
95–96, 99–103; and patriotism, 19–20,
130
Federal Bureau of Investigation (FBI),
126, 178n60
Federal Communications Commission
(FCC), 21
Ferge, Zsuza, 68
Ferguson, M., 182n17
Food and Drug Administration (FDA), 32
Forbes, James, Jr., 31
Fordice, Kirk, 72
Foreman, George, 56
Fotopoulos, Takis, 129
Fox News, xvii, 35, 109
Frank, Jason A., 183n36
Frank, Thomas, 184n40
Freedom of Information Act, 141
free speech, 7–9, 20, 120
Freire, Paulo, 109, 181n43
Friedman, Milton, xvi, 49
Friedman, Thomas, 2
Frum, David, xiv, 157n17
Fukuyama, Francis, 49

Gallagher, Charles, 64
Garland, David, 39
Gates, Henry Louis, 56
GATT. *See* General Agreement on
Tariffs and Trade
Geballe, Shelley, 98
gender issues, xvi, xviii, 32, 106
General Agreement on Tariffs and
Trade (GATT), 60
Geneva Conventions, 4, 26, 35

189

About the Author

ᴥ

Henry A. Giroux holds the Global Television Network Chair in Communications at McMaster University, Canada, and is the author of *The Abandoned Generation: Democracy Beyond the Culture of Fear* (Palgrave, 2003).